3 Godfathers – The age of innocence. Photograph by Alexander Kahle.

Company of Heroes

My Life as an Actor in the John Ford Stock Company

Harry Carey, Jr.

MADISON BOOKS

Lanham • New York • London

Published by Madison Books
4720 Boston Way
Lanham, Maryland 20706

3 Henrietta Street
London WC2E 8LU, England

Library of Congress Cataloging-in-Publication Data

Carey, Harry, 1921–
Company of heroes : my life as an actor in the John Ford stock company /
Harry Carey, Jr.
p.   cm.
Originally published: Metuchen, N.J. : Scarecrow Press, 1994.
Includes index.
1. Carey, Harry, 1921– . 2. Motion picture actors and actresses—
United States—Biography. 3. Ford, John, 1894–1973. I. Title.
[PN2287.C266A3 1996] 791.43'028'092—dc20 [B] 96–11359 CIP

ISBN 1–56833–068–5 (paper : alk. paper)

Distributed by National Book Network

⊖™ The paper used in this publication meets the minimum requirements of
American National Standard for Information Sciences—Permanence of
Paper for Printed Library Materials, ANSI Z39.48–1984.
Manufactured in the United States of America.

For Marilyn

Contents

Acknowledgments

It wasn't until I finished the first draft of my manuscript that I realized it takes more than one person to write a book.

It takes an energetic and gifted editor-friend like James Pepper to pull all the pieces together and decide what to "cut" and what to "print."

It takes someone to give you a push. That push came from dear friend, director, writer, actor, Lindsay Anderson.

It takes an unbelievably devoted wife like Marilyn Carey who gave me continued insight through my several drafts.

Grateful thanks to my son Thomas Carey for all his valuable input, and to computer wizard, Betty Leonard.

Also, to my beloved mother, Olive Carey, who kept after me to write. I'm sorry she didn't live to be one hundred instead of ninety-two so she could read this book. But, like Eric Clapton hopes—I too hope—that she sees it in heaven.

In the Beginning

People need landmarks. They tell us where we are, where we've been, where we want to go. And if you live in one place long enough, you begin to acquire quite a few of them. I've lived in the city of Los Angeles for 70 years. Some of my landmarks still exist, haven't been knocked down, plowed under or covered with asphalt.

If I look north from our home in Sherman Oaks, California, I see the hills where I was born. If I look west, I see the hills where my dad died. East is Universal Studios, a company my father, Harry Carey Senior, helped to put on the map by making two-reeler westerns. To the west is Thousand Oaks, Simi Valley. I've made so many TV westerns out there that I've lost count. It's all houses now. I'm moving out of Los Angeles—too crowded. Maybe this book is my attempt at a kind of "portable" landmark. My journey has been that of a character actor. I've worked with the great and the not-so-great. But mostly I've worked with men and women who loved their profession, and who like me, had kids to raise, and houses to pay for. I've worked with many people, but I've only had one teacher. That man was John Ford. He was my nemesis and my hero. There were times when I was not an admirer—but when the day's work was done—I loved him. He once introduced himself by saying, "My name is John Ford. I make westerns." He sure did.

One afternoon my father and I were sitting in his bedroom in a house my mother had rented in Brentwood, California. Brentwood is a very fancy suburb of Los Angeles, and this was a beautiful and comfortable house just north of Sunset Boulevard. It was 1946, and L.A. was a far different place to live then. The neighborhood was quiet and peaceful; almost a rural atmosphere. Just east of my dad's house, right across Sunset Boulevard, there were two polo fields bordered by the Riviera Country Club. And a little further down the road was the "turn-in" to the Will Rogers Ranch. We were having a drink together; Bacardi rum with a little water, no ice; and we were talking about the movies. I asked him how come he had not worked for John Ford in so many years. Now I was certain that he would launch into his usual twenty-five-year-old tirade about John Ford and his faults and egomania, but he surprised me. He took a big drag on his cigarette and blew a column of smoke through his nose. That made him cough, which made him blow his nose and wipe his eyes with one of his huge specially made handkerchiefs. Then he said four simple words, "He won't ask me." And then he added something which would have given John Ford a stroke, had he known how well my father knew him. He said, "But you will—not till after I croak—but then you will. You can bet on it." My father was absolutely on the nose with that one.

A few months later, my folks (well, my mother—she did all the money stuff; my dad earned it, and she handled it; sometimes foolishly, but always to make him happier and more comfortable), moved a mile or so up Mandeville Canyon Road in a house built by Cliff May, a popular architect at that time who built large rambling ranch-style homes. My wife Marilyn and I, and our two little babies, Steven, a year-and-a-half, and Melinda, six months, moved into that great big place with them. We had an entire wing to ourselves.

Anybody who was anybody lived around there. Robert Taylor lived just up the road. So did Jean Arthur, and John Charles Thomas, the great baritone. Shirley Temple and her handsome husband, John Agar, were just a mile away—and so was Joan Crawford, Gary Cooper, Claude Rains, and Pat O'Brien. On Tigertail Road, you could see Henry Fonda with little Jane riding behind him on his tractor as he plowed his land. Gregory Peck was up on the hill, and Rex Harrison and Lilli Palmer lived further up on Mandeville Canyon.

It was absolutely wonderful out there then. The only thing that put a damper on it was that Pop was sicker than hell, and no matter how hard I tried to make him laugh, and I really knew how to do that, it was short-lived—always followed by that gut-wrenching cough. He was miserable because he couldn't ride his old horse, Sunny, anymore—well, he couldn't do much of anything any more. He was only going on 69—not too old, even in those days, but older than we figure it today. The doctors said he had emphysema, and not much was known about it then.

I had been in three movies that year: *Rolling Home* with Russell Hayden and Jean Parker; a big feature for Raoul Walsh with Robert Mitchum and Teresa Wright called *Pursued,* and after that, *Red River.*

I was lucky as hell to have been cast in *Red River.* It was my first movie with John Wayne, and he was the reason I got the part. Howard Hawks mentioned to Duke that he didn't know who to cast as "Dan Latimer," the kid who, after singing a lullaby to the restless cattle, tells Duke that he wants to use the money he will make on the drive to buy a pair of red shoes for his wife. Shortly after that scene the kid is trampled in the cattle stampede started by a cascade of pots and pans set off by a "sugar thief." Duke told Hawks that he didn't know if I could act, but I sure looked the part.

The scene with Wayne is longer than originally written. While we were rehearsing, Howard Hawks added some more stuff. He wouldn't give you more than you could handle, but he started improvising, and juggling it around, and pretty soon he had a good scene. It was a process shot. They had the cattle sedated I guess, because they were all lying around on the ground inside this big soundstage. I'm singing to them and Duke rides up. Well, we're doing the scene, and while I'm talking to Duke—I have one fairly long speech—he's going on like this—he's smiling, which is totally out of character for that role. So Hawks said "cut it." I thought, 'oh gosh, I did something wrong.'

Hawks said, "Duke, you're smiling. You like this kid, but you're a hard guy."

Duke said, "I wasn't smiling."

And Hawks replied, "Yeah, you were."

"Waal," Duke said, "I guess it's because I'm glad the kid's doing a good job."

Then I thought I had the world by the tail.

Today, *Red River* is rightly considered a "classic" western film. My father had completed his role down on location before I got the job, so even though we are in the same picture, we never worked at the same time. It was the last film he ever made.

September 21, 1947 was a beautiful, cloudless day. It was midafternoon, and again, I sat in my father's bedroom, this time holding his hand because he was dying. There were only four of us there. A wonderful young nurse; Doctor Arthur Harris, who was a personal friend; John Ford and me. John Ford, his wife Mary, and John Wayne had flown in from Catalina Island that morning after they heard that Pop was nearing the end. Duke Wayne worshipped my dad. He came in and out of the bedroom. I think he had appointed himself errand boy and news carrier to the many people who were in the other part of the house. God, it was a terrible day. Duke brought me a tumbler of whiskey. I think it was the first time I ever turned down a drink. I don't know why—Pop wouldn't have minded, but I guess I thought God wouldn't approve. No one should have to go through the agony that my father went through those last weeks. Dr. Harry Brandel, our old family doctor who, when I was a kid, would drive 40 miles from downtown Los Angeles to make a house call at the ranch, had dropped by for a visit about six weeks before. He had taken one look at the X-rays and had said that awful word, *cancer.* None of the hotshot Beverly Hills doctors had ever mentioned it. My mother was furious. She said he was nuts. But here we were, exactly six weeks later, and my father was dying.

Then something happened that I'll never forget. His suffering finally ended, and Doctor Harris reached over and closed his eyes. In a matter of seconds, the sky turned purple-black, the wind whined and howled, the draperies on the open French doors stood straight out—flapping like loose sails. The cottonwood and poplar trees on the patio bent almost in half from the force of the wind. A huge gush of cool air roared through the room; then all of a sudden—in an instant, it was all back exactly as it had been before; sky bright blue, trees upright, curtains limp. I know, I know, people were dying all over the world at that same instant, but that's what happened.

Then the wake began. It went on for about a year. I'm serious, it did. Mary Ford had Chasen's Restaurant in Beverly Hills send over piles of food and booze. Later that afternoon, Uncle Jack, as I would come to call him, sidled up to my mother and told her he was going to remake *3 Godfathers* with John Wayne playing my father's role, Pedro Armendariz, the fine actor from Mexico who had worked for Jack in *Fort Apache,* and me as "the Kid." He and Pop had made this movie in 1919 as a silent picture called *Marked Men.* I'm sure John Ford thought this was a wonderful surprise for my mother; that it would take away some of the pain of her loss. However, I never felt that it had quite that effect because she never wanted me to become an actor. For that matter, I don't think it made a big hit with Duke, either.

February 1st, 1948, was the date of John Ford's 54th birthday. Mary had arranged a small dinner party for him at their home on Odin Street in the heart of Hollywood. They had lived there for many years with their two children, Patrick and Barbara. Where the house stood is now a parking lot for the famous Hollywood Bowl. I guess that's progress. I will never forget that damned birthday party. It was a harbinger of things to come. He kept saying to me, "You're going to hate me when this picture is over, but you're going to give a great performance." He kept saying it and saying it. Mary had invited just a few close friends, Duke and his then wife, Chata, Ward Bond, my mother, Marilyn and me. Patrick, Barbara, and others of his family were there also. I was very nervous. Even though he had known me all my life, I didn't really know him at all. The few times I'd seen him as a kid, I didn't like him. He was scary, and I scared easily. I was always a little timid, and it didn't take a John Ford long to pick up on that. He knew his subject well, and had the scenario all planned starting with that damned birthday party.

"You're going to hate me when this movie is over, but you're going to give a great performance."

I said, "Okay, sir," and he replied. "What?"

I said, "That's fine, sir," and he replied, "Uncle Jack, you call me your Uncle Jack!"

I said, "Yes, sir."

Uncle Jack never cheated on the grog at his house. In truth, he actually encouraged everyone to drink. It was only on location that he would not tolerate any consumption of alcohol by anyone in his "stock company." This night, I hit the sauce pretty hard, but the more I drank, the more sober I got.

Then I got the first lesson in what I shall dubiously call my "schooling." You have to learn to *listen*. I was not good at listening, and on top of that, I was panicking. He muttered something about cutting the birthday cake, and then dashed out of the room. He suddenly reappeared with a huge saber, probably from the Civil War and handed it to me saying, "Melwood, cut the cake." Now "Melwood" was the name of the whiskey he and my father had gotten drunk on at the ranch the night I was born. It became a running gag between him and my father. Thank God, that tag only lasted a few more weeks.

Anyway, in taking the saber from him, I almost put his "good" eye out with it. "Jesus Christ," he said, "don't you know how to handle a saber?"

I replied, "No, sir, I was never an officer."

"Thank God for that," he said, "or we'd have lost the war."

The next few minutes were pure hell, but I did finally whack the saber through the cake in a way that satisfied him and we all had a piece. On the way home later that night, I told Marilyn that, "This trip to the location in Death Valley might be my last anywhere."

3 Godfathers

The filming of *3 Godfathers* was rapidly approaching. Thank God I had the script. I memorized it backwards and forwards. My God, I was going to be co-starred with the number-one box office attraction in the world and Latin America's greatest star, Pedro Armendariz. The memory of the birthday party was wearing off, and I was once again in my own mind, anyway—a promising young actor.

In the meantime, my agent called to tell me that I had been offered the juvenile lead in one of Gene Autry's pictures. I wonder what direction my career would have taken, had I done that instead.

During my first visit to Uncle Jack's office, I learned that he hated agents, even though he had one himself, Jack Bolton, whom he liked. He also hated producers. He once told his grandson, Dan, who at the time was thinking of becoming a movie maker, "You have to start at the bottom and work your way up—so be a producer." In reality, of course, he realized producers were necessary, at least during the preproduction activities, but once he began shooting, they had best stay away. On one of his movies, *The Informer,* he asked the producer to come down to the set and then called for quiet.

"I have an announcement to make," he said. "This is your producer, Cliff Reid. Take a good look at him, because it's the last you're going to see of him!" Whereupon Mr. Reid went back to his office for the duration.

Uncle Jack never ran dailies or rushes, the scenes that were shot the previous day. He always knew exactly what he had on film. He actually cut or edited the picture as he shot it. The film editor didn't have fifteen or so cuts to choose from, as is usually the case. This technique didn't work as well for him at the end of his career, but by then, it was too late for him to change—and who would want him to? Even at his worst, he was still one of the best.

Every actor has to have an agent, if only to dicker about the money. Walter Herzbrun was my agent at the time I was given the role of the Kid in *3 Godfathers,* but I had to bid him farewell. A few weeks before the movie started, Jack said to me, "Why don't you let Lester Ziffren handle you? He's honest, and he's the only agent I'll allow in here, other than Bolton." So I signed with Lester. I then found out that for years and years, Ford's agent had been Harry Wurtzel, and that Lester was married to Harry's daughter, Edie. Anyway, it worked out well, and everybody was happy.

But not even Lester approached Jack for work. What you did was simple, once you caught on. When word got out that the Old Man was going to start a picture, you simply went over to the office for a visit, and he'd tell you whether you were in it or not. That's the way it worked. No one ever asked him anything about the picture—not John Wayne, not Victor McLaglen, not Ward Bond—not anybody. You sat there until he told you, and when he did, he usually told you a little about the story and a little about your part in it.

Most of the major studios had bungalows on the lots for their very important writers and directors. So it was at RKO Pathé Studios on Washington Boulevard in Culver City. These bungalows were all pretty much the same. They usually had a little porch, a small outer office with enough room for a secretary, and a couple of chairs for nervous actors to sit in while waiting to go into the inner office. The first thing that struck you when you went over to visit Uncle Jack was the smell of coffee. There was always a large urn in the front office filled with fresh coffee and huge mugs to drink it from. With Uncle Jack, you didn't have to wait long. Once he found out you were there, he would yell for you to come in, even if there was someone very important with him. He always introduced me as Harry Carey, Jr., not Dobe Carey, and he was the only person to do that. Even today, MC's sometimes introduce me as Dobe Carey, and nobody at the function knows who the hell I am! Dobe is the nickname my father gave me the night I was born. I had a thatch of red hair the color of the adobe bricks our ranch house was made of. If I had to make the choice again, I would use Dobe Carey as my professional name and escape all those remarks by shop girls and gas station attendants about Japanese suicide. Although Uncle Jack called me "Ol' Dobe," he never once suggested that I drop the "Harry Carey, Jr." for films. In fact, he introduced me in *3 Godfathers* as Harry Carey, Jr., even though it was my fourth film. He never liked any of his actors to speak about other movies they were in.

That old white colonial building on Washington Boulevard is a real landmark for me. A happy one, for sure, because everything that happened to me there was good. That is where I really got to know Uncle Jack, and really got to know Duke Wayne, and started to get to know about the movies. There was absolutely no chain of command with John Ford. There was him, and there was us. There was no star except him, and he treated us all the same. If you got your ass chewed out, not to worry—it might be Duke's turn on the next go-round, or Ward Bond's. But I think Ward liked it. I think he liked to get Jack riled up, just to see the fireworks. Ward was the biggest glutton for punishment of any of the Ford actors. To quote Jack on Ward Bond, "Let's face it, Bond is a shit. But he's my favorite shit!" He pronounced Ward's name with his State of Maine accent, "Wahd Boned." When Duke saw Ward coming, he'd break out laughing in the way Duke had and he'd yell, "Thank God, fellas, the heat's off. Here comes Ward!" And then he'd laugh some more. Of course, Ward never let us down.

For openers, right in front of "himself," Ward would greet the day with, "This would be a helluva picture, except Wayne's playing my part!"

Ford, hearing this, would say, "Well, there goes my day. I thought the son-of-a-bitch had the day off!" He always used him, though. Ward was great at his work, and Uncle Jack loved him. In fact, it is hard to guess which of those two big guys he loved the most. Few people realize that Ford's political beliefs were not aligned with those two men. His politics fluctuated, depending on who he would like to see as president of his country, and, God, how he loved his country. The "liberals" in this town always called him a "right-winger" or a "reactionary," but he was simply a true patriot. Later on during the shooting of *Yellow Ribbon*, he and I were the only ones in the company to vote for Truman.

3 Godfathers began filming the latter part of May 1948, so from about the first of April, my trips over to old RKO Pathé became more frequent. Most of the time, Duke was there, too. I had only seen Duke a few times since *Red River* at some social functions, and he was always sort of distant and hard to talk to. I hadn't gotten to know him as yet. No matter how many times you worked with him, unless you were totally alone with him and therefore, had his complete attention, you never felt quite sure he heard a word you were saying. It was like he was high-hatting you, and he really didn't mean that. He never consciously high-hatted anyone. This trait of his, this sort of, "I don't really know you're here," expression used to drive the people he worked with—and worse yet, the people who worked for them—absolutely bonkers. It made them butter up to him, which annoyed him and often caused him to insult them in some way. He couldn't bear reticence.

If someone told him off on the set, he would most likely say to a friend, "Jesus, I'm kinda glad the guy showed some guts."

That was Duke, but I didn't know any of these things about him at this time.

This day when I walked into John Ford's bungalow, there wasn't much room in the outer office, because John Wayne was in it.

"Hello, kid!" he said. Then he kind of chuckled and gave me the real John Wayne grinning look over the top of his eyebrows. "I guess ya' know that yer in for it, dontcha?"

I said that, yes, that had been made very plain, and told him Ford's "You're going to hate me" line.

"Oooohhhh Yeaaaah," he laughed. And he laughed some more. Then he got real serious. "Listen," he said, cutting his hand across the air, "I think yer gonna do real fine [God, that sounded good], but I don't give a damn how good ya' are—he's gonna—be on ya' really bad—so ya' gotta—make up yer mind ta' tell him you ain't gonna take it—or jes' grit yer goddamn teeth an' do yer best. Ya' hafta' make that decision on the very first day. Or—ya' kin make it right now in there an' get it over with."

"Oh, I want to make the picture, Duke. I mean this is a helluva chance for me."

Then he got that wise-ass grin again, and his eyes sparkled when he said, "Ya' may wanna—eat those words in a few weeks." He laughed, and we went into the inner sanctum.

It surprised me to see that Duke acted almost as subservient as I did. At least at first, until we settled down. I never settled down, but I was smart enough to keep my trap shut unless spoken to. First, there was just mostly gossip between Uncle Jack and Duke—kind of "inside the family" stuff. They both made it plain that I was welcome, however, and I was not excluded from their conversation.

Finally Ford said to Duke, "You're going to be working with Pedro Armendariz, the world's greatest actor, in this movie, so you'd better be on your toes." I couldn't understand this, because Laurence Olivier was around then too, but of course, he was giving Duke the "business" for my benefit. That's when I first realized that, perhaps some of the time, I wouldn't catch all of the hell. I don't know why he acted as if Duke didn't know Pedro, because Pedro had been in *Fort Apache* with him a few short months before.

Ford was with actors like some guys are with girls. Every so often, he'd "discover" someone new—new to him, that is. It didn't matter if this person had been around for years; to Ford he was a brand-new discovery.

In 1948, his discovery was Pedro Armendariz, the "Clark Gable of Mexico." That was a perfect handle for Pete, too, because he was the most magnetic and colorful actor I've ever worked with. He was flamboyant and extremely articulate. I remember Ford also saying that afternoon, "He's one of the most magnificent actors I have ever directed." I couldn't wait to meet him, but that wouldn't happen until we got to the location, because Pete was finishing a movie in Mexico with Maria Felix.

Although Pedro hated to be reminded of this, the truth was that he was born in Texas. His mother was English, and he had been educated in the United States. He was a citizen of Mexico, however, and lived there with his wife, Carmen, and two children, Pedro Jr., and Carmella.

I drove home after this visit to the studio, feeling not too bloodied and a little more relaxed about the whole adventure. The next call I got was from Ford's long-time secretary, Meta Stern. "Mr. Ford wants to see you in your wardrobe." Now, things were really starting to percolate.

On this trip, I met some of the regulars: Uncle Jack's brother-in-law and first assistant director, Wingate Smith. Wingate had earned the Purple Heart in both World War I and World War II. Almost everyone called him "Unck."

Also in the office was a guy who was bigger than Duke, Mickey Simpson. Mickey always played bad dudes. They all welcomed me like one of the family. There was wardrobe everywhere, all over the office. I don't remember that ever happening again. There was a long rack of Western clothes hanging out on the porch, and two or three cardboard boxes of hats and neckerchiefs in the outer office, awaiting the Old Man's selection. The two men who wrote the wonderful screenplay were there, too. That caused me some anxiety. I wondered if any of my part had been changed.

The Mecca of motion picture wardrobe was the Western Costume Company, which backed up to Paramount Studio on Melrose Avenue. All of this stuff had come from there. Pretty soon, a harassed-looking little man named Mickey Meyers emerged from "in there." He was our wardrobe man, and he began to show me some of the clothes he had picked out for me. He was just being friendly. We both knew he had nothing to say about my wardrobe for this movie.

Then Duke arrived. "Hi ya'," he said. "Well, where's yer boots an' hat?" He said it like a drill sergeant. "Ya' must have a favorite pair of boots, dontcha?"

How did he know? "Well, yeah," I replied.

"Well, where the hell are they?"

"In the car," I said.

"Well, Jesus Christ, what the hell good are they in the goddamn car? Go an' get 'em an' throw 'em in there with the rest of the wardrobe. He'll pick 'em out."

"He will?" I asked.

"If they look right, he will," promised Duke.

So I ran like hell for the car.

Uncle Jack loved wardrobe fittings. He loved the western clothes of the 1870s. He loved them in his hands and actually helped you put them on, especially the bandannas and the hats. If he had an actor he hadn't used before in the show, he found out a lot about him during the wardrobe-fitting routine.

Duke reminded me once more, "Fer God's sake, kid, keep yer mouth shut and yer ears open! And don't make any suggestions, no matter what the hell he does. An' be careful, 'cause he'll try to suck you into it."

I was apprehensive. I'm a people-pleaser at heart, so I was a perfect target for Ford's sarcasm. Heaven knows, he loved my dad very much; he was dedicating this movie to him. He was paying a debt he felt he owed, but he was also getting back at my dad for something, through me.

In we went. He didn't even say hello. He did introduce me to Frank Nugent and Laurence Stallings, the screenwriters. He was thoughtful in that way. He never treated you like you were unimportant. Believe me, I was very important. There'd be no game without me. I was the goddamned ball!

There was a long sofa across the room from his desk. He pointed to the far end of it on his left and said, "Stand over there and let me look at you." So I did.

He looked at me and winced. "Put that shirt on," he said. The wardrobe man was holding out a shirt, so I undressed to the waist and put it on.

"I can't tell without the pants. Put on the pants." I took off my shoes and pants, put on the faded pair of Levis that Mickey handed me, and tucked in the shirt.

"Now lemme see the boots," he ordered. I put on a large pair of period boots called "rough-outs."

"Holy Christ! Are those really your feet?" he exclaimed.

"Yessir," I said.

"Where did you get such big feet? Your father didn't have big feet."

"I guess from my mother's side of the family," I said.

"The boots are lousy and the shirt is lousy," he said. "Don't you own a pair of boots?"

"Yessir," I replied.

"Where are they?"

"I think they're around here someplace," I said innocently, and I ran out and got them.

"That's the idea," he said, "but, Jesus, I don't know where you got those big feet."

Then he got up and found a shirt that suited him and had me put it on. He tried about five different bandannas on me. On a couple, he cut the corner and tore them to make two triangles. I thought Mickey Meyers would have a heart attack. He finally decided on one. Hats came next. I was worried about my hat. He peered into the box of hats and started throwing them around until he came to a big black one just like my dad used to wear. I was afraid of that. I was six foot, one and one-half inches tall and weighed 146 pounds, stripped. I had a thin, half-starved look in those days, and I knew I would look stupid in that broad-brimmed hat. So, did he, but I hadn't figured that out. I plunged. "It's kind of wide in the brim, isn't it?" Deadly silence. Duke turned and faced the wall.

Finally, "Oh, so you're going to direct the goddamn picture."

"Oh no, sir," I cried helplessly and looked at Duke, who now was staring right at me. I think he was madder than John Ford! Ford was having a good time! The game had started. I had made the first of many blunders, but, just as Duke had predicted, Jack rummaged around in the hat boxes until he found my hat. He placed it on my head and said the magic words, "Yeah, that's the idea. Wear that hat." He backed off, giving me the once-over, and said, "It's your own hat, isn't it?"

"Yessir," I said. He looked at Duke and grinned. I wonder if he knew that I had worn it in *Red River.*

After that he and Mickey put a pair of suspenders called galluses on me, and I was finished with the first important phase of the movie. He allowed me to stay while he fitted Duke, so he could see how we looked side-by-side. Duke was treated the same way I was. He wasn't allowed to put his two cents in, either. I remember he hated his pants. I don't blame him. He despised pants with a high rise. They come all the way up to your rib cage, and after you move around a little, they fall down around your hips where pants should be, and your ass looks like you were a little late in getting to the john. Of course, that's what the Old Man fitted him with. He did have galluses to keep them up, but he hated them. What he really liked was a rust-colored denim pant called "booger reds." The boots were a different story. Duke wore a size ten and one-half, and his arch was so high that he could never get a pair of factory made boots on. The wardrobe man would keep hauling in size ten and one-halfs, and he'd get them on just up to where his instep hit the top of the boot, whereupon he'd get very mad and throw the boot all the way across the fitting room. I don't know why they kept trying; they always had to make them special for him. On noncavalry pictures, we all wore our own boots. Ford was supposed to have been a stickler for authenticity. Well, perhaps he was, but when it came to boots, nine times out of ten, you wore your own. *3 Godfathers* was supposed to be set in the 1870s, but the boots I wore were ones that I had worn on the ranch when I was nineteen. When I knocked the heels off my boots in the sequence on the desert just before I die, the audience never noticed I didn't have on period boots. One of Uncle Jack's favorite lines was, "If they're looking at your feet, you're in deep trouble."

In 1948, although Duke was number one or two in popularity at the box office, he wasn't the legend he became fifteen years later. Luster Bayless became his top costumer in this later period and made the outfits that really fulfilled the image of Duke that America came to idolize. The clothes he wears in all the memorial prints and photographs we see of him on our vacation trips in all the little eateries across the United States are the ones Luster Bayless designed for him. He knew how Duke wanted to look in his "September Song" years.

Harry Carey, John Wayne, Tom Mix, Roy Rogers, Gene Autry—none of them would have made a dime without a horse! The two biggest suppliers of horseflesh in the golden days of westerns were the Fat Jones Stables and the Hudkins Bros. Stables. Fat's place was away out in the northeast San Fernando Valley. It was considered really out in the sticks then, but now it's "in town." The Hudkins stable was near Warner Bros. in Burbank, and it's a cemetery now. Their huge barns and corral not only held horses of every breed, shape, and color, but they had every type of horse-drawn vehicle imaginable; everything from stagecoaches to chariots.

There are basically two kinds of horses in movies: good ones and lousy ones. A bad horse can made the best of riders look awful. Don't tell a wrangler you can ride, or you'll get a ringer for sure, to prove you can't. Wranglers are usually darn good cowboys and will help anyone who doesn't come on like he knows it all. I can count on one hand the movie actors who know how to ride a horse really well. It's like anything else; it takes a lot of practice to do it right.

It was out at Fat Jones' spread that I first met Ben Johnson. No one has ever looked better on a horse than Ben Johnson. John Ford found that out when he saw him double John Agar in *Fort Apache*. He turned to Duke and asked, "Who's that kid doubling Johnny?"

Duke said, "His name's Ben Johnson. He's married to Fat Jones' daughter."

I drove into the big yard at Fat's not knowing why I had been ordered to report there. Uncle Jack certainly knew I could ride a horse. It was the first time I had been there since I was a little kid. What a place! I had never seen so many horses and so much equipment in my life. Ben was sitting there on a stocky bay horse. Uncle Jack and his driver, James, pulled up in his station wagon and he got out. He greeted Ben and the other cowboys, and ignored me. After some banter with them, he turned and said, "Oh—Dobe—climb up there behind Ben, will you, kid?" So I shook Ben's hand and got on behind him.

"Gallop around," the Old Man said. So we did.

Then he yelled, "Haven't you read the script? Ben is Duke, and you're supposed to be wounded, so be half falling off!"

I put my arm around Ben's waist, hooked my thumb under his belt and sort of hung over the side, half on and half off. In a little bit, the Old Man said, "Okay. That's enough."

Ben kept on galloping, so I straightened up and put my hands on my hips so the old bastard could see that I could ride without hanging on. He made believe he didn't notice. The whole process took only about twenty minutes.

We all said our good-byes, and Uncle Jack said to me in a kidding way, "Ya done good kid. But you're going to hate me by the time this picture's over."

I didn't know at that time that Ben was under contract to Argosy Productions, a company founded by John Ford and Merian C. Cooper, the man who had created and produced the original *King Kong*. I also didn't know we would become lifelong friends.

About a week after my twenty-seventh birthday, May 16, 1948, we left for the Furnace Creek Ranch in Death Valley, California. There was also a Furnace Creek Lodge, but the ranch part had two-room cabins, and the cast stayed there. Some of the camera crew and makeup were there, too, but the rest of the company were somewhere else nearby. There was no air-conditioning, but that was not uncommon in those days.

The next two days were actually kind of fun—the rest period before the storm. My ass remained unchewed that weekend. We got there on a Saturday, the same day that Pedro Armendariz, "the world's greatest actor," was due to arrive. I was rooming with Ward Bond, and Uncle Jack exclaimed when he heard that, "Oh God. You poor kid!" That had been arranged for my benefit, though, because in spite of all of his braggadocio, Ward was a calming influence.

All of us—Jack Ford, Duke, Ward, and myself—greeted Pedro out there in the driveway between the green cabins and the date palms. Pete was in his early thirties, in the prime of his life and his career. He had just recently completed the Spanish version of John Steinbeck's *The Pearl,* a film classic superbly photographed by Gabriel Figueroa and directed by Emilio Fernandez, whom they called "the John Ford of Mexico."

Pete was very handsome and had the greatest eyes: deep brown with lashes that looked like they were store bought. He had on a white silk shirt, tailor-made beige gabardine slacks, and brown and white shoes. Pete was sharp! He hugged us all, Mexican style, and right away I felt that I had known him for a long time. He was extremely kind and polite. This was Saturday. Sunday was another story. Sunday was Armendariz's wardrobe day!

On a Ford picture, you never knew ahead of time what was coming, but on awakening Sunday morning, I figured it would also be a day of rest. Time to review my dialogue; perhaps ask Duke or Pedro to run over the lines with me. Either of them would have been happy to do this. In spite of all my fears, in the true spirit of youthfulness, the role didn't seem all that big a deal. It was the man in the dark glasses I was worried about.

We'd had a rather late breakfast and were sitting around the lobby when in walked Wingate with orders that we were wanted, pronto, in the auditorium. For some reason, there was an auditorium there, like they have in high schools. It had a large stage with footlights and everything. We were to report there for more wardrobe sessions.

Pedro had a very colorful way of speaking, and he had announced to Jack the day before, "Jack! Jack! I have brought to you from Mexico the most fantastic outfit for this picture you have ever seen! I had eet especially made for thees role!" He phrased his sentences like bursts from a Tommygun.

Ford stared at him for one moment, then said, "Oh, really? Well—I mean—Christ!"

We three Godfathers marched into the auditorium. Duke and I changed into our wardrobe, but immediately Pete was all over the Old Man like a blanket. He repeated, even more fervently than the day before, that he had the perfect costume for this picture. And he added, "You see, Jack, you have to understand the people of my country! I am to them their symbol of Mexico! I have an image, Jack—that I have to maintain in my country. I cannot wear the wrong clothes!"

"Okay, okay," said Jack. "Let's see the outfit. Go put it on."

"Oh, fantastic, Jack," said Pedro. You will not be sorry." He happily ran off stage.

In the meantime, Ford noticed that everyone was there, except Bond! "Will somebody *please* get that horse's ass Bond?" ordered Jack. Two assistants rushed out. Wayne was smiling. I wanted to, but thought better of it. Ford came up on stage, fiddled with my outfit, and decided that it was okay as he had remembered it. He had another look at Duke's wardrobe, too, and then returned to the front row seats to await Pete's entrance. He didn't have long to wait. In came the Symbol of Mexico! As inexperienced as I was in the motion picture business, I was appalled by what Pedro Armendariz thought he should wear in this legend of the Southwest. He looked like a rider from one of those early California hispanic groups riding down Colorado Boulevard in the Pasadena Rose Parade. Jack Ford's expression never changed when in crisis; this day was no different. He pushed his dark glasses up onto his forehead. This rendered him totally blind, which is probably what he wanted at that moment.

Pedro: (All smiles) "Well, Jack, what do you think?"

Ford: (Never changing expression the whole time) "Pete, it's beautiful! Just beautiful!"

Pedro: "Ah hah! I knew you would like eet, Jack! I had eet made especially for this part!"

Ford: "That's great, Pete. And you can wear it in a movie. But not in this movie."

Pedro: (Starting to go wild) "What? You must be kidding, Jack! I *have* to wear this outfit! I have to dress for the people of my country! Also the people of Latin America! They expect me to look like this. It's my goddamn image for Chrissake, Jack."

Ford: "Pete!" Then softly, "Jesus Christ, Pete. Don't you know the story? You're not playing the symbol of Mexico. Please forget you're a goddamned Mexican. Make believe you're a Guatemalan. I mean—get this straight, for Christ's sake. In this picture, you're playing a saddle tramp. You're one tough son-of-a-bitch who becomes a half-decent guy after the baby's born. The clothes you wear are the clothes you've stolen off guys you've shot in gunfights. Comprende? Jesus, Pete, that outfit. I know you spent a lot of money on it, but wear it in the goddamn Santa Barbara Fiesta!"

Pete stormed around the stage, his huge Spanish spurs clanging, and cussing in Spanish. Then he tried one more time. "Jack, don't you understand? In my country I'm a star! I must dress like a star!"

Ford had had enough. He paused a moment and looked helplessly at Pete. Finally he said, "Wardrobe!" (meaning Mickey Myers) "fit this guy in a tuxedo! He's going to play a pimp in my next movie!"

Well, that about ended it. Pedro kept on stomping up and down the stage, and when Mickey handed him the wardrobe Jack had picked out for him to try on, Pete threw the clothes across the stage. The two of them remained very good friends until Pedro's death in 1962, but he never made another movie with Jack.

I've sat on many movie sets and listened to many actors talk about John Ford. I've heard them say, "I wouldn't fall for that game he plays! He makes them all kiss ass! Wayne—all of them. I don't go for that shit! He'd try that sadistic act on me just once, and I'd tell him right in front of his whole gang of ass-kissers, 'Mister Ford, stick your picture up your royal ass!' "

I wish I had a buck for every time I've heard those words, but I never saw it happen in any of the nine movies I did with him. I've seen actors refuse to do something, but when that happened, he'd just get someone else to do it. He wouldn't fire the man off the picture; he simply wouldn't hire him again. He never put a person down to another director, either. He didn't believe in blacklisting. Now I'm not saying that Ford never got angry, but this time, he acted as though he was enjoying Pedro's histrionics, and I believe he was. Maybe that wasn't even the day he made a decision concerning Pete's future with him.

There were rules to follow when you were working for Ford. Let me point out something significant about that. The rules were only for the actors he truly loved; those of us who were fortunate enough to be one of his regulars or what was later known as his "stock company." He was foxy. He directed some of the most gifted actors in the world, but I only know about the company that I was lucky enough to work with. Yes, he truly loved us. Not because we were Oliviers or whomever, but because we did what he asked in the very best way we knew. And that made him supremely proud and happy. On the other hand, there were many actors who could get away with stuff we could not. They could come and go as they pleased. That's the way he was. But they didn't see him between pictures, or go to his parties, or drink his whiskey when work was done, or sit by his bed to talk, or pray with him on Memorial Day.

3 Godfathers was cinematographer Winton C. Hoch's first film for John Ford. That first afternoon, Winnie Hoch came to a decision. He decided to be one of the team. It only cost him one horrible moment. Jack had heard raves about Winnie's skill with color film, so he was in a little trouble right there. I don't think at that time Jack was as comfortable with color film as he was with black and white. After lunch, we were all driven out onto the famous sand dunes. Winton Hoch was an extremely nice, no-nonsense man with wild, bushy eyebrows and the bearing of a field general. He had a patrician nose on a handsome face, and was the very best at what he did. I remember hearing that he had a Ph.D. and knew more about color photography than anyone else in the business, but he was about to fall into the Ford trap.

We stopped on the desert when the driver couldn't go any further without risking getting stuck in the sand. Uncle Jack gazed around for a moment from the front seat of the station wagon and then, like he'd suddenly made up his mind, he leaped out and began wading across the deep mounds of freshly blown sand. The way he was striding across those dunes had all the theatrics of MacArthur's return. Come to think of it, they were a hell-of-a-lot alike—both hams to the core. We all jumped out after him, Ford in the lead, and the rest of us marching dutifully behind; a ritual that was repeated every morning on location. He walked with great purpose; long strides, and everyone must be in step. "You're out of step," he'd yell, and you had to do a quick-step to catch up.

Finally he stopped on top of a dune. Winnie, who was second in line, came up and followed Ford's point of focus as best he could. Then Ford dangled the bait. "Winnie."

"Right here, Jack."

Then Ford, acting like he'd just discovered that Winnie was on the picture said, "Oh—there you are! You know, this could make a hell of a shot." He had put his right hand up to his eye, making a lens out of it.

"Jack," said Winnie, "what I would suggest is that you put your camera here, and from this angle, you can . . . " That's as far as he got.

"*What!* I mean, did I hear you right?"

I'll give Winnie credit; he took another run at it. "I was only going to say, Jack, that it would make a beautiful tracking shot if you . . . "

Now Uncle Jack Ford was becoming disturbed. We could tell because he pulled out one of his huge white handkerchiefs and shoved the corner of it into the side of his mouth. The rest of it hung down the front of his shirt like a big windless sail. This was the first time I saw this happen, and I was to learn that it was an ominous signal of bad things to come. If that tendon on the right side of his neck began to pump in and out, well, hell! Everybody overboard; man the lifeboats! It was really scary, and it wasn't even directed at me.

"I was only going to say, Jack . . . " Winnie said lamely.

Uncle Jack, Pappy, Coach, Old Man, Himself—all of them turned on Winnie. He took the handkerchief out of his mouth, and without raising his voice said, "Do you want to go home right now? Who in the name of Christ do you think you are talking to? I mean, Jesus, you're going to lecture me about your pretty goddamned picture postcard shots? Well, we're not having those kinds of shots in this picture! And I tell you where the camera goes."

Winnie said blandly, "Sorry, Jack," and they never crossed words again. The next year, Winnie won the Academy Award for his second Ford film. Uncle Jack never tried to take any credit for that. And so Winton C. Hoch had been tested and passed. It was still only Sunday.

Ford and his new cameraman calmly discussed the work that lay ahead and wandered around a little longer. He had Duke, Pedro, and me walk over some of the dunes while he squinted through his "lens" again. He looked right at me when he warned us to watch where the hell the camera was pointing so we wouldn't mark up the virgin sand before the camera rolled. Jack had put the handkerchief back into his jacket pocket, and it wasn't long before we all got back into the car.

If you went out on location and caught Ford in action, this is what you would see. He was about 6 feet tall, 175 pounds. He wore expensive dress shirts, usually blue, with French cuffs, but no cufflinks, so the sleeves hung down over his hands. They were usually a little soiled, as were his cream-colored flannel slacks. Sometimes he wore a real belt, but if not, he used a necktie tied around his waist with the knot at the side. Many times, his socks didn't match, and his shoes were old brown-and-white saddle shoes with the laces untied so they flopped all over the place and sometimes tripped him. I swear, sometimes he tripped on purpose so that somebody would have to catch him. He wanted to see if they were paying attention. He always wore a jacket, no matter what the weather: a windbreaker or a khaki military combat jacket with a patch of some sort on the shoulder. Sometimes he wore a scarf around his neck. The hat would be a well-worn and pretty dirty slouch hat of the very best quality, when new. He cocked it to the right side, with the brim turned down all the way around. Periodically, he would pull the brim down even further and follow that by pushing his dark glasses up the bridge of his nose. At times, he wore a St. Louis Cardinals baseball cap. Stan Musial once gave him one, but it was too small. Once in awhile, he would wear a tweed cap, like Duke wore in the *Quiet Man*. He rarely chewed on his handkerchief when he had on a cap, and I quickly learned that the cap meant that he was in a better mood. He had a pipe between his teeth most of the time, back then.

Uncle Jack always wore dark glasses. They weren't ordinary dark glasses. They were so darkly tinted you could barely see his eyes. You never knew where he was looking, or at whom. This was before his eye operation, and before he wore a patch over his left eye. He was even more mysterious with the patch. He loved that patch. It was only when he took off his glasses to clean them (usually on the tail of his shirt, which he never bothered to tuck back in) that you got a really good look at him. He had kind, soft eyes. They were warm and friendly Irish-blue eyes, with not a trace of the sadism he could display. Maybe that's why he never took his glasses off when he was mad.

He wanted everyone to think that he had once been a tough Irish street brawler and football player. He could be very cruel, and he could be dearly loving. He had a quality that made everyone almost kill themselves to please him. He had a way of thanking you for your effort that was unlike any other director. He did it in a strange way, but he did it wonderfully, and you slept really well that night. People ask me how I could work under all that tension. There wasn't any tension. He was a great commander.

Monday morning! The first day of shooting! We're not anywhere near the sand dunes. With Uncle Jack, you never knew. Not too bad a day, except that I thought I took too long to mount my horse, but he didn't reshoot it, so I guessed he wanted it that way. That first scene taught me one thing, though. My concept of my role as William Kearney, the "Abilene Kid," was directly opposite of Uncle Jack's. The minute I said my first line, he gave me a line reading. Students of the acting profession seem to be of the opinion that great directors do not give line readings. I found this not to be true. Ford, Hawks, and Hathaway all did. And it worked. At least they did so with novice actors. Ford would even give Duke a reading, but not Jimmy Stewart or Richard Widmark, years down the road. Anyway, he sure did it with me.

I had it figured out that this "Abilene Kid" was a juvenile delinquent—a really bad, cocksure-type kid of that period. Why else would these two tough hombres take him along on this bank job? I sure didn't figure they would take an altar boy with them and take a chance on getting caught because he got scared. So when Uncle Jack made me sort of whine, "I ain't backin' down" in that scared way, I thought, *Oh shit, I'm off to a bad start here.* I sure kept my mouth shut though. The most important thing I found out during this first week of shooting was that Jack did not always mean exactly what he said. He would mumble some piece of direction, and it could really be a puzzle. Like, "Dobe! (very harshly), when Duke leaves, you're holding the baby. Walk over to the rear of the wagon and lean up against the big wheel! Yeah, that's the idea. Now, you got that straight?" (Then sotto voce) "Don't forget to be at the front wheel. Okay—we're rolling!" He always said, "Yeah—that's the idea," meaning that he approved of what he had just said.

Now, what the hell does he want? Am I at the front wheel or the rear wheel when Duke leaves? I had better not ask, but I'm confused and beginning to panic. This made him truly furious. He had a form of body language that I had to learn to read. Duke and Pete knew how to do this, and Duke would try to help me behind Jack's back. "Jesus, kid," Duke would plead with me, "I know the old bastard is scary and confusing—but ya' hafta jes' clear yer brain an' really listen hard—and watch every move he makes!"

"But, goddamn it, that was deliberate, " I complained.

"Ha—ha—He's just giving ya' the business. He's breaking you in, Ol' Dobe" He went on to tell me about some things Jack had done to him ten years earlier, on *Stagecoach*. That made me feel a lot better.

I had a basic flaw that drove Uncle Jack insane: a lack of energy in my acting. I had this maddening habit of underplaying everything. It really wasn't from fear or shyness. I still haven't figured out why I was so totally relaxed in front of the camera, when he could be so vicious. Maybe I was still fighting that altar boy thing he wanted from me. I mistakenly kept thinking I was right. Now that I think back on it, I should have gone for it! Shown him what I was made of! I was furious when I first read a Ford biography and the author said that he had "bullied" a performance out of me. The author was right, but there were a few times I think I would have done a better job if he had let up on me a little.

This was not the way John Ford usually directed a movie. I was only seeing the "Mr. Hyde" side. There were times when I know Duke or Pete wanted to say something to him about getting off my back. Even some of the crew wanted to. They told me so later, but they said that every time he let me have it, the scene got better. He used all kinds of little tricks, and I guess I did act awfully dumb. He was getting tired of pumping me up before every shot. One time, I'd be okay dramatically, but I'd be hidden from the camera. An actor has to "feel" the lens. Then I'd miss my marks and wind up with a shadow over my face. All this will drive any director nuts, not only Ford.

3 Godfathers is considered by Ford and Wayne buffs to be one of their classics, but when it was released, the critics were not kind. A lot of emphasis was put on the long, drawn-out sequences of the three of us walking, then plodding, and then finally staggering across the endless sands and salt flats. Ward Bond, who played the sheriff, had put a bullet in the canvas water bag attached to Wayne's saddle. This was our supply of water, and it was supposed to last until we could reach Mojave Tanks, where we could refill our bags and make good our escape. The story is simple and beautiful.

I do not remember the Old Man being nice to me for one whole day during location shooting in Death Valley. He was bearable or unbearable—never nice. I'm sure my dad could have warned me about this, but maybe he decided to spare me the worry. I did not call him "Uncle Jack" on that movie! I rarely asked him a question, but if I was truly stuck, I either addressed him as "sir" or just "Jack." I was damned if I was going to call him Uncle Jack, and make him a relative. It would hurt him terribly to hear me say that now, and I wouldn't, because I came to love him dearly. He didn't give much indication he thought too much of me then, either. He kept telling me. "My God, Audie Murphy begged me for this part!"

As one day followed another, there came to be a kind of unspoken dialogue between us. He knew when I was looking at him, and I was able to sense when he was going to start letting me have it. This made him worse. "Get your ass over here, goddamn it!" he'd yell. "Now, for God's sake, try not to screw this up." The treks across the desert were the worst. We were more or less in a line, but you had to be careful not to block one another from the camera. I couldn't seem to manage this, so he finally put me in front. I was the leader! Oh my God!

It was a bright, sunny day out on a place called the Devil's Golf Course, not too far from Badwater, which is the lowest point below sea level in the Western Hemisphere. Jack had set the camera just where he wanted it and exclaimed, "Oh my God, Dobe has to be in the lead." Now I was nervous.

He said, "Hold up your right hand," so I did.

"Okay," he said, "see that big rock to your *right*. And then there is a smaller one to the left of the big one on *your right. Right?*"

"Yessir."

"Now, hold up your *left* hand." I did this.

"Now, head out towards the big rock until I yell 'Dobe' and then veer off to your *left* towards that little rock. Got that?"

"Yessir."

"We're rolling!"

Off I went in the lead. At least I didn't worry about covering Duke or Pete. They had to clear me. I knew Duke wouldn't have any trouble, but I wasn't so sure about Pete. He was still fussing and fuming about his goddamned outfit. We had only gotten about a quarter of the way, when the Old Man yelled "Cut!"

Back we headed toward the camera. I was terrified. He was yelling all kinds of terrible things at me. He pantomimed masturbation with an expression so loathsome that even in my teen years, I could never have looked that demented. Everyone giggled.

In the middle of this tantrum, Duke said very loudly, "He went right where you told him to!"

Well, that was really something—John Wayne riding to the rescue.

Ford stared calmly at Duke, and then with phony surprise said, "Ah ha—I forgot. Mr. Wayne here once produced a picture. So now he's decided to direct this one." Duke just wiped his face and looked exasperated, but I could have kissed him. Nothing more was said.

"Okay. We'll try it again." and he told me to go to a different rock.

Near the beginning of the story, the Kid gets shot in the shoulder and infection sets in. I had to keep remembering that I was slowly but surely dying. That was the last thing I had to worry about. Ford had that all mapped out! Jack never explained the reason he did things. He just did certain things to get results. So he made sure I died a little each and every day.

After about ten days or so, he thought up a little gag. He wasn't angry when he did this; in fact, it was a sort of signal that maybe there were better times to come—but don't depend on it. It started with the "baby" we carried in our arms. The doll was pretty worn-out, even when we got it. Some of the paint was beginning to wear off—it was a well-used baby. It was hard to keep believing this doll was really alive, and it was doubly hard to keep the top of its head from being exposed to the camera. It seemed as though I was always the one with the baby, and one day, Harvey Gould, the camera operator, said that he could see the doll's head above the blanket.

Jack pulled one of his surprises. He said, "Dobe. Come over here, kid."

So with the symbolic "Christ Child" in my arms, I walked over to him, expecting to be humiliated again, but he said, "Kid, Harvey says that the head shows. You have to remember to keep the head covered so he won't get sunstroke."

That's it? That's all there is?

Then he said, "Bend over."

What in the hell is this? I thought. But I did as he asked, and he gave me a swift, hard, kick in the ass. When I turned to look at him, he was smiling. "That's to keep you on your toes," he said.

And that's all there was to it. Thinking back on it, it seems a degrading thing, but I assure you, it was a bright moment and was done in fun. Sometimes he would have Duke do it. It embarrassed Duke.

Jack would preface it with, "Do you think Dobe needs waking up?"

No one would answer. Then he'd say, "Maybe we'd better give him a kick in the ass, just to be on the safe side." I accepted it like a schoolboy in the principal's office. I was sure as hell his student. I'm sure Audie Murphy never would have put up with that. Years later I worked with Audie and liked him very much. I'm sorry I never told him that story.

There were some unforgettable experiences on those sand dunes— some funny and some sad. One tragicomedy happening could have turned out to be very serious. In the film, there is a tremendous windstorm. God only knows how many shots we did trudging through it. The studio had sent up two huge, wooden airplane propellers. I'd guess they were each about eight feet from tip-to-tip, and they were encased in thick steel cages to keep us from getting our heads lopped off. They kicked up one hell of a storm when in operation. Sand was everywhere—in our eyes, ears, boots, our pants, everywhere! And on top of that, there was an honest-to-God natural sandstorm. Ford's Irish luck. And hot? It was hot—at least 130 degrees. Ford said it was about 85.

"It's not hot, for Gods' sake! Not hot enough!"

I thought, *Bullshit.*

In this sequence, the sand completely covers the three of us. Nothing shows but dunes. We had made little openings in the bedroll canvas to breathe through. The grips had a hell of a time with the reflectors, which raised the temperature even more. Every time this scene had to be reshot, one of the grips or propmen (I'm not sure which department shoveling comes under) had to shovel the sand back over us again. Then, with a piece of brush, he would smooth out the sand, and they would turn on the wind machines. The audience is not to know we are there. One take—it had to be one take, it took so long to get us ready. Ford was well-known for his "one takes," anyway.

In the story, our horses have run off during the storm. All's quiet, storm's over, the tableau is: nothingness. No life anywhere. The director shouts "Action!" Duke sits up first, wakes Pete up, then Pete sits up. They are both unaware that the horses are not there; they're just grateful to be alive. They both try to awaken me.

"Kid! Kid!" They shove me a few times, afraid I might not be alive. Then, I, very dizzy, in a daze, finally sit up, very groggy, holding my arm. They ask me if I'm all right, and I say something to the effect that "Yeah, I'm okay, but my arm throbs." *Then*—in the first take, I look around the campsite and, panic-stricken, shout the question, "Where did you picket the horses?"

Duke and Pete have a big, almost comedic argument and shouting match. End of scene. Aha—we did not get that far.

The handkerchief was in place in Jack's mouth. The neck tendons were pulsating in and out. I couldn't imagine what was wrong. It had felt really good, but instead of that wonderful word, "Right," he yelled, "Cut it, goddamn it!" just as I get out the word horses. He looked at Duke and Pete, making that awful face and gesture I hated so much.

"Dobe," he said, "after you say your first line, do *not*, I repeat, do *not* look all over Death-goddamned-Valley before you say, 'Where are the horses!' You know where the horses were tied. So just look at where they were supposed to be. See! (pointing) At that spot! Christ!"

And the handkerchief went back into the mouth.

"Here we go again. Say your first line, then the horses line, then look at where the horses were tied—not all over the place. Jesus! We're rolling! Okay, action!"

All is quiet. One—two—three—Duke and Pete sit up. They wake me up. So far so good. I sit up, answer their question about how I feel, then look around and say, "Where are the horses?"

He went *nuts!* He was ready for a straitjacket! Here comes the guy with the shovel. The whole routine again. Duke and Pete were being extremely sporting.

We go again. Action—one—two—three. Duke and Pete sit up. They wake me. I sit up. Answer their question about how I feel. Now, this time I *did* look to where the horses had been tied, and *then* I looked around for them. Isn't that logical? Not finding them at the place they were supposed to be, you would look to see if they were someplace else.

Pete and Duke were standing. I was still sitting down. Jack Ford picked up a very jagged rock about the size of a cantaloupe and threw it directly at my face! He was about twelve feet away, and directly on target, too, but I ducked. It didn't hit me, it hit the "Symbol of Mexico" about four inches from his cajones. He was almost an instant soprano. It broke the tension, and the whole crew started laughing hysterically. Pete went into a rage! It took a long time to get him under control. I got out of it that time, but more was to come later.

The full impact of the rock throwing didn't set in until we were all cooled off and back in our cabins. I must say that it was the cabin times that made the location bearable. After the work out there on the hot sand, we would head for the station wagon and hurry back to the oasis of the little green cabins. The Old Man would sit in the front seat, of course, with a very silent driver. Rarely did he turn around and say anything, and if he did, it was not to me. Duke and Pete and I would sit side-by-side in the backseat. No special car for Duke on a Ford show. Great big Duke, all six-four, 225, and Pedro, six-feet and 180 and constantly fighting his weight. He was a certified gourmet whom Jack called "Gordo" on occasion. Of course, I sat between them. I was the perfect middleman; six-one with my boots on and 150 wringing wet. I'd sit in that backseat and stare at the back of Jack's head and think to myself, *God, how I'd love to shoot that mean, sadistic bastard right between those Irish ears.* I knew he was thinking up stuff for the next day, because I hadn't broken and run yet. I didn't know what he wanted from me. The last thing he would usually say to me was an insult.

So the little green cabin was a welcome place. No cold beers, of course. Only the crew was allowed that. Duke always had Poland Spring Water from Maine sent up to location. Plain, not sparkling. He filled our ice boxes with it. For some reason, Duke and Pete always chose my cabin to congregate in after the day's work. Even though Ward shared it with me, he was usually off someplace, because he didn't work every day. Ford always took a nap before dinner, so the three of us had a couple of hours to ourselves. No, not the whole evening.

The three of us would sit on that screened porch, and it was wonderful. After all that happened each day, we would still laugh and laugh and drink Poland water with more joy than if it had been gin and tonic! Neither of those real pros ever attempted any coaching. I didn't get any sympathy, either, just warm compassion, and love, and understanding.

Duke would say, "Well, yer finally startin' ta'—catch on, aren't ya?"

"He ees doing a fantastic job! Pedro would say to Duke, and Duke would reply, "Yeah, but he sure as hell ain't gonna hear it from that Old Man! Ha, ha, ha."

"Will I ever?" I asked.

"Probably not," said Duke. "I wasn't too sure those first couple a days, 'Ol Dobe.' No—he won't tell ya.'—He won't ever tell ya'." Then the Wayne grin. "But ya' jes might work fer the old bastard again."

I couldn't believe my ears! "He likes me?" I couldn't believe it.

"Sure he likes ya'—Jesus—can't ya' tell?" Duke collapsed into roaring laughter, and so did Pete. I just sat there with my mouth hanging open.

One of the things I have been blessed with is my total inability to play cards or any "board" game, either, for that matter. During the first year of my marriage to Marilyn, she trounced me every single night at cribbage. That set the seal on what I already knew was a fact. Because of this, I didn't have to play cards with Jack Ford. Duke did. He had been playing cards with him since *Stagecoach*. Duke really loved to play cards; chess even more. He was good at both. But even between pictures, Duke was on call at any time to come to Ford's house for a game with him and a couple of his cronies. It cost Duke one hell of a lot to pay Jack back for what he did for him on *Stagecoach*. He never forgot what that movie had done for him and how Jack had fought to use him.

On this picture, though, it was dominoes. On the very first day Pete arrived, he had announced, "I am without question—oh, yes—the greatest domino player in all of Mexico." That got Ford's attention. "They say down in my country," Pete continued, "that it is wiser to fight the bravest bull at the Plaza de Toros than to play dominoes with Pedro Armendariz! Hee, hee, ha, ha, ho, ho, ho!" His laugh was right from the gut, sonorous and contagious. You could not help laughing when Pedro, with those huge, bright, brown flashing eyes and polished white teeth let himself go. Only Jack looked at him like a gunfighter at a prospective victim.

"Amigo," Jack said, "You are on. Every evening starting Monday after dinner. Me and you and Duke and—My God, I guess Bond. Melwood here (indicating me—I was not Dobe yet) can be water boy."

And so it was dominoes every night after our Poland Water, a shower, and dinner. And I was water boy! I had to keep their glasses filled with ice water, just like a waiter—back and forth from the kitchen. I thought about draping a towel over my arm, but decided it might not be too wise a move.

It was fun, though. First off, I found out that the Old Man cheated. He peeked at other players' tiles whenever he could, and used other forms of "gamesmanship." Once Duke asked Pete to please let Jack win so he'd be nicer the next day.

Pete's answer, of course, was, "Are you keeding for Christ's sake! To hell with heem!"

My roommate, Ward, played "Pearly" Sweet, the sheriff who headed the posse that was after us. Some of Ford's regulars were in that posse: Hank Worden, Fred Libby, and future star Ben Johnson. If you had told Ben back then that he was going to win an Academy Award someday, he'd have sure called you plumb crazy. We saw very little of Ward and his posse, except at dinner time. They only come into the story off and on, so they spent their days up at the big pool at the Furnace Creek Inn. There was no pool down where we were. The Old Man referred to the posse as the "brown-assed" boys. On the few days that they were to work for him, rather than the "second unit," Jack would say, "Well, well, tomorrow the 'brown-assed' boys have to work." He didn't count the second unit as work. Ben was not included in the "pool bunch." He hung out with the stuntmen and the wranglers.

Supporting actors often take a lot of ribbing from the stars because of the frequency of their days off. That's one of the most common conversations in the picture business. There you are on a shooting day, already in the bar, two or three drinks ahead when the company gets in from shooting. That is, of course, on a non-Ford movie. Some of those movies were not worth going to see, either. On a Ford film, there was never any doubt. Everyone was always "on call."

One day after work, Duke and Pedro were in my cabin drinking Poland Water and shooting the breeze, when we heard a car sliding to a halt on the gravel driveway. Like a shot, Duke was at the porch screen, peering out. After a couple of seconds, his face alive with anticipation, he quickly motioned for us to join him, putting his finger to his lips for us to keep quiet. Lo and behold, there was huge, bearlike, ex-football tackle Ward Bond, in a silk Japanese kimono, sitting behind the wheel of a station wagon as though he owned it. Beside him was a blond, very frail young girl, wearing rimless eyeglasses. She looked to be about twenty. I would cast her as a kindergarten teacher. It was worse to see than Fay Wray with King Kong. Without warning, Ward made his move. He gathered her up in his arms. All you could see was the top of her head! Bending the poor girl back over his lap, he smothered her face with his ample lips. Her glasses were long gone.

Duke looked at us like he was going to vomit and exclaimed, "How can she *kiss* that son-of-a-bitch?" Then he yelled out really loud, "What are you doing, Ward?"

Ward, who hadn't figured us to be home from shooting yet, shoved the girl back up into a sitting position, snapped a quick good-bye, and rushed into our cabin.

"What the hell are you assholes doing here?" he shouted.

"I live here, Ward," I said.

"I don't mean you, you red-headed pisspot" (he always called me that, even when he wasn't mad). "I mean these other two asses!" He was boiling mad, and I knew he wanted to take Duke on right then and there. It would not have been the first time. He was Duke's closest friend.

"Who the hell are you calling a ass, you ugly asshole?—and how can a poor decent girl even kiss such an ugly bastard?" yelled Duke back at him. He was doubled over with laughter and having a marvelous time because he had caught Ward off-guard. He'd made Ward look stupid, and that was one of his favorite sports. Ward huffed and puffed some more, called Duke a few more horrible names, but Duke waved him off, and Ward let it go.

Nat King Cole had a big hit record out while we were filming, called "Nature Boy." Ward sang it all day long. I am sure Ward thought he sang it better than Nat, but he sang it in the style of Louis Armstrong. He actually did a pretty good rendition. Hearing that song always makes me feel like I'm back in Death Valley.

The after-dinner domino games were picking up in intensity. The pairings were always the same: Jack and Duke against Pedro and poor Ward. I should not find it necessary to say "poor Ward." You never had to feel sorry for Ward Bond. He was as indestructible as an army tank. Ford's barbs and salvos just bounced right off him—stinging shots that would have withered anyone else for the rest of the night. And being the partner of "the greatest domino player in all of Mexico" was no cakewalk, either. If Ward made a wrong move, he got blasted from Pete. I was really beginning to look forward to the evening wars. Uncle Jack was saying things to me like, "That's a good boy," or "Ol' Dobe knows how to do it," when I brought the water. For the first time, he was calling me "Ol' Dobe." Maybe what Duke had told me was true, after all! He wasn't just trying to boost my spirits.

One night they were in the middle of a really hot game. Pete was sitting to the Old Man's right. I noticed with amusement that Uncle Jack, pipe in mouth and his ever-present dark glasses on, making it was hard to tell where he was looking, was leaning back in his chair sneaking a peek at Pedro's dominoes. This time, Pete caught him red-handed!

"Ah-hah!" he shouted. "You want to see my hand? You want to see my hand? Well, have a good look at eet!"

And with that, he threw the whole rack of domino tiles at Uncle Jack and made direct hit on his chest. All movement stopped in the room. Everyone waited to see what Jack would do.

He looked at Duke and said, "This goddamned Mexican has gone completely nuts. First he doesn't like his wardrobe; then he doesn't like his horse; then he doesn't like his goddamn dialogue. Now he doesn't want to play dominoes anymore because he's losing. For Christ's sake—I mean!" And he got up and went to bed. I thought for sure that would be the end of the dominoes, but no, they were hot and heavy at it the next night, as though nothing had happened.

Getting aboard a horse in a scene can sometimes be the biggest problem of the day when shooting a western. Even with experienced riders, there are many reasons why this happens. In the first place, movie horses get the smarts real quick about the cue "flee the scene." One situation that drives directors crazy is the classic scene where guys come flying out of the saloon or sheriff's office, mount up, and ride hell-bent-for-leather out of town. Ninety-nine percent of the time, depending on the number of men flying out of the door, some of them don't manage to get mounted. The director better "print it," if by some miracle he gets it the first time, because he may never get the shot again. The basic cause of this age-old western problem is this: horses are creatures of habit. If a horse learns how to do a certain thing, it takes a trainer ten times longer to make him unlearn it. Now he's learned that when you run toward him from the door to the tie-rail, he's supposed to run off with you. And he's right. But if the other riders are quicker and beat you getting on and taking off, your horse won't wait for you to get on. He wants to go like hell and catch his buddies. You have to try to keep him still while you get on and the others are roaring down the street or you have to get on him on the fly. That's mighty hard to do, and takes a lot of luck, no matter how good a rider you are. I used to hate being in those scenes, but they are fun to watch. One or two of the horses usually farts, and if it happens to be your horse, for the same reason you always feel like it was you who did it.

The day after the domino fiasco, Pedro had to get on his horse in the scene, and he had a horrible time. He looked like he was trying to climb the Matterhorn.

Ford asked, "What seems to be the problem?" He was smiling, "I suppose you're going to tell me it's your pants."

"Yes, yes, yes," screamed Pedro. "You have heet the goddamned nail on the head this time, Jack! I can hardly walk een theese damn pants you're making me wear. Can't you tell I have a hard time walking and keeping up? I cannot take normal steps!"

"Well for now, just get on your horse, for Christ's sake. And shut up—I mean—Jesus, Pete!"

"Ah-hah!—that ees another thing, Jack! I am a *walking hardware store!* You have so much crap hanging on theese bloody harse." Even though Pete spoke excellent English, he always pronounced "is" as "ees" and "horse" as "harse." With each complaint, Ford would find something more to hang from his saddle.

"I can't get my leg over theese bedroll," he'd yell. Another pot was added. The heat was off me for awhile because of Pete's antics.

Pedro was an authority on the history of Mexico. A few years later, I saw his very impressive library in his beautiful home in Mexico City. He used to lecture about Mexican history during our leisure hours. It was never boring. Nothing Pete did was ever boring.

There was this piece of dialogue in the middle of the big windstorm. Pete had to say to Duke, referring to the wind, that it was, "What they call in my country a Santana, from the clouds of dust that follow the cavalry of the illustrious General Santa Ana." This is a wind that comes off the Southern California desert. The weathermen on TV say "Santa Anna." It was named after the infamous Mexican President-Dictator, General Santa Anna. He is remembered by Americans for his part in the Battle of the Alamo. Politically, Pedro considered himself a liberal, not only concerning his government, but ours as well. He used to say to me, "Don't ever discuss politics with Duke. Eet screws up the whole party!" It was good advice.

So—the big problem was not the wind machines breaking down, not having to smooth out the sand, not me hiding from the camera's "eye." No. The big problem was Pedro! He did *not* want to say the line and speak of the General as "illustrious." Over the howling wind, he told this to Jack.

"What?!" screamed Jack.

"Jack, Jack," Pete screamed back. "I cannot say theese line. And—hah—I weel not say theese line!"

"Let me hear the line," screamed Ford.

"No. I weel not say eet."

Ford got up from his chair and yelled, "stop the goddamned wind machines. I mean, Jesus." Then he asked Pat Kelly, the script supervisor, to read him the line.

Pat read the line again out loud.

Ford turned to Pete, "You're trying to tell me that you won't say that line?"

Pete replied, "That ees right, Jack."

"Why not, for God's sake? I mean, that's in there for a reason. That's what the guy would say. I don't give a shit what you *want*. That's the line, so shut up and say it!"

"Jack, you do not seem to understand. That Santa Anna was a shiiiit! He was a no-good bastard!"

Ford, never raising his voice said, "Pete, that's your line. You're costing the studio a goddamned fortune, for Christ's sake. So say the goddamned line."

But Pedro would not be denied. He started stomping around in circles. He shouted in Spanish. He threw up his hands in despair. "You do not understand, Jack. My people weel not understand! That line makes them think Santa Anna was a nice guy. To name a wind after heem—it's an insult to my country!"

Then Jack, with great patience and sincerity, said, "I love your country, too. Mexico is a great country with great people. I used to say you were a great actor. Now, I'm going to say that you are the biggest pain in the ass I ever directed! You're worse than Bond! Now say the goddamn line the way it was written! All right. We are rolling. Action!"

Pete read the line perfectly, with great feeling, but he muttered to whomever would listen to him all afternoon.

Later on that day, during a quiet moment, Ford came up and tickled him under the chin. "Thank you, Gordo. Tonight you do not have to sneak a milkshake. You can have one on me for the 'Santana' line."

"Ha-Ha. Great—terrific!" Pete answered, but there was no joy in his exclamation. He had a milkshake as soon as we got in.

Along with the trials and tribulations of being a player for John Ford, there were woven into the fabric of his artistic endeavors many moments, and often whole days, of great joy. Upon arriving on the set, you would feel right away that something special was going to happen. You would feel spiritually awakened all of a sudden, a kindred spirit with Uncle Jack. That feeling has never happened to me again on any set. There was always music coming from the accordion of a little Italian-American named Danny Borzage. He played the accordion on every John Ford picture. I have no idea on which movie Danny began with the Old Man. He had a sort of childlike quality; almost ageless. He never complained about anything. He certainly was not a particularly good accordion player, but his music moved you. It wouldn't be a Ford set without his sound, a plaintive sadness that pulled at your heart, that made you feel, "Thank God I'm here to do a scene for that Old Man in the chair by the camera."

It was one of those days that I arrived out there on the hot sand dunes. Because of the heat, we would shoot from 8:00 in the morning until 11:00, go back "home" for lunch, back out at 3:00, and work until 5:30 or 6:00. June, the month with the longest days, we could easily have worked till

7:30. Any other director would have, but not Uncle Jack. He wanted his nap.

Uncle Jack sauntered up to me with a hint of a smile on his Irish kisser and said, "Do you know the 'Streets of Laredo'?"

"Of course," I said. "I mean, yessir, I—I—I—know it, yessir."

"I hear you're scared to sing in front of people," he said.

"Uh, sometimes. Yessir," I said.

"Well," he ordered, "climb up on that parallel. Go on kid, get your skinny ass up there, and sing 'The Streets of Laredo' for all of us here!"

Thank God he didn't tell everyone to be quiet and listen. Danny started playing it on his accordion while I climbed up onto the platform.

"My God, you know it!" Ford teased Borzage. "That the right key?"

I said, "Yessir," cleared my throat, and nodded to Danny to start again from the beginning. I sang the hell out of that old song! The Old Man had made me do it just when he knew the moment was right. I had sung in a movie before; part of a cowboy song in *Red River,* just before Duke rides into the scene. But that was nothing like this, up there in front of the whole crew. I gained confidence as I went along. The song has many verses, but I only sang the first and last that Burl Ives had taught me in 1940. When I finished, everyone on the set applauded.

Now it was time to film the scene. In it, I ask Duke if I can hold the baby. It's the first time the Kid wakes up to the fact that he will die soon. He sits on a little chair in the shade of the wagon and reaches out. Duke gently places the child in the Kid's arms. The Kid looks at his godson for a moment and starts to hum a tune. Then he rises and begins to sing the song as he walks unsteadily around the camp area. It was pure Ford. The moaning wind, the canvas slapping at the rear of the wagon, Duke and Pedro transfixed, worrying about their godson until they're taken over by the sadness of the song. It was beautiful! Except, dumb me, kept using up the real estate that was outside the focus of the lens! Jack had carefully mapped out the exact route I should take. He did not have his handkerchief in his mouth, and he was not mumbling. I should have understood him easily, but I was so overcome with the moment and the singing of the song that I didn't pay attention to where I was going. The shot, though emotionally moving, was worthless.

"Oh my God!" he cried. "Where's Audie! He knows how to take orders! Do you see that black thing right there with the glass pointing at you, dumbbell? I mean—film, by the time it's developed, costs thirty-seven cents a foot, and I'm wasting it on you!"

I distinctly remember the 37 cents. I can't imagine what color film must cost today. I was getting paid $350 a week. At least I was cheap. He was mad at me again, and I don't blame him. Even Duke was mad this time. He told me so later, in no uncertain terms.

"Kid, when you were doin' that song—geez, I mean, the first time ya' did it, it was terrific! But, Christ, you were outa' the goddamned picture half the time! The second time you were *thinkin'* too much! Stop thinkin' so much an' jes *do* it, goddamnit. Let that Old Man do the thinking. Yer not gettin' paid ta' think—yer gettin' paid ta' act! You were wanderin' all over the friggin' set!" He gave me a punch on the shoulder. "You were too wide on the turns, Ol' Dobe." He sure was right.

If the Old Man had thrown a rock during that scene, I wouldn't have blamed him. But he didn't—he just got meaner after every take. Every time we had to reshoot the scene, I'd ask Danny to lower the key. I was seething mad at myself and Ford, and as a result, my throat was closing up shop. By the time he said the magic word, "Right!" I sounded like a record winding down. The movie critic of the *New Yorker* magazine wrote, "Harry Carey, Jr., croaked a western dirge." That scene is still painful for me to watch.

There is one scene in *3 Godfathers* that is so overpowering, it's worth renting the movie just to watch that scene alone. Duke returns to Pete and me, having discovered the lonely covered wagon with the woman inside.

"She's gonna' have a baby!" he gasps. "She's gonna' have it now!" It was a privilege to be able to share that scene with him.

Now a word about whether John Wayne was really an "actor" or not. I know he once said, "I'm a re-actor." Well, he was that, too, but Duke was a terrific actor. You only had to play one reasonably well-written scene with him to find that out. How does one define an actor? In the true sense of the word, an actor is a highly trained individual who, through the use of makeup and a characterization, becomes someone other than himself and makes the audience believe it. My little dictionary says simply: "One that acts," or "one that acts a part." So there you have it. Impersonators today don't have the screen personalities to imitate like they did when Gable, Tracy, Bogart, Hepburn, and Cooper were in their prime. It's hard to do a take-off on today's leading men and women. Duke became one of their favorites to imitate. He had his own very special persona, and he is still being imitated today.

There is a scene where we are well into our trek and have only a few drops of water left. Duke says that the little that is left "goes to the Kid." He takes his machete and begins to lop the top off of a barrelhead cactus, and he reaches in and pulls out some of the pulp. He starts to squeeze it into the canteen I am holding. Duke was a pretty good squeezer with those huge paws of his, but alas, nothing was dripping into the canteen. Before Ford could even make a comment, a voice filled with authority came from the back of the set. "You can't get any water out of that kind of cactus!"

Jack slowly turned in his chair and asked, "Who in the hell said that?"

The same voice answered, "I did, Mr. Ford. That barrelhead cactus has some moisture in it but you'll never get it to drip into that canteen."

The man who came forward turned out to be the park ranger of Death Valley, Stan Jones. He was a husky man of medium height, with a friendly smile.

"Who the hell are you?" said Jack, "and what makes you a goddamn authority on cactus?"

"It's my job, sir," replied Jones. "No water in that cactus." Jack asked his name and was very polite to him. They talked for awhile and Stan left, but it would not be the last we saw of Stan Jones.

Jack moved on to the next setup and left the cactus. In this scene, I read out of the baby book written by the Dr. Spock of the 1870s. The three godfathers are really in a jam in this sequence. We're out there in this blinding heat, and we have a newborn baby on our hands. Fortune smiles on us a little, though, because Pedro has found a small trunk in the wagon with baby supplies, including canned milk. We start the first rehearsal. We all have lines and it's going well, then we come to the part where I find the page in the book titled "bathing the baby." Duke's holding the "baby," Pete is listening, and I'm reading haltingly out of the book. There are two more rehearsals. All is going well. No problems.

The Old Man says, "All right, we are rolling. Action!"

Now the words that I have to read are neatly typed and pasted to a page on the inside of this old prop book that's supposed to be the baby book. Very thoughtful of the prop man, and very easy for me. It's going too well.

Ford yells, "Wait a minute. Stop! You're not reading that, are you?"

I replied, "Well—heh—heh—heh—sort of. I mean, I can't help it."

Duke says, "Oh, shit."

I could barely hear it, but it didn't help my morale. He and Pete exchanged glances of pity and turned their backs. Jack yanked the book from my grasp, turned to another page, and said to me, "Now read!" He stuck his handkerchief into his mouth and sat down to have some fun. "Start again. Action!"

This time I fooled him; I had the whole passage memorized! Something had told me to learn it when I was still at home, working on my lines. It didn't surprise him—nothing ever did. We finished the scene, and he said the magic word, "Right." He and Duke exchanged a smile.

The next day we returned to the cactus. Same deal. I'm holding the canteen; Duke reaches into the cactus, gets a fistful of pulp and squeezes. The water, gently but steadily, starts dripping into the canteen. We finished the scene. The Old Man yelled, "Right Where the hell is that ranger who said there wasn't any water in that cactus?"

Standing away off in the distance, smoking a Camel, was Stan. Jack acted surprised to see him when he arrived at his chair.

"Oh my God," he said. "I mean, I'm really thrilled you're here Ranger Jones. Duke—Dobe—do that scene we just shot for Ranger Jones here." So we redid it, and Jack said, "Did you see that, Jones? There's *water* in that goddamn cactus. You told me yesterday that there wasn't any."

Jones was smart enough to laugh it off with a smile and a shrug. He knew full well that Jack had had the "green man" soak the cactus in a bucket of water all night. In truth, however, many a dying man's life has been saved by sucking the sticky fluid out of the barrelhead cactus. It just won't drip the way Ford wanted it to.

Duke was a terrific swimmer. So was Pete, and so was I. One night, the Old Man said to us, "Tomorrow I'll be using the 'brown-assed' boys, so you have the day off."

The next afternoon we got a studio car to take us up to the pool at the inn. We were like kids—Duke was 41, Pete 36, and I was 27. We splashed one another, pushed one another under water, and shoved one another off the diving board. We had a hell of a time, laughing and talking about all the crises during the shooting. In those days, everybody smoked. You were either odd or in training, if you didn't. But Duke! He lit one Camel off another all day long. We used to raise hell with him about it.

"You're not patting me down already? It's only ten-thirty in the morning, and you're already out?" He'd start toward, you patting the pockets on his vest or pants with a big grin on his face, trying to make you think he'd forgotten his.

"Hell-ooo, Ol' Dobe," he'd say. Then he'd start searching you like a detective looking for dope in one of today's TV shows. When I'd give him one, he'd say, "Jesus, how can you smoke these (meaning the brand) goddamn things? I'll give you a pack tomorrow."

He never did so, but I found a remedy for that problem. One day I was passing his dressing room—the kind that is on coasters and is on the sound stage. The door was open, and I looked in. He wasn't there, but his cigarettes were! Right there on his dressing room table were five cartons of Camels. He'd posed for an ad for them. I just took a carton to my own dressing room, and then, when he wanted a cigarette, I gave him one of his own! He finally said, "Ya' finally learned to smoke the best cigarette!"

The reason I bring all this up is because I thought I was some sort of champ at staying underwater a long time. I figured that because of the way Duke smoked and the fact that his only exercise was playing cards, I could easily beat him swimming underwater. So, as we were splashing around, I said to Duke, "I'll bet I can swim underwater in this pool longer than you can."

"What? Hah—hah—hah. You have ta' be kiddin,' friend! You are *on!*" I really did think I could beat him; after all, I was younger, and I exercised a lot more than he did. I played golf and tennis, and rode horseback. It was a very big pool. My turn first. I swam up and back twice and then another half. I ran out of air and surfaced.

"Not too bad, for a skinny guy," he commented and jumped in. He then went almost twice as far! I couldn't believe it! He didn't razz me or brag—he just knew what he could do. It never occurred to me that his lung capacity was over twice mine and that he'd been diving for abalone off Catalina Island for years.

Well, we were coming down the home stretch. Location shooting was almost ended, but my dying scene was yet to come. Under any condition, the movie acting business is never a walk in the park if you are playing one of the leads. It's a hit-or-miss proposition. If you're a hit, you're off to the races. You get a brand-new contract, a brand-new car, a brand-new house—sometimes even a brand-new wife. The one who went through hell with you won't do anymore. All of this can happen to you, if you're a big hit in a picture with a superstar like John Wayne. But if you're simply good or not bad, forget all that. It's back to earth again. Back to calling your agent, back to interviews and screen tests, back to waiting for days while "they" make up their minds. "Shall we use the kid we've already got under contract or go with this young Carey kid? He was good in the test, but his agent wants five bills a week. Our kid's sitting on his ass, plus we're only paying him seventy-five." All of these thoughts were going through my head as we drove out to the Devil's Golf Course, 200 feet below sea level and 126 degrees under the beach umbrella where the camera sat patiently waiting to photograph me dying.

I was ready for it. Bring on the old bastard! He had even been nice the day before, after Pete almost pulled out all of my hair in the scene where he tries to make me drink from the canteen.

"Well," I thought, "I ain't giving you one chance to be mean and sadistic today. You think you have to beat it out of me, Mr. Ford? Put your handkerchief away. I'm ready. One take!" I really couldn't wait to do it! "Wait till you see the first run-through."

Here we are! Out of the car! There's the music! Thanks, Danny. "As I walked out on the streets of Laredo" I'm already starting to cry. There's Jack pointing to "the spot." The camera's ready! Everyone is ready! I'm ready!

He yells, "Lie down. Right there!" I did what he told me. He put Pete on his knees beside me with the Bible. Duke is standing, legs wide apart, holding his western hat up in the air to shield my face from the sun.

"All right, let's hear it! Let me see what you're made of!"

I must admit that was a good punch. I felt that one, but no matter; I took it well. I was still ready to surprise him.

It is an incredible tableau—the three of us in this inferno—starkly beautiful. I did the scene for John Ford, the greatest director in Hollywood, with John Wayne, the biggest movie star, shading my face with his hat!

When I finished, before anyone had a chance to move, the thought sped through my brain, "I had no idea I could be this good! God, that was fantastic!"

What I heard from *him* was, "Well, Jesus-H-Christ. Now we are really up shit creek! Well, it's too late to get Audie. I mean—what are we going to do with you kid? Huh? I mean…"

It was never really what he actually said to you: it was the way he said it.

"My God, son, we're trying our damndest to make a good movie here! This is the high point of the whole goddamned picture!"

I was so flabbergasted that all I could say was, "I'm sorry. I thought…"

"You're sorry! And you thought what?" he screamed "Jesus, I'm the one who's sorry! *You're sorry.* Christ—I mean…"

In truth, I believe any other director would have been happy with my work that morning. Duke said later that day, "You didn't think you could get away unscathed did ya'?" Jack had been waiting for this day, and he was not to be denied, no matter how good I was. I had had his wrath brought down on me before, God knows, but never like this day. Never like this big scene. He started calling me everything he could think of—accused me of everything he could think of.

Then he said, "You haven't got any guts. You're a coward, and you're yellow!"

I sat up and said to him, "You can call me a lousy actor, but goddamn it, don't call me yellow!"

"Then lie back down there, goddamn it, and die like a man. Goddamn it, I want to see you die. So die for me, for Christsakes, and make us all right here believe it!"

Then he turned around. The whole company was there, watching. I felt like I was in the middle of some early Roman games, and it was thumbs down.

"Walk away from him," he yelled to Slim Hightower, who was bringing me a drink of water.

"Leave the bastard the hell alone. Let him lay out there in the sun for awhile and think about the goddamned scene. Then we'll come back and see if he can possibly do it. Leave him lay. Walk away. That means everybody!"

So everybody walked away—way back to where the location trucks were parked. I lay there, squinting up at the bright sky. My mouth got so dry I couldn't swallow. My back was on fire. That salt flat was so hot I felt I was in a frying pan. I was there about 30 minutes, and by then, I didn't care if I did die, but I still wanted to be very good for him! There we were, just me and the camera. It looked lonesome. They must have unloaded it. At 130 degrees, the film would melt into a glob.

Finally—finally, here they came back. I heard later that some of the crew had gone over to Wingate and threatened to quit if Jack didn't let up, but the Old Man was boss, and they had to go along.

"Okay, okay, let's get this thing over with." He leaned over me. "How do you feel now, huh? How do you feel now, kid? Are you going to play the goddamn scene, or are you going to chicken out on me? Maybe it would be better to just say, the hell with it, and send you home, eh?" He kicked me on the hip with the side of his foot, just to get my attention. He yelled out, "Quiet on the set! This will be picture!" He was enjoying himself. "Everybody ready? We are rolling!"

The voice of the soundman, "Speed."

Ford: "Action!"

At last. It wasn't me talking. I heard a voice I'd never heard before, the voice of a dying young man. Who was this? It was like I was outside myself. The broken sentences went on, one after the other, until the last, "God bless Momma and Poppa, and make me a good boy. Amen."

It was over. Duke lifted me to my feet. He had his arms around me, holding me up. Ford took my face in his hands. He was smiling, "Why didn't you do that the first time? See how easy it was? You done Good! That's a wrap!"

I wandered around, delirious, until Pete pointed me to the station wagon. I knew I had passed the test. From now on, it would be different.

Every evening, on any film, the assistant director hands out the next day's shooting schedule. It's loaded with information. It can make you feel happy, and you love the rest of the evening, or it can give you the "yips." This is on an ordinary film, not a Ford production. The next day's schedule has it on the time of your call, if you're working, or "hold," which means no work. With "hold" you can take off and do what you want. Then there are the letters WN— "will notify." This means that Production must know where you are at all times. If you want to run to the store, call the office so they won't wet their pants when you don't answer your phone. With Uncle Jack, they printed those things, but we never bothered to look at them. With Ford, you were always on call. He'd suddenly get an idea and say "Get me Bond. God help us."

So the day after my "death," Duke and Pete and I were coming out of the restaurant, calmly picking our teeth after breakfast. We were heading for makeup. Out from his cabin comes Jack. "You guys going home dressed in those dirty old clothes?" Wow! We couldn't believe our ears. Uncle Jack said, "Tell Wingate that you guys can go home. Give my love to everybody. I have to go over to Lone Pine and shoot a sequence with Bond, God help me, and the rest of the 'brown-assed' boys. That long sequence with the sheriff's posse at the train station." He said all this to Duke, like he was our leader—which he was.

In less than an hour, we were in the limo with a studio driver; a great big Lincoln Continental with "factory air" conditioning and all the other fancy extras. I couldn't believe it. I thought I was dreaming. As soon as the driver shifted into high, Duke let out a cowboy yell, just as he did years later, as Rooster Cogburn. The miles ticked off and we were yapping our heads off. Duke suddenly turned to the driver and said, "Listen, friend. If ya' come across a little store or somethin' that looks like it jes' might have some drinkin' whiskey, waal, how's about pullin' over an' lettin' me out?"

It wasn't long before we stopped. We got out; Duke signed a few autographs, bought some Camels; and the nice lady put a bottle of "Who-hit-John" in a brown paper sack. Off we started again. Never, ever, in all my born days has a drink of booze tasted so good. We only had a pint, so it went pretty fast, but it was just the right amount. The girls were waiting for us at home.

The rest of the company returned home in a couple of days, and shooting resumed on the old RKO Pathé lot in Culver City. I look back now on this time as one of the most proud and satisfying periods of my life. I will never forget my first day on a John Ford set inside of a big soundstage. As I opened the heavy door and stepped inside, I felt as though I were entering a sacred place. Danny Borzage's music was floating over the top of the controlled bustle. "Something beautiful is happening here." You didn't have to see him to know he was there. In all the years I worked for him, that feeling never changed.

I knew immediately that this was going to be different from location. This man with his Irish cap and his pipe; a trace of a smile; rarely the handkerchief, was a John Ford I had never seen before. He was much more relaxed—a different man. He kidded around a lot. You really had to screw it up for him to get nasty on the soundstage. However, if a producer or studio head came on the set, he stopped shooting. He was neater and cleaner, too. He was never in a lousy mood when he wore that 1930s tweed cap. I loved to see him wear that.

He had small, delicate feet and hands, and was amazingly graceful. He also had eyes in the back of his head. Ben and Duke and I always kidded about that. You'd never see him look at you. You could be yards behind his back, and he'd catch you fooling around with a rope or whispering, and sure as shootin', he'd call out your name.

"Why don't you hang around the camera? You might learn something."

I never let him out of my sight when I was making a picture with him.

Duke used to say, "Jesus Christ, what a football coach he would have made. He'd make a damned high school team beat the Rams!"

It's almost the truth. Even when I was a boy and he made his periodic pilgrimages to the ranch, I only remember his wicked wit and sarcasm. But now! This was truly "Uncle Jack." This was the reason he wanted me to call him that.

When shooting at the studio, Uncle Jack always had lunch brought into his office: pastrami sandwiches with all the trimmings. He never went to the commissary. A few of the principals in the cast would have their lunch there with him, and many times there would be some other star besides Duke, visiting the Old Man. Boy, did I feel like a bigshot! I was all swelled up on myself, actually, but I didn't know it at the time. This was heady stuff for a young actor with hardly any experience. Jack would say something lousy to Duke occasionally, for the benefit of the guest, as if to say, "Look how I handle this big guy I made a star of." Well, at least it wasn't me. Duke could take it. He wasn't embarrassed. He was used to it.

About the third day of interior shooting, I had a big scene to do with Duke and Pedro. The day before, the wonderful actress Mildred Natwick had done a fantastic scene as the dying mother of our godson, and Uncle Jack had been knocked over by it. I felt it was a hard act to follow. I was just wiping the mustard off my fingers, there in his office, when he said to me, "Know your words?"

"Yessir."

"Well, let's hear 'em."

So I did the whole speech just as though I were in front of the camera. He looked right at Duke (I'll never forget this), and they exchanged big smiles.

"That's fine," he said. "Let's go shoot it."

The soundstage was covered with sand, brush, tumbleweed, cactus, and everything else needed to make it look like a desert. There sat the old covered wagon with a lantern shining from within. They don't bring the outside inside much anymore. It's too expensive. Nowadays, they leave the outside outside and actors go to it. The "inside" is usually a private home in whatever town they are shooting the "outside." Not many sets are built today, except for a successful series.

One day, I went over to the set, even though I knew I was out of the story; but you never knew, and besides, by now, I really didn't want it to end. I felt like I was going to be a movie star. I'd made a movie for Raoul Walsh called *Pursued,* a couple of years before, but not much had come from that. And then I did *Red River.* This was different. I was truly grateful for the opportunity of a lifetime. Very few young actors get the break I had been given. Now Marilyn and Mom wouldn't have to worry about my future. Yep! I was the Star of Tomorrow! What a wonderful world it was! I wished I could put on some weight and muscle and look more like a real leading man.

"Well," I thought, "Jimmy Stewart is skinny, and he's doing all right. Sure, he's handsome, but can he sing?"

Composer-conductor Richard Hageman was doing the score for the picture. Strangely enough, Maestro Hageman had given me my first voice lesson. No less a personage that Kurt Weill had sent me to him. Uncle Jack had him playing the piano in the saloon when Duke comes staggering in on Christmas Eve with the baby. Duke turns around from the bar, greets Ward, who has just come in to arrest him, and passes out from exhaustion. In the version Jack did with my father, he dies there and that's the end of the movie, but the Old Man gave this one a happy ending. I liked the first ending better, and so did Duke; but what the hell, folks all over the country still love that movie. It plays a lot during the Christmas season.

Anyway, this afternoon I had been on the set a very long time and nothing was going on. This wasn't normal procedure. It was very relaxed: guys were telling jokes, throwing the baseball back and forth, and generally horsing around. I was on about my fifth cup of coffee, and still Uncle Jack wasn't on the set. I went out the stage door and into the narrow street that separates the sound stages, headed for the men's room. Suddenly I stopped dead in my tracks! There, parked by the entrance, was a pickup truck and horse trailer with the Fat Jones' logo. There, tied to the trailer, was a stately and proud old buckskin horse with a long, black mane and tail. He was beautifully groomed, the dapple marks shined through his summer coat. It was Sunny, my Dad's last and best horse. He said hello to me the way a horse does when he's glad to see a friend—a couple of low, snorty rumbles from deep inside. I went over and leaned against him and patted him on his breast. Old Hank Potts was there, with a stiff brush in his hand. In a moment, Uncle Jack came up from behind. Cliff Lyons was with him, and he was dressed in clothes like my father wore.

Uncle Jack turned me around by the shoulders and gently said, "Go home, kid. You're not supposed to see this." Those were his last orders. I was finished with the *3 Godfathers*.

I simply said, "Okay. Thanks, Uncle Jack," and headed for the car. Then I began to cry. I couldn't stop. It was a while before I could trust myself to drive down Washington Boulevard. Sunny, very old—in his mid-twenties—doing his last movie—with Cliff on his back. What Jack shot that day was Cliff riding to the crest of a hill. He pushes his hat back on his head and leans back with his right hand on Sunny's rump. He looks off into the sunset. On the screen appears:

TO THE MEMORY OF HARRY CAREY
BRIGHT STAR OF THE EARLY WESTERN SKY.

Myself When Young With Cowboys and Navajos

My father didn't know anything about movie stars, because he didn't give a damn about the movies. He said he just made them for money to buy things. I'm sure in the early days, twenty-five years before, when he and John Ford were writing and shooting films together, it was fun for him. He always said when I was growing up, "You kids go to the show. I've got a hell of a good book. You should read more books and learn the truth about the West. The movies screw it up. They make Billy the Kid a goddamn hero. He was nothing but a juvenile delinquent."

Pop was a Western convert from the East. If he told you something about Western lore, he was usually correct. He had read every book on the West he could get his hands on. When he was sixteen, he saw Pawnee Bill's Western Tent Show. I think it even predated Buffalo Bill Cody and his show. It was the first time he had ever seen a Western saddle or anyone wearing a cowboy hat and carrying six-guns. The bug bit him.

My father's real name was Henry Dewitt Carey, and he was born on January 16, 1878, on 116th Street in New York City. It's Harlem now, but at that time it was a rural neighborhood. His father was a Judge of Special Sessions in White Plains, New York, and also president of the New Home Sewing Machine Company, so they were pretty well off. When my father was six, the judge moved the family up to City Island, which is above the Bronx near Pelham Bay Park. It was a wonderful life for my dad, growing up there. City Island's trades were boat building and fishing. He learned early that if you needed a little pocket money, you dug a bucket of littleneck clams and sold them to a housewife for her old man's dinner.

After grammar school, my father went to Hamilton Military Academy, where he graduated as Cadet Captain. He had an appointment to West Point, but went to New York University instead. He got expelled, though, because he ran the "picnic bloomers" of the madam of the local whorehouse up the campus flagpole. That probably wouldn't get a kid kicked out today. He made it into law school anyway, and was in the class with the infamous future mayor of New York City, James J. Walker, "Beau James."

Pop never took the bar exam because he fell overboard from a schooner he had in Long Island Sound and almost died from pneumonia. In fact, his lungs never fully recovered from that long battle for his life. It was boredom from lying in bed that got him writing. He wrote a play called *Montana,* and then toured with it for about three years. He played the lead, of course, and he had a live horse on the stage. He made a quarter of a million dollars before he was thirty. He was a Western star who had never been West. Years later, a writer named Max Miller called him the "Bronx Cowboy."

In the meantime, he and his first wife, Honey, had divorced. He wrote another melodrama called *Heart of Alaska,* but it was a huge flop. He was totally broke. One afternoon in 1911, he was sitting in a bar in New York, and in came his friend Henry B. Walthall. It turned out that Henry was working for director D. W. Griffith. He offered to introduce Pop to him, which he did. Griffith liked his athletic ability, and my father made many movies for him, both at Fort Lee, New Jersey, and when Griffith moved his company to Hollywood.

My mother was a young actress of sixteen at Universal Studio at the same time Jack Ford was working there as a combination propman-stuntman for his brother Francis Ford, who was a major star there. Her father, George Fuller Golden (christened George Michael Fuller), had been a famous monologist in vaudeville. He, George M. Cohan, and Jim Corbett were the founders of the first actors' union for stage performers, the White Rats of America. All of us Careys are very proud of that. Olive Fuller (Golden was added by her father as part of his stage name) was born on January 31, 1896, and John Ford was born on February 1, 1894. Pop was pushing forty before Mom and John Ford were able to vote. All the young people at the studio hung out together, so it was my mom who first introduced John Ford to Harry Carey. Pop was responsible for Ford being a director. He convinced the head of Universal, Carl Laemmle, to let Jack direct his next movie, which he did, but they both took a cut in salary.

The two of them would pack up camera, cast, and crew and make silent movies in the desert wastes of Southern California. They were a fantastic pair until they split up in 1921.

There was always a sort of "time gauge" in our family, like B.C. and A.D. All the while I was growing up, I remember hearing my mom say,

"That was before Harry and Jack split up," or "That was after Harry and Jack split up." She always said the split-up was caused by Joe Harris, an actor who had been in my father's play *Montana,* and J. Farrell McDonald, an actor whom Jack Ford used in all of his movies. They were a couple of old busybodies who were jealous of Jack and Harry's friendship. Each had a load of dirty gossip which, unfortunately, my dad and Jack believed. Mom never really forgave Joe for that, even though he came to live on the ranch as a sort of foreman, and stayed for thirty-five years. This was the end of the Ford-Carey films. They never recaptured the warm friendship they had had in the early days, even though Pop did work for Jack once more, in 1935, as the prison superintendent in *The Prisoner of Shark Island.* My father was terrific in it, and it makes me wonder what great films they could have made, had they continued together. The split-up was the reason John Ford made *3 Godfathers* for the third time. It was a tribute to his old friend, Harry Carey.

Saugus, California, is approximately thirty-five miles north of Los Angeles. Five miles north of Saugus was my father's 1,000-acre ranch, which he and my mom had homesteaded. It was about as wild and western as any cowboy could wish for and was still only a forty-five minute drive to Universal, the nearest movie studio. An old white frame house sat about three-quarters of the way up into a big canyon. I was born there at one o'clock in the morning on May 16, 1921. We didn't have any electricity in that old place, so my mother, while in labor, yelled for somebody to tell the hired hand to bring the Model T Ford truck around and shine the lights in the window so the doc could "see what the hell he was doing." My beautiful mother looked like the most proper lady, but she swore a lot, and probably said more than "hell." My father was in the next room with John Ford (which is why in later years he always wanted me to call him Uncle Jack) and the then-current mayor of New York City, "Beau James," Jimmy Walker. Jimmy Walker was a famous afterdinner speaker, so I don't suppose it was his habit to get too sloshed of an evening, but my father and Jack Ford managed to get some whiskey called Melwood. They proceeded to get plastered; not weaving-around plastered, but feeling no pain. From then on, every time Ford saw me with my father, he'd say, "Melllood . . . lilill Melllood," alluding to how drunk he and my dad were that night at the ranch. I hated it. I really hated it when they'd do that. "Not funny, not funny," I'd say to myself. So these were the first two of a long list of famous personages to visit the ranch during my lifetime.

I remember Jack Ford's visits to the ranch while I was growing up, because he scared hell out of me. There was cockiness about him that reminded me of the kids I'd wind up getting into fights with at school. He and my father were not working together anymore. I remember Pop being very happy about that. This was in the thirties, and Ford was very successful. He had directed some great movies with the greatest stars. My father never went to his movies. Jack knew that, and it had an effect on their relationship. I sensed the bitterness between them, and even with my ten-year-old mind, I wondered why they bothered to keep this visiting business going. Of course, I knew nothing of their collaboration on movie scripts and the laughs they had shared. Sometimes a movie they had made together would pop into the conversation. Ford would say, "When I wrote *Hell Bent,* I was—and my father would exclaim, "Jack, for Christ's sake, I wrote most of that!" Ford would smile because he'd scored a point and gotten my father sore. I didn't like him and wished he'd get back to the boat he kept bragging about. I had no idea what these two men had done together.

In fact, fifteen years later, when I worked for him, I had no knowledge of the history they had made at Universal. I was at least fifty before I became interested in Pop's film career; before I realized what Ford meant when he would say, "Harry Carey was a great actor"; before I realized what a genius Ford himself was. You have to live that long and work for other directors before it hits you how lucky you were to have been in his films.

We usually had about fifteen head of horses at the ranch. There were two hundred head of whiteface cattle, six hogs, six milk cows, two goats, a herd of sheep, a very horny midget pony from a circus, and lots of dogs. My father would pick up any poor stray dog he found wandering along the road. People were having trouble feeding themselves, let alone dogs, so they would come out to our part of the country and dump them. They found a friend in my pop. He loved dogs and gave them a home for life. About once a week my mother would bring home meat scraps and bones from the local butcher shop and cook a mess of porridge in a huge copper kettle to feed them. Roaming the mountains and flatlands were coyotes, mountain lions, bobcats, and all the small game they hunted. There were many varieties of birds, from songbirds to the predators, and lots of lizards and snakes. It was a place my father never wanted to leave. He always threw a fit when my mom told him he had to go to town.

Pop was at the height of his fame as a western star in the late twenties. He and my wheeling-dealing mother created a first-rate tourist attraction

at the Harry Carey Rancho. "Rancho" was painted on the two, two-story
high water tanks that loomed above the pump house on the east side of
the house. The "Harry Carey Trading Post" and tourist cabins were about
a forty-five-minute drive from Hollywood, and people would flock out to
see their favorite western hero. The term *trading post* has a western ring
to it, but in our case it was a sort of misnomer, because it was more like a
country store. However, it was a special country store, because you could
purchase goods there you could never find anywhere else. There was a
post office and the usual stuff you find today in the trillions of convenience
stores all over the country.

What made their country store unique and really wonderful were the
rugs and jewelry that were made by the Navajos right on the ranch. If you
walked straight back through the store, you would see a shedlike building
where two or three Navajo women were weaving. They tended the sheep,
spun and dyed the wool, and wove glorious rugs, just as they had learned
to do on the reservation. The silver and turquoise jewelry was made by
Striker (that's all we knew him as). He had his little workshop under
another shed where the "dudes" could watch. It all sold like hotcakes.
Weekends were really a sort of carnival. How I loved to ride on my horse
beside my father all the way down from the corral to the Trading Post. I
was about five years old, but I really thought I was grown up. I wore a big
hat, spurs, and toy six-guns.

I grew up with the Navajos. Some time before my memory of it, my
father brought about forty Navajos—men, women, and children—to the
ranch. My sister, Cappy, and I spoke Navajo before we spoke English,
because we had a Navajo nurse named Zani. My father could speak the
Navajo lingo pretty good himself, and we still have the little "dictionary"
he carried with him with pronunciation marks. He trusted the Navajos
more than he trusted the caucasian help. He knew their ways and beautiful
humor. He always claimed that the Navajos who hadn't been to the
missionary school were the best. "That's where they learn about stealing,"
he'd say, "at the goddamned missionary school."

I remember them as great horsemen. Of course, history tells us that.
The men I remember were Bahee, Friday, and Billy Day. They were very
athletic, on or off their horses. It was an incredible sight to see them riding
bareback, hell-bent-for-leather, over a hill, singing at the top of their
voices. The most American sound in the world, really. Friday was my hero
because he could run so fast and ride the bucking horses. Until the Navajos
left the ranch, they dressed in traditional garb. The women wore full skirts
and velveteen overblouses with lots of turquoise jewelry. The men had

their hair wrapped with wool into a bun and a bandanna or "jah" around their head.

There was a small canyon just west of the main ranchhouse that was fittingly called Rodeo Canyon. It got that name early in the spring of 1925, after someone from the Newhall-Saugus American Legion Post called and asked Pop if he would consider putting on a rodeo for charity. He came up with the idea of having an all-Indian rodeo. He spoke to them about it, and they got as excited as kids at Christmas. Grandstands were built on the hillsides of this little canyon, and Pop had a circular one-quarter mile track graded, with the infield loosened up so the falls wouldn't hurt too much. Then he bought four bucking horses and three teams of good horses that Friday and Bahee trained for "Roman Riding." The show was such a huge success that they put it on every Sunday and made a lot of money for charity. At the time, I didn't find exceptional all the famous people who came to visit and the special things that took place during my childhood. I thought our way of life was normal. It wasn't. Remembering it now, I find it quite astonishing.

During the teens and twenties, there were still a number of people alive who had been part of the real West. Dad, Uncle Jack, and myself as a young boy were fortunate to meet some of these characters. Jack Ford, in his later years, would tell me with pride how Wyatt Earp came on the set to watch the shooting of one of the Ford-Carey westerns and talk with him and my dad. Uncle Jack would sometimes embroider the story a little in the retelling, but the meeting was true, and that link and other links to the old West that they were portraying on screen were real.

In 1926, when I was five years old, the great Western artist and sculptor Charles M. Russell passed away. I have heard that most children cannot remember very much about their lives before five or six years of age, but I remember him. He was a little boy's dream, with his stories of his life as a real cowboy in Montana and his magic artist's hands. He, like my father, always had a roll-your-own Bull Durham cigarette hanging out of the corner of his mouth. Some of his ample grey hair fell on either side of his forehead. I would always sit beside him. In those days, presliced bread was unknown, and a whole loaf would sit on a platter in the middle of the dining room table. He would nudge me with his knee and ask, "What kind of animal shall we make this morning?"

I would usually say, "A horse."

With that he would reach into the center of the loaf of bread and pull out a hunk from the middle, dip a hand into his glass of water, and knead the bread to make it more pliable. Then he put both hands out of sight under the table, and when he brought them back up, there would be a little white horse that he would place in front of me. He could use up a whole loaf of bread in a short space of time making coyotes, goats—all kinds of little animals.

Charley and my father would sit at that big dining room table drinking coffee and swapping out-West stories from about six in the morning till lunch. In the afternoon, Charley would go down to paint in the adobe cabin my father had built for him. The next morning, there they both would be once more, talking—talking—talking, until my mother finally ran them out.

Charley had a stepson who was twice my age, about ten. His name was Jack. He loved to put his hand in my face and push me over, which always made me cry. One day Charley and my dad were sitting in the den when I came in crying. They wanted to know what happened, and I told them what Jack had done. Maybe Charley didn't really think it out when he said to me, "Well, hit him over the head with a piece of firewood."

Right away, I thought that was a super idea, so that's what I did. I was laying for him when he came around the corner and put a terrible gash in his skull, but he never pushed me in the face again.

Like most kids, I carried a cap pistol on my hip. I would ambush Charley and make the sound of gunfire by going "Bing, Bing, Bing" at him. Not long before he passed away in 1926, he sculpted me a barnyard billygoat out of beeswax. He stood it on a rough wooden base on which he wrote: "To Dobe from Bing-Bing Charley—don't let nobody get your goat." I treasure that goat.

I always felt very comfortable around Charley. He was a very generous man. Back in his drinking days, before his wife, Nancy, made him stop his carousing, he gave away most of his artwork. But he had been sober for years when he gave my folks two huge watercolors and two bronzes. My mom sold them in 1952, but we still have the goat, a steer made from plaster of Paris, a sorrel horse made from papier maché, and a wonderful letter he wrote to my dad about a cache of booze hidden up the canyon. He illustrated it in watercolor, with cowboys galloping toward my father who's holding up the missing bottle.

William S. Hart was a western star at the same time as my father. Actually, he was a bigger star, but with all due respect, I could never figure out why. Every so often, they would run his movies down at Newhall School. All of us kids thought he was a terrible "hamola." He had been a Shakespearean actor on the New York stage, and maybe he didn't want

Harry Carey, Sr., and my mother, Olive Carey, in the early Universal Picture, *Knight of the Range*, released in 1915.

John Ford in his early twenties directing middle-aged Harry Carey, Sr.

The Harry Carey ranch where I was born on May 16, 1921 in the room hidden by the large tree.

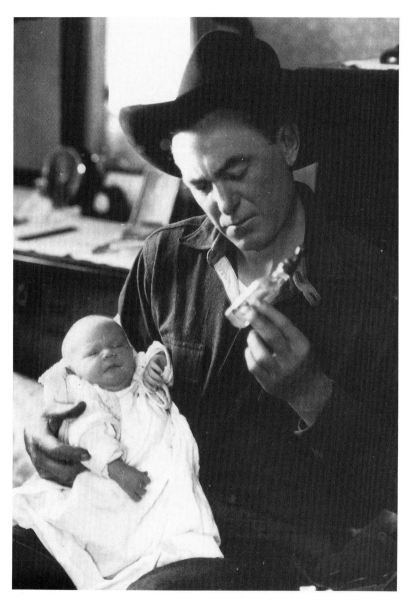

Harry Carey, Sr., getting acquainted with his new son.

A party at the ranch circa 1923. Front row left to right: Charley Russell, Harry Carey, Sr., Harry Carey, Jr., Fred Stone, Henry Herbert Knibbs. Middle row: Otto Meyer, Dick Winslow, James Rogers, Will Rogers, Jr., Mary Rogers. Back row: Frank H. Spearman, Sam DeGrasse, Edward Allen, Clarence Sovern, Spearman's driver, Will Rogers' aide, Spearman's son.

My first horse—Sikis (*My Friend* in Navajo)

Roman-riding Navajo style on the Carey Ranch long before Uncle Jack thought to have Ben Johnson and me do it in *Rio Grande*.

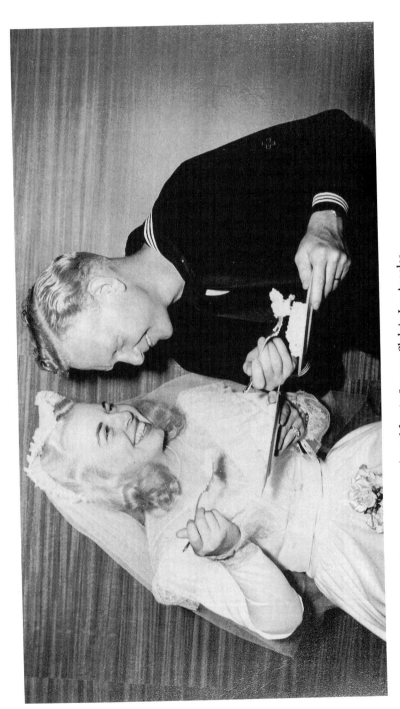

August 12, 1944 – Our wedding reception at the California Country Club in Los Angeles.

3 Godfathers – My death scene. The toughest day of my motion picture life.

3 Godfathers – Riding into town. The beginning of the picture but one of the last scenes shot out on the RKO Ranch after returning from location. Photograph by Alexander Kahle.

3 Godfathers – By this time I knew I was in for it. Photograph by Alexander Kahle.

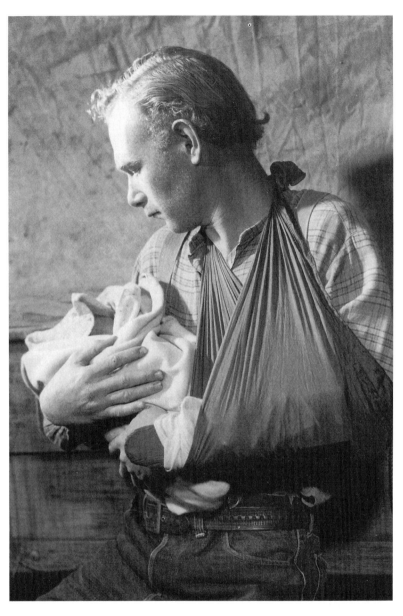

3 Godfathers – Just before the "Lullaby". Photograph by Alexander Kahle.

3 Godfathers – When this scene was over Pedro had a fistful of my hair.
Photograph by Alexander Kahle.

3 Godfathers – "You're not reading that, are you?", Uncle Jack said to me. Photograph by Alexander Kahle.

3 Godfathers – Our first look at Death Valley. Photograph by Alexander Kahle.

3 Godfathers – I'm looking off camera because Uncle Jack is screaming at me, again. Photograph by Alexander Kahle.

anyone to forget it. He was a very tall man, but he rode this teeny-weeny paint horse. His feet were so close to the ground it made us kids laugh. I think he was afraid of falling off.

My father respected Bill Hart and liked him, even though, you couldn't find two more different men. Right above where my sister, Cappy, and I went to school in Newhall was the Hart Ranch. Now it really wasn't a ranch, it was a huge estate. He lived in a house that resembled a castle in Toledo, Spain. It was on top of a mountain and overlooked the town. It's a state park now, and hundreds of people visit it every year.

The two made it a point to get together socially at least once a year. I remember one visit to his awesome place when I was twelve years old. He had a very deep, booming voice, and he asked me, "Young man, do you know your Shakespeare?" All I knew about Shakespeare was that Romeo had the hots for Juliet. It was a long night.

It's Bill Hart's visits to *our* place that I remember the most. One day during the Christmas holiday season, he came up. Prohibition had not yet been repealed, so my father always went to an Italian family who lived somewhere in the hills behind town to buy his booze. What they made there was the Italian equivalent of "white lightning" called "grappa." It was very powerful stuff. I was much too young to know what it was like, but I saw what it did to folks.

The minute Bill came in, he started acting real "western." "Waaall by God, it's good to be here, Harry! By God, yes."

My father asked him if he wanted a drink.

"By God, yes," he answered.

Pop went to the cabinet in the dining room and brought out a gallon jug of the grappa and two water glasses which he set down on the table in front of Bill. My father didn't fool around when he decided to drink.

"You have ta' kinda' go easy at first with that stuff, Bill," he warned, "it's got a wallop like a mule."

Hart laughed as he grappled with the cork, "Don't worry, Harry. I was weened on this stuff!"

He filled the glass a little over half full and took a big swallow. Suddenly, there was a great transformation. All the blood in his body went to his head. He couldn't get his breath. Noises came out of his constricted throat, and great tears fell on the copper-topped coffee table. Pop didn't laugh, and neither did I, because we were really worried. Finally, Bill straightened up and said, "Jesus Christ! What in the hell is that stuff?"

Things settled down, and they were having a pretty good time when it was time for dinner. A Mexican family by the name of Corrall lived on the ranch at the time, and the grandfather grew and canned little light-green chili peppers. The were so hot the top of your head would come off. I used to carefully bite off the end and take out the seeds before I ate one. My dad, however, chewed the whole thing without batting an eye. They were always in a bowl on the dinner table, and as luck would have it, were right in front of Bill Hart. He immediately grabbed a handful.

Pop again said, "Ah, Bill, ya' better go easy on those. They're hotter than..."

That's as far as he got. Again Bill was purple, again sweat was glistening on his forehead. He tried his best, but it wasn't good enough. I guess he couldn't think of anything else to do, so he blew them all over the dining room table. Cappy and I were so doubled laughing we had to leave the table. I don't know how my dad handled that one.

Hart didn't go into any more wild-west stories that evening, but he seemed less formal than any other time. I remember I liked him, and except for the two painful bouts, he enjoyed himself.

"What are you doing with all those goddamn mares?" That's what Will James used to say every time my dad took this world-famous writer and artist up to our corral. We only had three mares in our remuda of sixteen horses, but he spotted them immediately. Now, you don't get to be famous Will James without being sober some of the time, but, though I hate to say it, except for one visit, he was always either half drunk or already there whenever I saw him. He had a beautiful wife, Alice, who I remember cried a lot. No one knew back then that alcoholism was really a disease and not just some character flaw. Had there been recovery programs like there are today, perhaps Will would have lived longer.

He used to put on a wonderful show for me, though. He'd sit in the den in Pop's big writing chair, find a pad and pencil, and ask, "What animal shall I draw?"

"A mountain lion," I would answer.

"Where do you want me to start? At his tail? One of his feet? Where?"

"His tail."

So he'd start drawing a mountain lion from the tip of his tail. He did it just as easily as he would have had he started with the head. Within a minute or so, there would be a hungry mountain lion crouched for the kill. He was a wonderful animal artist, especially with a plain old lead pencil. I loved his horses. He always drew them with that little Arabian dip in their nose.

When he was really in his cups, there wouldn't be any drawing. He'd get sullen and ornery and grab me by the hair. "Com'ere," he'd say, nearly jerking my head off. It's too bad that most of my memories of Will James are those of a dedicated booze-fighter, but I have to remember that when he came to see us, he was on a sort of nonworking vacation from his home in Montana. And I do remember the time he spent at our ranch cold sober. A kinder, more gentle man I have never met. When a man's really into the booze, he can only stand the demons of being "dry" so long. Relief is only a swallow away.

My father always said that only one man knew Will Rogers well, and that man was old-time vaudeville great Fred Stone. But all of America felt they knew Will Rogers, and so did I. I had never seen him in a movie, but I knew he was somebody very special. Even the first time I met him, he didn't seem like a stranger to me. Like Charley Russell, he was my friend right off the bat.

When I was about nine years old, we were living in Brentwood, California. Pop was finishing M-G-M's epic *Trader Horn.* We would ride on horseback from our place over to the Will Rogers Ranch, which was about five miles to the west of us. Pop liked to visit with Will, talk about horses, and kid about the picture business. Will teased my father about "ridin' that plow horse." This was before the days when riding a stocky quarter-horse was considered "in." Will would always be fiddling with a rope. He was so expert with it that he'd gotten bored with roping calves, so he began roping goats. Goats are smarter and very hard to catch.

Polo was Will's favorite sport, so he had mostly thoroughbreds on his place. What I remember the most are the polo matches at the Riviera Country Club. Will's two sons, Will, Jr., and Jimmy, played too, and also a big husky Texan who became very popular in movies, Guinn "Big Boy" Williams.

My mother's younger sister, Mignonne, lived with us the whole time I was growing up. She took care of Cappy and me when my folks were on location. We loved her dearly. Mignonne was a great athlete, a fearless and superb horsewoman. She'd take Sunny, the "plow horse," over to the private polo field Will had on the ranch and "stick and ball" with the boys. Will thought she was terrific. It was usually Mignonne who drove us to watch the Sunday polo games. The spectators parked their cars around the perimeter of the field, sat on the running-boards, and watched. Between chukkers, Will would wander over, leading his horse, to where our car was. He was always chewing gum. He never smoked or drank in his life.

Behind that easy-going "down home" manner was a physically and mentally powerful man. In retrospect, he seemed to have a whole world within himself. What he had, and most celebrities don't have, was approachability. He'd stand there twirling a rope, chewing gum, and rambling on to Mignonne, Cappy, and me.

One day, Mom, Dad, and I were having dinner at the Brown Derby Restaurant on Vine Street in Hollywood. We were going to the Friday-night fights at Legion Stadium. Will was in the next booth, and he came over and sat next to Pop. He kidded Pop again about his horse, and then in a serious but excited way, he spoke about his upcoming flight to Alaska. He talked about the thrill of flying. Pop replied that sixteen hands was as high as he wanted to go. A few days later, I was in study hall at Black Foxe Military Academy. Over the public address system came the announcement of Will Rogers' death in a plane crash. I leaped up from my desk without permission and ran down three flights to the bathroom. I locked myself into a stall, and then I cried, and cried, and cried.

She Wore a Yellow Ribbon

The eight movies I did with Uncle Jack after *3 Godfathers* were almost a walk in the park by comparison. I say "almost," because Jack always had something going on. He made a point of that. He made life an adventure, and every day was one not to be forgotten. That is why I have almost total recall of every one of the films that I worked on for him, even though it was many years ago. The most recent was in 1963.

She Wore a Yellow Ribbon was made in Monument Valley in 1948. It was my first trip there. It was late in October. Today, it is fairly easy to get there. It's just a few hours drive from Flagstaff on a very nice highway. In 1948, it was damned-near impossible, and if the weather didn't cooperate, it *was* impossible! I can't imagine how they did it in 1938.

We took the train to Flagstaff. It sure was different from that long ride by car to Death Valley in May of that year. I remember thinking, "I'm a seasoned veteran now. Uncle Jack can't pull anything out of the hat that will be a shocker now." Then I remembered that, with him, you never knew. I'd heard that he was hard on Victor McLaglen.

Old Victor was in the club car, getting nicely sloshed. I was at a table down at the other end with Uncle Jack and Duke. The Old Man was watching Vic with an amused expression on his face.

"Why don't you guys go down and whoop it up with Ol' Uncle Victor? We don't start shooting until day after tomorrow."

"No thanks, Coach," replied Duke, genuinely laughing. "I ain't that dumb, an' neither is this red-headed kid here. Right, Ol' Dobe?"

We got off the train in Flagstaff and wandered into the Harvey Coffee Shop. There was one of them in every railway station of any size. They were a wonderful part of America then. All towns look alike now—shopping malls with Sears, McDonald's, Pizza Hut, Osco Drugs. Flagstaff was wonderful. After a huge breakfast, we were assigned to our station wagons, and off we went to work in that glorious red land on the Navajo reservation.

I had only seen Monument Valley in black and white—*Stagecoach* and *My Darling Clementine*—and anyway, I had paid little attention to the scenery, focusing on the action and the gunfights. As far as I know, no one had photographed a movie there in color yet, and even Jack had reservations about it. He liked the shadows, and the light and shade effects of black-and-white film.

John Agar and I were sent off in a car with Uncle Victor. We were in the backseat, and Victor was up front with the driver. There's a sort of unwritten rule in the picture business that the Old Guard always sits in the front seat with the driver. In his younger days, Victor had been a professional boxer and had the distinction of "going the distance" with the great fighter Jack Johnson.

"He never knocked me down, lad," he told me, "but he sure beat the livin' be-Jesus out of me." Uncle Jack called him Uncle Victor, so I did, too. He was still very huge and strong.

It took most of the day to drive into Monument Valley. Thank God, the weather cooperated. The roads were just dirt and very rutted. The scenery was so fantastic that it didn't seem such a long ride, and I got to know John Agar. He had worked in *Fort Apache,* and we did a lot of note comparing on the Old Man. Victor spent most of the trip snoring away the miles, though between naps, he would turn and talk to us. He seemed genuinely interested in our young careers. The first thing he asked was if I had worked for Jack before. When I said yes, his big bashed-in face got all wrinkled up like a schoolboy who's telling you a secret behind the schoolhouse. It went something like this:

Vic: Tell me, lad. You've worked for him, have ya'?

Me: Yessir. Last summer.

Vic: Mean to ya', was he?

Me: Oh God, yes. Very mean.

Vic: Yeah-yeah-yeah. I know, lad, I know. He's a sadist, he is. A sadist. A big part in this one, have ya'?

Me: Oh, yes. I'm Lieutenant Pennell.

Vic: Ah, yes. Well, I haven't read it yet, lad, but he's a bad one. A fucking sadist, he is. But ya' can't let it bother ya', lad. You mustn't let it bother ya'.

His warning was not exactly comforting, but on the other hand, I already knew that.

John said, "I don't take him seriously. I don't give him a chance to really get to me. If he gets nasty, I just kid him out of it. I laugh it off. Then he gives up and goes after someone else. He isn't that bad. Just don't take all his crap seriously."

Well, Johnny's Johnny, and I'm me. Johnny doesn't rattle, and when the Old Man discovered that, he turned his attention to those of us who do. Uncle Vic made the trip a joy. He had a wonderful childlike quality and a don't-give-a-damn-what-happens attitude.

And so, we made our way into what was to be known later as "Ford Country."

Harry Goulding and his wife, Leona (everyone always called her Mike), owned and operated the Trading Post there on the Navajo Reservation. It was Harry who first brought photographs of Monument Valley to Uncle Jack before the making of *Stagecoach*. Harry made all the arrangements with the Navajos who worked on the movie. Jack always used the same bunch. Harry spoke Navajo, and he was the one that the production office contacted before shooting began. The Gouldings were wonderful people, and Jack could not have made those films without their help.

I've always been an awful fussbudget about where I live, how I dress, and yes—even how I smell, so it was a rude awakening when I first saw my living quarters. The living conditions there at Gouldings' were very "out West." There were five special cabins for the stars of the movie. Duke and Uncle Jack each had a cabin to themselves, but the rest of us doubled or tripled up. The crew was housed in the beautiful Anderson Camp down about a mile below. They had hot water and showers and marvelous food. We "special" folks in the cabins had to share the toilet and shower. None of the cabins had a bathroom. They were mostly glorified hogans. The floor was swept, hard dirt with a Navajo rug on it. Everything was uneven; the floor sloped down toward the valley. There were two little chests of drawers, a chair, and three cot-sized beds, each with a quilt and a Navajo blanket on it. In the middle of the cabin stood an old-fashioned kerosene heater, like the kind we had on the ranch when I was a boy. It kept the place nice and warm, and we took turns being the first one up in the morning to light it. It was beginning to get cold up there, and would get a lot more so before we left.

When Joanne Dru and Mildred Natwick arrived, they stayed in the Gouldings' home above the Trading Post. They had hot and cold running water. There was no running water in our cabins, either. There was a washhouse up the hill on a rise. The Navajo women did the laundry there, and we also took our showers there; Duke and Uncle Jack too. The shower was an old five-gallon oil tin with holes in the bottom. It hung from a wooden beam, and the hose that ran into it carried cold water! You stood under this shower and asked some sadist to turn on the water. I'll tell you, you didn't stay under long—just a smidgen of soap and a little water to get the red dust off. Our cavalry blue uniforms stood up in the corner after about a week. We did change our longjohns every other day or so. We never did figure when Vic washed. No one ever saw him go near the shower.

My roommates were Pat Ford, Jack's son, who was my age and a good friend, and Arthur Shields, a wonderful character actor. I always admired Arthur. His brother, Barry Fitzgerald, was one of the greatest scene-stealers of all time. Both were graduates of the famous Abbey Players. Jack Ford so respected Arthur that he was the only man he would allow to coach his actors off the set. The second night there, Uncle Jack ordered me to go back to my cabin to "work with Arthur on your part."

The first day of shooting! A cold crisp morning. We were in our "dirty shirt blue" uniforms, astride our cavalry horses. We weren't really "dirty shirt"; that was just an old cavalry expression. We were shiny and polished. Gouldings' Trading Post served perfectly as the battalion headquarters. Duke loved this role; he always said it was his favorite. On many occasions in later years, I would rave about how magnificent he was in *The Searchers,* and he would always counter with, "Christ no, Ol' Dobe. That wasn't my best work. The part I'm most proud of is *Yellow Ribbon.*"

Duke made his entrance into the picture, coming out of battalion headquarters to address the troops. It went perfectly. Agar in front of his company, and me in front of mine, Duke's arrival, some dialogue—bam— bam—bam!

"Right. Cut. Print it!"

Beautiful words. There was no, "Well that would have been all right, but Dobe forgot to . . . etc. . . . etc." Man, the world's a beautiful place. Could it be I got through the first shot unscathed? If I do as I'm told, I'll be okay? Is the baptism over? I rode a horse, I said a line, and I didn't get chewed out!

Duke smiled and winked at me like, "See, I told ya'."

That was also the day Ben Johnson got broken in. I know that Ben had made a couple of other movies and had handled dialogue successfully before. He played the lead in *Mighty Joe Young,* but he had never really been directed in a scene by Jack.

In this scene, Ben explains to Duke what kind of arrow it was that killed the poor fellow in the stagecoach. Ford sensed that Ben was a little uptight. Not too much, but just not as casual as he wanted him to be. Well, it was just as Duke had said on so many occasions: if you have something minor to do, Ford can be a pain in the ass, but if it's an important scene, he handles you like a baby. That's what he did with Ben in his first scene.

Uncle Jack had him standing beside the stagecoach with the arrow in his hand, giving Duke, Captain Nathan Brittles, the lowdown on what happened. It's hard to explain what Jack did without acting it out, but he had this "body language" and these bizarre expressions he used to show nonchalance and confidence in a character. That was why he never wanted photographers snapping his picture when he was working. He used to warn them, "Ask me when I"m not busy, and I'll ham it up for you."

"You know," Ford said, "you're not really a Yankee at heart, Ben." Ben liked that. "You're a Johnny Reb who fought with Jeb Stuart, and now you're in the Yankee Cavalry, but you were an officer in the Confederate Army. You respect Brittles, but you're not afraid of him like these other guys," and he waved in our general direction.

"Understand, Ben? That's your job, and you're damn good at it. You're one hell of a scout. Okay. Yeah, that's the idea, kids."

He clapped his hands, smiled behind his cigar, and said, "Yeah—that is well—that's the idea. Now let's go through this scene real easy. Get your props. Makeup!"

He always did that. If he really wanted Makeup, he'd yell, *"Wardrobe."*

"All right, here we go. Nice and easy now. Ready, Ol' Ben. You're Johnny Reb giving these guys the lowdown, okay?"

"I'll try Mr. Ford, but I'd sure rather fall off a doggoned horse or come flat-out down one of them hills than say this here dialogue. You jes' point out the hill you want me to come off, an' let some other actor say them words."

Ford loved it. "Here's my Tyree." From then on, Ben had it made.

Uncle Jack knew how to relax an actor, just as he knew how to rattle one. In a few moments, he had Ben acting like a veteran of a hundred movies. Ben has had that "Ben Johnson" technique ever since. He is a much more versatile actor than a lot of people realize, definitely not a one-dimensional artist. He can go many ways. For instance, he can play one of the scariest villians you would ever want to encounter, but he's all cowboy inside.

Jack was a man for all seasons, but not a man for all actors. He was kind to the tough and cruel to the fainthearted, paternal and gentle to the girls. They *loved* him, but he was afraid of them. He knew the guys he could be tough on, like me, and even Duke. Had he "discovered" Duke later on in Duke's career, it would have been the same. The Old Man would have had his number at any age. Ben Johnson did not fit into this category. He was the product of the Oklahoma range and the rodeo circuit, a fledgling actor who took special handling. He was not too crazy about the picture business in the first place (he just liked the money), and he wasn't too anxious to become an actor.

Uncle Jack did take big chances with Ben on horseback, though. If he had gotten hurt (and it happens to the best of horsebackers), I don't know what he would have done with the part of Tyree. But, what the hell. Ford knew—he *knew*—the gods wouldn't dare do that to him.

On *Yellow Ribbon* the afterdinner activity was cards, not dominoes. I wasn't expected to hang around, but I watched a few nights, just to see the feathers fly. Sometimes they played Hearts, but 90 percent of the time it was poker, and guess who had to win? If himself didn't come out ahead at the end of the evening, there was hell to pay the next day. He'd always arrive at the table with a sackful of silver dollars, and they'd better still be with him when he went to bed.

Since Ward wasn't on the picture (Victor McLaglen played the only part he would have been right for), Cliff Lyons had to fill in for him at the card table. Cliff hated it. Cliff was doubling Duke (this was before the days of Chuck Roberson and Terry Wilson), but he didn't have much to do, because Jack made Duke do nearly all of his own riding, even if it was "really Western."

So, the afterdinner card game was Uncle Jack, Duke, Cliff Lyons, and Wingate Smith. When I think back on it, it must have been pretty hard on Duke. Here's a man who's carrying the whole picture on his shoulders, who has to know his lines perfectly, never miss his mark, and play cards every night, and lose. Everyone caught it but Wingate. Wingate was a relative, and Ford never picked on those in his family. If for one reason or another Wingate was unable to play, Jack would send for a little banty rooster stuntman named Frank McGrath.

From the first day I walked on a movie set, I had heard the name Frankie McGrath. He had doubled Pedro on *3 Godfathers,* but it was on *Yellow Ribbon* that I really got to know him. We spent so much time sitting out on the range on our horses waiting for the word *action* that I got to know all the stunt guys better. Thank God I got along well with him, because he could make life a real pain in the ass for those he didn't care for.

Ford would say, "That's it. I'm not going to use him anymore. He's too goddamned much trouble." But he always did use him because he needed him, and he was the best at his job. Frankie was half American Indian and half Irish; a wiry and sinuous five-foot-seven, with jet black hair, a dark complexion, good looks. He had been extremely handsome in his younger days, but he was so nuts and impulsive that his looks were secondary. He drank gin most of the day, and never missed a beat. Drinking never interfered with his work.

I'll never forget the poker game I watched when Frankie was one of the foursome. I couldn't believe my ears!

"Hey, One Eye!" Frankie addressed Ford. "Stop peeking at my damned hand." As he said that, he kicked Ford in the shins. I thought Duke was going to faint.

It didn't bother Ford much, though. He just said, "Hey, Useless! You're drunk. I don't know why in the hell I put up with you. Well, Lyons talked me into it."

Frankie replied, "Go ahead, Boss, send me home. DeMille wants me, anyway." He always had a comeback. It went on like that all evening.

The following morning, Frankie said to Cliff, "Hey, Mother, (McGrath called Lyons Mother a lot of the time, and he was the only stunt guy who could get away with it), why is the Old Man riding my ass today?"

Cliff answered, "Well goddamn. Goddamn. Don't you remember the way you talk to him when you're drunk?"

Yellow Ribbon was the first time I really became aware of the importance of stuntmen and discovered what far-out characters they are. I'm not around them too much anymore, but from a distance, they seem to me to be a far different breed from back then. In the first place, today they are more like professional athletes, and they work a lot harder at staying in top physical shape. Today there isn't much horse stuff, so they are more geared to car stunts and chases, motorcycles, explosions, and "high falls."

Dar Robinson was the greatest stuntman ever in the high fall category. He was killed riding a motorcycle, and the stunt was not even a difficult one, compared to his other feats.

Of course, Ford had the very best cowboy and Indian stuntmen in the business. He used other men for his non-Westerns, such as Dave Sharp and Harvey Perry, but the majority were the Western type. The guys I'm talking about usually trained in a saloon, and their sweat was eighty-proof, but they did it right and were never out of a job, because they were the best at their craft. Uncle Jack loved them for all those gifts—whether it be in the saloon or on horseback. He wasn't strict with them as he was with his actors. He loved to tease them, and he was very proud of them. His favorite stuntman was a very shy and very quiet New Mexico cowhand named Slim Hightower. Duke's character in *3 Godfathers* was named after Slim—Robert Marmaduke Hightower.

These men toiled under the strong hand of almost-legend Cliff Lyons. Now when I say "almost-legend," I surely don't mean to cast a shadow on the good name of Cliff Lyons, but history tells us that poor Cliff already had a shadow cast over his able body by none other than the Babe Ruth of the stunt profession, Yakima Canutt.

The exploits of the great Yakima Canutt have been recorded many times, and Western movie buffs know him well. Yak was the granddaddy of all stuntmen. He did for stuntmen what Arnold Palmer did for golf. When it came to horses, tame or outlaw, he had no peer. He made more movies with John Wayne than anyone in the picture business. He doubled him, and he played parts, too. He and Duke literally invented and developed the "movie punch," which every actor must learn if he has to do a fistfight in a scene, and make it look believable. Yak doubled Pop a few times. The one that sticks in my mind the most was a serial called *Devil Horse*. The outlaw horse of the 1930s was called "Rex, the Wild Horse," and he was truly wild and dangerous. I heard, as a kid, that he had killed one of his trainers. In the *Devil Horse* serial, Yak told the prop guys to tie his wrists and ankles around Rex's neck and let 'er rip. It was horrifying to watch. Yak didn't think it was too tough. Pop said that absolutely no one else would have even dared to try that. To my knowledge, the only time Yak worked for Uncle Jack was on *Stagecoach*. He did that marvelous stunt where he was dragged underneath the stagecoach worked his way up hand-over-hand between six horses, and then climbed back up to the top of the coach. Yak was different looking, he had a great face, and, he could handle dialogue well. Cliff Lyons didn't have any of these attributes. Ford used to give Cliff dialogue to say, anyway, but it was God-awful when he did it; and if Cliff were still with us, he would not take exception to that statement. What Cliff was superior at was being in just the right place at the right time when the going got dangerous. He was Ford's head stuntman or the "stunt gaffer."

Duke idolized Yakima Canutt from the old days, but Duke had tremendous respect for Cliff Lyons.

"God, I'd hate ta' hafta' fight that son-of-a-bitch," he used to say. And he was right. His workforce used to say of him, "To whip him, you'd have to kill him." Boy, they were right on that score. Ford never made a western without him. I think he found out on *Stagecoach* that Yak didn't scare or play the game. Cliff did.

On *Yellow Ribbon,* we had Frankie McGrath, Fred Graham, Slim Hightower, Billy Jones, Bobby Rose, and Post Parks. Post Parks was probably the greatest "six-up" driver who ever lived. He could take a stagecoach pulled by six horses hell-bent-for-leather down a narrow path that would make a mountain goat be careful and stop them within six inches of where the cameraman had put his mark. That is almost impossible for any teamster to do when coming in at full clip, but Post did it time and again. Ford loved Post.

When you worked for John Ford and made the inner circle, so to speak, you were on call or at his beck-and-call from the time you woke up until you went to bed. At any time after work you could get a message—the words were always "The Old Man wants you." On *Yellow Ribbon,* the whole feeling of the picture was different than it had been on *3 Godfathers.*

I saw a lot of Duke in those days, and I never heard him complain any more than a mild, "Christ, I gotta' be at Jack's again tonight." It wasn't just gratitude, either; Duke really worshiped him. He never ceased to be amazed at how easily Jack could construct a scene and film it in one take, without a hitch. He never ceased to be amazed at the immense power of his leadership. Duke had a thorough knowledge of film-making, but no matter how many movies he made with Jack, he was always surprised by his genius. The minute he heard the Old Man yell out, "Right! Print it!" he'd look at me with a huge grin and say "Jesus, he makes it look so goddamn easy, and it ain't—ha—ha—hah!"

The second week on *She Wore a Yellow Ribbon,* we filmed inside the fort. Uncle Jack and cinematographer Winnie Hoch had the camera low to the ground over at the stable area, shooting out across the parade ground. All of Wayne's troopers were in perfect formation, standing at attention, listening to Victor McLaglen making a spiel to them.

Victor always made me laugh until my sides split, and he had the same effect on Ben. Vic was, in real life, a lot like the role he played as Sergeant Quincannon. With that guilty-little-boy quality inside of that huge body and smashed-in kisser, he was a real scene-stealer without trying to be one. Vic never reverted to sly tricks to get a laugh; he just played himself. He never really knew his lines word for word (at least in his later years, when I knew him), and it worried him not in the least. You don't fall asleep on a Ford set if you're a bundle of nerves, and Vic fell asleep all the time. Many times, his snoring would ruin a scene in progress.

Uncle Jack would cry, "Somebody wake Vic up, for Chrissakes!"

This morning, old Victor came into the scene striding up and down in front of his troopers. He informed them that he had an important announcement to make. Ford stopped him. This was a first rehearsal, and he wanted to insert an idea he had. Since Vic didn't know too many of his lines, it didn't bother him a bit. Ford knew that, so he started again, from scratch. A great many of Ford's scenes were constructed in this manner.

At Victor's left, toward the end of the formation, was a Navajo mongrel dog lying peacefully asleep, caring nothing about the action going on about him.

Ford shouted, "Do you know your lines, Victor?"

"What's that, Jack?" Vic stopped walking and cupped his hand around his cauliflower ear. That started the troops giggling.

"Shut up! No laughing, goddamnit!" Ford shouted again, "Do you know your lines, Victor?"

Vic answered, "Of course, Jack darlin'. Of course I know me bloomin' lines!"

"Good. Then go!"

"What?"

"We are rehearsing, Victor! So action. Go!"

Vic walked in and shouted to his men, "Now men, there's a very important announcement I have to make!" Then he thought for a moment. ("What the hell is the next damn line?"—Oh, yeah.) "Now there's going to be women on this trip! Uh—uh—uh. ("Now what in the hell is the rest?")

Ford cued him. "And I want you to watch them words. Watch them words!" Then a big smile from Victor, and he repeated, "and I want you to watch them words! Watch them words!" He thought that was the end of the scene. The dog was still lying there asleep.

Ford yelled, "Victor! Victor!"

"Yes, Jack?"

"See the dog? Lean over and pet the dog! Then look up at the men and say, 'Who's dog is this? Who's dog is this?' Then pet the dog once more and say, 'Nice dog. Irish setter!' You got that?"

More laughter from the troops. I mean, it was funny.

"Shut the hell up!" Ford yelled again, "No goddamn laughing, goddammit!" After two or three more rehearsals, Jack decided to go for a take.

"All right," shouted Ford. "Quiet, quiet, quiet. This will be picture! Victor do you have all your lines and your business?"

"Oh my, yes, Jack," was the answer.

"All right. We are rolling."

"Speed," yelled Pop Crain.

"All right, good and loud, Vic, and don't forget the dog. Action!"

"Now men, I have a very important announcement to make. There's gonna be ladies on this trip—and . . . " He sees the dog, who is still sound asleep. "Whose dog is this? Whose dog is this?"

No answer.

"Nice dog. Cocker Spaniel!"

Ford yelled, "No. No! Jesus Christ! Russian wolfhound, goddammit! Oh, the hell with it."

There was a moment of silence, and then I thought Duke was going to have a stroke from laughing. "Oh, Christ. Oh, my God!" He covered his face with his hands and bent over and staggered around, out of sight.

Ford stood up, took off his hat, put it on again, walked around his chair in a small circle, and finally said, to no one in particular, "Cocker Spaniel? Jesus Christ, he didn't get the gag!" Then to Victor he said quietly, with gentleness, "Victor," as he tickled him under the chin, "it was fine, but we have to do it again. You didn't get the right dog."

"But Jack, I petted the same bloody dog as in the rehearsal."

Then Ford explained it to him with great patience. "Just say, 'Irish Setter' the next time, Victor. All right, kids. One more time for Uncle Vic and his dog."

No one had moved an inch, and that Navajo dog was still there. God bless all who were at that fort when the leaves were turning in 1948.

Then came the day to film the "picnicking scene." I had had very little trouble with the Old Man's trickery up to this point, so I felt secure for some reason. I cannot believe that I was stupid enough to think I'd get through the picture without wounds of some kind. I didn't see any storm clouds ahead.

Uncle Jack was cheerful when he told me to get into the buggy, which was being pulled by two well-bred-looking horses. He stood on the spot with his hands on his hips, his pipe jutting out of his mouth, and said, "Dobe! Drive them over here to this spot where I'm standing." I did. So far, so good. Then he helped Joanne Dru get into the buggy seat beside me. Duke was standing there, and so was Johnny Agar. In the scene, Agar stops me just as we are driving toward the gate and tells me I cannot take Joanne off the premises on a picnic because of the danger of hostile Indians. Duke comes in there somewhere while John and I are having one hell of an argument about Army "regs," and says his now-famous line, "Picnicking, Mr. Pennell?"

Then he takes Joanne away and sends me on the picnic all by myself, looking like an ass. It was a good scene, and funny too, when all was said and done.

The gate of the fort was right in front of me, and all I had to do after the dialogue was drive the team out through it. Nothing to it! I could have driven four horses, let alone two. Then came the curve ball. Jack saw that I was having a good time with this rig, so he had a wrangler turn the team and buggy so they'd be on an angle facing the fort wall. Then he told me to back the team up before I headed out the gate. We went through all the dialogue perfectly, and then I tried to back up the team, and because they were jammed at an angle, he knew I would not be able to do it. The right front wheel jammed up against the wagon bed and the horses started to panic, rearing up and leaping around. I had backed up hundreds of wagons on the ranch as a kid, but on this day, it was hopeless. I ruined about four scenes, and I was embarrassed.

Now the front gate was open. Ford finally cut out the backing up and had the wrangler face the buggy back the way it was in the first place. All was going well, but I was really furious, so as soon as the last line was spoken, I yelled, "Yaaaaaaaaa!" at the team and let them have their heads. Unbeknown to me, during the scene, Duke had taken it upon himself to throw a huge rock at the horses at the same time as I let them go. You don't see that in the movie. I'm here to tell you, we were on our way to kingdom-come. Outside the gate, there was about 100 yards of level ground, and then it dropped off at a 45-degree angle all the way to the floor of the Valley. I had runaways on my hands, and I saw where they were headed. There was nothing to pull, because the hack was running up their heels.

No brakes—just me, standing straight up "sawing" the lines and pulling with all my strength. Those horses were flat out! I was a goner! I thought of bailing out, but it was all cactus and rocks.

"You bastards!" I yelled. Then, out of the blue came a rider scorching across the rocky hillside. He was at the team's head in seconds. He practically jerked their heads off as he grabbed the right wheeler's headstall, and stopped them dead still, like they had hit a wall. I fell back on the seat, dead-tired, and looked at my saviour for the first time. It was Cliff Lyons. Good old Cliff. He literally saved me from the hospital in Flagstaff that October day in 1948.

One day Uncle Jack was shooting the sequence in which a wounded horse soldier (beautifully played by old Western star Tom Tyler) was being operated on by the cavalry doctor (Arthur Shields) assisted by an officer's wife, Mrs. Allshard (Mildred Natwick). It's a wonderfully blended scene of comedy and drama. She gives the wounded man a few shots of whiskey to help ease the pain and gets drunk along with him. This interior shot was done in the studio later, but part of the sequence was "interior-exterior," and that was what Jack was shooting this day. Uncle Jack's Irish luck held again. The sky was ominously dark and threatening. Duke rides back, looks into the lantern-lit wagon, and reports to his men that the wounded trooper will be okay. The sky was getting blacker and blacker. It was late afternoon, and along with the purple-black clouds, a cold wind came up with a smattering of rain and lightning. As I think back on it, it was a scary experience. One place you don't want to be when there is lightning around is near a horse. Many are killed every year. The whole Ford Stock Company was out there in the storm. Many Ford films have a special scene that stands out from the rest of the movie. Victor McLaglen getting his dirty money in *The Informer;* Henry Fonda's "I'll be there" scene in *The Grapes of Wrath;* John Wayne's sad and poignant walk away from the cabin door at the end of *The Searchers. Yellow Ribbon* has its storm scene.

This is the shot that every lover of Ford films asks me about. It's after the operation on Tyler, and the troops are leading their horses away from the camera.

"Did the cameraman (Winton Hoch) refuse to shoot it because it was too dark?"

"No, he did not refuse."

Jack was ready to call it a day. The weather was too bad. There was no light, except for flashes of lightning, which were getting so close you could smell them—loud cracks of thunder and a freezing, misty rain. We were all heading for the station wagons to go back to Gouldings' to get warm, when we heard, "Hold it! Hold it! Go back to your horses. Go back to your horses!"

Ford had called a wrap, and then he looked around and said to Winnie, "Winnie, what do you think?"

Winnie answered, "It's awfully dark, Jack. But I'll shoot it. I just can't promise anything." He was being as honest as he could.

Jack said, "Winnie, open her up (the lens on the camera) and let's go for it. If it doesn't come out, I'll take the rap."

"Fair enough, Jack. Let's go, boys."

It sure as hell came out! It was a Technicolor breakthrough. Back in those days, the film was not nearly as sensitive to light as it is today. Now, over 40 years later, the cameraman would have no problem.

So there's the cavalry walking along, leading their mounts, the saddles and harnesses creaking, the sabers and canteens rattling, and the horses snorting and coughing under that black, eerie sky, with lightning flashing.

Winton Hoch won an Academy Award for his tremendous talent—not only for that famous shot, but for all of them.

Actors are a strange breed. We are in seventh heaven when our agent tells us we have come to an agreement with a movie company and will be on location (we don't care where) for X number of weeks, for X amount of dollars. Then, after a few weeks of shooting and judging the town on its merits or lack of them, we can't wait to hear, "That's a wrap" for the final time. We want to get home! After two weeks of unemployment, we start screaming at our agent again because we're not working. Home is hot and smoggy, and we long to go someplace where it's either too hot or too cold, the restaurants are lousy, and the rented car doesn't run right! How spoiled we have become.

When Uncle Jack yelled the magic words, "It's a wrap," we had been in Monument Valley exactly three weeks. Most of us figured it was just a wrap for the day. Even though we knew location shooting was winding down, none of us knew which day would be the final one.

Duke had been leading us across the valley—all dismounted—when Uncle Jack called out, "That is well. Cut it!" Then he turned toward our really fine production manager, Lowell Farrell, and in a lighthearted, phony, surprised voice said, "Oh, Lowell!" like he'd just discovered Lowell was there. "We've finished everything haven't we?"

Lowell was a cool customer, and the Old Man respected him. He replied, "Jack, you're the Boss. If you say we have completed shooting here in Monument, then it certainly is a wrap."

Jack took the bullhorn, fiddled with it until he found the clicker, and shouted at the top of his voice, "Thank you, boys! Thank you all for your hard work. My best to your families, and have a Happy Thanksgiving! Let's go home!"

Little Danny Borzage played "Red River Valley" as John Ford and John Wayne climbed into a station wagon, and off they went toward Gouldings' in a cloud of red dust. They'd be back—both of them—and me, too.

Our arrival in Flagstaff, after spending three hard weeks in Monument Valley, was the equivalent of arriving in, say, San Francisco. Flagstaff seemed like a metropolis. Jack would have hated to hear me say this. He hated complainers, (none of us did complain while we were up there). We had fun bitching about all we had been through, though, there in our cozy hotel room in Flagstaff.

Lowell Farrell (probably under orders from Jack) had done a very thoughtful thing. We had a three-hour layover before the train left for Los Angeles, so he booked rooms at the hotel, so we could relax before train time. Ben and I went up to our room to take our first real shower in three weeks. We had that red dust in our hair, our ears, our eyes, and ground into our skin. One shower wasn't going to get it all, but it would make us presentable.

We dried off and started getting into our dress-up clothes. In those days, when you left your house to go *anywhere*, you dressed up. The clothes you came to location in were either a suit and tie (also necessary for all social occasions and to get into a good restaurant), or a blue blazer, grey slacks, and loafers. I liked Bass Weejuns because they made my feet look smaller. You didn't wear prebleached designer blue jeans with holes in the knees, or running shoes, or a T-shirt which said "Fuck Off" or some other inspirational message. You didn't carry a canvas bag with the name of an athletic company on the plane with you, containing everything you would need for the six weeks you would be gone.

Ben was different. He wore a western-cut suede jacket, a cowboy shirt, and a tie. He had on $50 boots and a $50 cowboy hat. Those last two cost way over $200 each today, and Ben still dresses the same way. I dress Western style nowadays, too. For some reason back then, I thought you had to be a champion roper to wear Western clothes. Ben used to call my clothes jelly-bean clothes. But no matter, you had to have a coat and tie. I kind of miss that old dress code. I like it.

George O'Brien showed up, called room service, and ordered us some beer. We knew it was okay by the Old Man, if George ordered it. He was sort of like our priest. He kept us on the straight-and-narrow. We felt safe with George. "Immune" is a better word. We were immune in the company of George. That first beer in Flagstaff was almost as good as the first drink with Duke and Pete after *3 Godfathers*. It didn't have to release as much tension, but it was ice cold, and even George O'Brien, who wasn't a drinker, had to admit, "Boys, I've never had a beer taste better!"

George started chuckling. He'd take a swallow of beer, a puff on his cigar, and laugh again. Finally I asked, "What's so funny?"

He laughed again and asked. "Boys! Are we through shooting this picture? Now tell me? Are we?"

Ben and I both looked puzzled, and then I said, "Hell no, we've got a week or more left at the studio back home."

George answered loudly, "Yes. That is correct! That is very correct. We have more filming to do back in Hollywood! Ha—ha—ha but ha—ha Victor McLaglen—ha—ha—as sure as hell does not know that! Ha—ha. He's, at this very moment, down in the hotel barbershop, getting his hair cut. He's sound asleep in the barber chair, getting nearly all of his hair cut off!" He went on laughing. Then he added, "What is today? Thursday? God help him if Jack sees him before Monday in town. He's got to see him Monday, though; we're shooting the big dance sequence in full dress, and Uncle Victor has a haircut that won't match a damn! You'd think that Victor, after all these years in the business, would know better."

It wasn't really surprising, though. It was very typical of Victor. Here he was, in from "patrol" (something like his real past, out in India), and the first thing you do is get a bath and a haircut. He just got fact and fiction mixed up. Uncle Jack must have understood that, and he never said one word to Uncle Victor about his hair, or lack of it.

We each had two beers and some sandwiches, then we got on the train and slept like babies all the way to L.A., me dreaming of Marilyn, Ben dreaming of Carol, and Johnny Agar dreaming of Shirley Temple.

Big limousines picked up the actors and the production people at Union Station in Los Angeles. Johnny and I rode out to Brentwood together. I was extremely happy and couldn't wait to get home to my 23-year-old wife and two babies. Johnny desperately wanted the same thing; he wanted Shirley Temple there to greet him. I will never forget those huge iron gates at the entrance and the long driveway up to their palatial home. But it was just Johnny and a collie dog took that long walk alone. His beautiful Shirley was in Reno, making a movie with Clifton Webb.

We finished the filming at Pathé Studios, and I thought I could rest on my laurels and await the release of *3 Godfathers*. Instant stardom, loads of money, and a house of our own. The dreams of a youthful actor are boundless. There were hundreds in Hollywood with the same dreams; now, there are thousands. Casting people have three Academy Directories, each as thick as a New York City telephone book. In 1948, there was just one, and it was about the thickness of a short novel.

The final week of filming went smoothly. Johnny and I did our scene where we start to have fisticuffs over Joanne Dru and Duke bawls us out. We also shot the scene where Duke and Ben and I watch the Indians massacre the bad guys. It was Duke's idea that Pennell take a chaw from Brittles. He suggested it to Ford, and the Old Man went for it. Duke could get away with that every now and then. He knew when Ford was in the mood and when he wasn't. The role of Pennell is that of a conceited ass, and Duke wanted to convey in that scene that Pennell might someday develop into a real man. The irony of the whole *Yellow Ribbon* story, where my character was concerned, was that Duke was so into the character of Nathan Brittles that he treated me, Dobe Carey, his old *3 Godfathers* pal like I really was that horse's ass, even off the set. I guess I must have been giving a fairly convincing performance. We didn't become friends again until the picture was over.

After you finished a Ford movie, there was a little ritual that was terrific and memorable. You drove down to his office to pay him a final visit and express once more your gratitude for the work. He was always very jolly, and seemed grateful, too. Then he would remind you that in the outer office were some still photographs you might like to have. With a final farewell to him (all location horrors were forgiven), you proceeded out to the table beside Meta Stern's desk, where there was a stack of beautiful eleven-by-fourteen matte-printed stills from the just-completed movie. You could take all you wanted. Each one was a story. Each one was forceful, filled with poetry, drama, pathos. You wanted them all, even the ones you weren't in. Duke didn't seem to get in on this, for some reason, because years later I showed him one from *3 Godfathers,* and he was very surprised when I told him how I had gotten it.

Uncle Jack's favorite still photographer was Alex Kahle. He was a master at his craft. But even so, Uncle Jack directed the taking of the stills. He staged them, placing each actor in perfect composition with the surroundings. Then he'd say, "Wet your lips, and don't close your mouth."—Bingo! True histrionics.

Paul Fix, the OSS, and Merry Christmas

On August 12, 1944, I married a gorgeous blond by the name of Marilyn Fix. Her father was character actor Paul Fix. Paul had worked with my dad many times, and they were pals. That's how I came to know Marilyn. Paul Fix was one of those guys that my friend Wendell Corey called a "blue-shirt" actor. To him, that signified an old pro who could do it all on a moment's notice. That was Paul, in a nutshell—an old Hollywood pro.

Paul had come to California to seek his fortune with his bride, Taddy, just before the advent of sound. No biographer of John Wayne has ever written much about Paul Fix, and Paul Fix had almost as much to do with Duke's success as a screen actor as did John Ford. Paul Fix literally taught John Wayne what John Wayne knew about acting. He was the man who gave Duke his first insight into forming the mold which was to be his persona. Most people give Uncle Jack the credit for this, but the first man to put the John Wayne image into John Wayne's head was Paul Fix.

Paul first worked as an actor with Duke in those early westerns. In those days, Paul had a sort of slinky, haunted look about him, like a man who might steal or lie, so of course he was usually cast as a heavy; not the head honcho, though, the sly henchman. He played a lot of gangsters, along with Sheldon Leonard or Barton McLane. Paul was very serious about acting, and he wrote many plays. He was always putting them on in the little theaters around Hollywood. He cast Duke in one of them, but Duke was so frightened of live theater that he overdosed on booze and made a total ass out of himself. His wife, Josephine, was so furious she screamed from the audience, "You're a *bum*—a drunken *bum!*" What a night in the theater! Little did they know that they were looking at the man who was to become the biggest movie star of all time.

Duke used to tell Paul that he felt awkward in front of the camera. He said he didn't know what to do with his hands; that he didn't feel natural. Not too many years later, Duke got his big break when John Ford cast him as the "Ringo Kid" in *Stagecoach*. Duke was overwhelmed by this good news but paralyzed with fear that he wouldn't be able to carry it off. He went to Paul for help. Without John Ford's knowledge, Duke went to Paul's house every night to go over the next day's work while they were shooting in town. Because Duke was kind of heavy-footed and used to trudge more than walk, Paul told Duke to point his toes when he walked, and the "John Wayne walk" was born. Try it yourself. Take a step and point your toe, like you're stabbing it into the ground—left foot, right foot. Your shoulders automatically move back and forth, and the hips follow, not unlike Marilyn Monroe's walk. When Duke first did it, it was ballsey as hell. As the Wayne legend began to form, the walk became more pronounced. *Rio Bravo* or any of the "Rios" are good examples.

I had two very active years as a Navy Corpsman. A year of that was at the Oakland Naval Hospital, where I was a surgical corpsman. Most of 1944, I was stationed at what was then the very new Point Mugu Naval Facility. Point Mugu is about a 45-minute drive up the coast from Malibu Beach. At the time I was there, it was nothing more than a bunch of tents and Quonset huts. The navy was forming Combat Aircraft Service Units there called CASU, and I was in one of those outfits as a corpsman. We were taking combat training there prior to being shipped out to the South Pacific. I would have to say that I was relatively happy. I was told many years later that I was a young man tailored for regimentation, such as that of the military. This man said I had the kind of mental and physical makeup that responded to that. He said the acting profession was all wrong for my type of guy; that I would be happier being a milkman. He was right, in a sense.

I had a lot of good buddies, and I was prepared to go overseas and get it over with. Of course, I would miss Marilyn like hell, but this was war. It was just like it was in the movies of that period. I must kiss her good-bye, tell her to be brave, and then go and whip the Japs. I'm sure I didn't realize that by then, the Japanese had just about had it. United States forces were taking back all of the islands that we had lost, and besides, I wouldn't be going for a few weeks yet.

Marilyn was working at Columbia Studio as a secretary, and we stayed at the famous Chateau Marmont in Duke and Chata's penthouse apartment, because they were away. They had been living at Paul and Taddy's house in Hollywood but had recently rented this apartment at the Chateau.

Chata was a beautiful Mexican actress whose real name was Esperanza Bauer. The Chateau Marmont is a Gothic-style apartment hotel at the far eastern end of the Sunset Strip. For years and years, it was the place to stay for East Coast artists.

On the few weekends we had together, we would go down to the big house my folks had at Corona del Mar, near Newport Beach. It was an incredible house, right at the mouth of Newport Harbor. When I was growing up, we always called Newport "Balboa," "Whoopie! We're going to Balboa." Mom and Dad had sold the old ranch in Saugus, California, while I was in boot camp and had moved down to the ocean.

On this particular weekend, I had gotten liberty from Point Mugu, and Marilyn and I drove down to Corona del Mar. That's where Marilyn got her first look at the famous John Ford. It was not a very pleasant experience: he scared the hell out of her. He was very drunk. One look at my dad told the whole story. He looked at me and shook his head—a look that did not go unnoticed by Ford. He was never *that* drunk.

Jack looked up at me and exclaimed, "Why the 'ell didn't you marry Barbara?" With that, Marilyn fled the scene, but the Old Man had me pinned in his gaze. Then I realized he was trying to make out the insignia on my arm. Ford would talk crazily when he was drinking. Much of the time he wasn't as drunk as he let on. I think he figured that if he acted really drunk, he could pick up on what people said about him and get a read on people. Pop was embarrassed for me.

Jack said something like, "Whas' the ra'ing bage on your ahm?"

I said, "How's that again, sir?" and he said it again, even worse.

He wanted to know what my "rate" was. I told him I was a corpsman third class. In navy terms, Pharmacist Mate Third Class. He just blinked at that, and finally, after what seemed an eternity, James, his loyal driver, came to the rescue and took him back to his yacht, the *Araner.* Dobe Carey was on his mind, but I didn't know that. I did know that he was a four-striper, a captain in the navy.

One day when I was back at Port Hueneme, which was just up the road from Point Mugu, they gave us the word: "After this liberty, guys, when you get back, you are secured. We're shipping out. Don't say a word." That was it. I'd only get to be with Marilyn one more time—maybe the last time, forever. Who knows? We had 6,000 miles of ocean ahead of us. So I drove to Hollywood to the Chateau Marmont, and we had the saddest dinner of our lives. We went to bed and waited for morning, so we could get it over with—get the good-bye over with.

Well, we steamed around the Pacific for 34 days. I think that was the most dangerous part of the whole time I was out there. There were still some Japanese subs roaming around, but a lot of us were in danger of puking ourselves to death. We finally got to Guam. The Seabees, God bless them, had made what seemed like a paradise out of that tropical island, which had only been secured two months before. Guam was heaven on earth after sloshing around the Pacific with 3,000 guys on a ship built for less than 1,000. I was on Guam about a month, just getting good and comfortable, when they split CASU 51 in half. My half went to the Caroline Islands. I settled into a routine there and was pretty happy. There were no Japanese and no war—just navy duties with a really good bunch of guys, many of whom had been at my wedding.

One day I was off-duty and lying in my cot reading a Western. It was mid-afternoon when a kid stuck his head in our tent and yelled, "There a Carey in here?"

"Yeah. Right here," I replied.

"H. G.?" he asked me.

"Yeah, that's me."

"Who the hell do *you* know?" he exclaimed.

"Whatcha' mean who do I know?" I didn't know what he was getting at.

"You're goin' back to the States, mate!"

I didn't know it was Ford. Ford never crossed my mind. I was sure there had been some mistake; how could I be going to the States? I went up to the personnel office, where my friend McNalley worked. He was more serious than I had ever seen him. In fact, I had never seen him this strange. He looked at me with suspicion and disappointment, then he said the same thing as the kid who came to the tent. "Who in the hell do you know?" Only he added "in Washington." He was looking me straight in the eyes, and I was taken aback. He wasn't my friend anymore; I could tell that. I wasn't happy—I was sad. It sounds crazy because I had with a chance to go back to my Marilyn, but I'd only been over there a little over three months, and in my deepest heart, I wanted to stay with the guys.

So I went to see my boss, Dr. Frank Thomas. "Doc, I have orders to go back to the USA, and I've gotten used to it here. I don't want to cause any trouble. Can you do anything to switch it around? Tell them you need me too badly here."

He looked at the papers I had in my hand and replied, "Carey, these are Bureau Orders. These come from the very top in Washington. You're going to have to go." Then he stood up and put out his hand. "Good luck in whatever it is you're going to do. You've certainly done a fine job for me."

I walked aimlessly around for a long time and, at dusk, headed for the chapel. I went into that grass House of God and fell on my knees. I did not want to leave my outfit. I missed Marilyn with all my heart, but I did not want to put anything over on these guys I had laughed and served with. I didn't want to leave until we could all go home together. When I left the chapel it hit me like a ton of bricks. The very last weekend that Marilyn and I spent at Corona Del Mar, a very, very long form had arrived from a government agency, and I had filled that form out. It took about three hours. I signed it and mailed it. This transfer had to be the result of that form.

I said good-bye to the guys. There were tears. I got on a C-47 (we know it now as a DC-3), and flew back to Guam. From there, I took another plane to Pearl Harbor. I was there a week until I was put aboard an old World War I ship and washed trays for eight days until we landed in Vallejo, California. Marilyn and my mother and father were waiting for me in San Francisco just across the bay, and believe it or not, the navy gave me 20 days leave. Then I was to report to the navy in Washington, D.C.

On the given date, I was there. Washington seemed like the craziest place on the earth to me. I went to the address I had been given. I didn't see anything on the doors that signified what outfit it was, but there were a lot of uniforms walking around—not only navy, but army and marine. I was supposed to see Lieutenant English. It was not what you would picture as a typical meeting with a naval officer. In fact, it was about as navy as an Abbott and Costello movie. My rate was clearly visible on my left arm, so that, at a glance, a regular navy man would know immediately what it stood for, but Lt. English didn't know what I was doing there, and neither did I. He was very pleasant, though, and didn't seem to care too much whether I went home or stayed there.

I felt I could have said to him, "Listen, sir, why don't I drop by in a couple of days, when the air clears, and we can discuss this then?"

But I didn't, and he looked at the papers I'd given him again and said, "Listen, Carey, uh—the—uh Skipper isn't here right now, and no one has left word with me what I'm supposed to do with you. So let me ask you this. Uh—are you a cameraman?"

"No, sir," I replied.

"A still photographer?"

"No, sir, I'm not."

He rubbed his head in frustration. "How about film editing? Are you a film editor?"

I thought I was in a game of Twenty Questions, but I said, "No, sir," to that, too. I said, "I'm a Medical Corpsman, sir."

"Well," he said, "we don't have a sick bay here. We send them over to the Naval Hospital just a few blocks away. So I don't know what to do with you, Carey."

After that, I decided I had better take the bull by the horns. I still had no idea of what branch of the service I had been assigned to. The papers I had been given didn't exactly spell it out. I had my leave papers and a letter with an address—that was it. Lt. English seemed a reasonable man, so I asked him, "Sir, what outfit is this? I mean what branch of the navy is this, sir?"

"Oh," he said, "I guess you're entitled to know that, young fella'. This is the Field Photographic Branch of the Office of Strategic Services—the O.S.S.—and our Skipper is Captain John Ford, but he's on an assignment." Of course, the OSS became what is now known as the CIA.

My Uncle Jack Ford had a hell of a lot of clout with Uncle Sam. I finally wound up in the film lab, developing classified government film and captured German film. I have a firm message to all anti-Semites who yell that the Holocaust never happened: it happened. We were some of the first people to see it on film. I served the last eleven months of my navy career under Captain John Ford. Now that sounds as if I might have seen him often, but I only saw him once. He served the country heroically. He'd been wounded while filming *The Battle of Midway,* and he served in two major invasions. The beach at Normandy was one.

When I arrived for duty in Washington, Jack was filming *They Were Expendable.* He had just completed this movie when he sent for me to come to his office in the Agricultural Building, where we were all stationed. By this time, I was well-trained in my duties and had been promoted to Petty Officer Second Class, the equivalent to a buck sergeant in the army. That helped my confidence somewhat. If anyone had told me then that just three-and-a-half years later I would be emoting in front of this same man, I would have sent for the men in the white coats.

I could tell right off he had been drinking. He'd just started, though, and wasn't too far gone, but his tongue was jutting in and out like it had at Corona del Mar. He looked at me a long time before he said anything. Finally he said, "Where the hell were you stationed before you came here?"

"The Caroline Islands, sir," I replied.

He just nodded his head. "How do you like the duty here?"

"Fine, sir," I said. "Just fine."

Then he stared at me some more. Finally, he said, "Ray says you're doing a good job here. I told your Maw and Paw. They're both fine. Okay, that's all kid. Get back to work."

I split really fast and headed for the comfort of the darkroom. God! What a scary man. That was the first time I remembered being alone with him.

The Ray he spoke of was Lieutenant Ray Kellogg, who was an officer in Field Photo and, in peacetime, the head of Special Effects at Twentieth Century Fox Studios. He was fearless, and good at his job.

There was a great big, tough, raw-boned man who was in all Ford films. His name was Jack Pennick. A more good-hearted soul never lived, but back then, I thought him as mean and tough as Ford himself. Anyone who loves Ford films will recognize Pennick right away. Later on, I was to learn that he had the unenviable job of waking the Old Man up every morning on location and handing him his coffee, which Himself might "accidentally" spill on the bedclothes. After Pennick woke him up, he'd sit there drinking the coffee and just stare off, not saying a word. Then he'd go to the toilet, come back out, pull on his clothes without bothering to tie his shoes, and walk out the door to the waiting station wagon. Water never touched any part of his body in the morning.

Jack Pennick had a good role as "Doc Charlie" in *They Were Expendable*. He had seen action in both wars, first as a marine sergeant and then as a navy Chief Boatswains Mate, which is the toughest rate in the navy, just like a topkick in the marines.

He had returned to duty in Washington before Ford did, and from the day he arrived—the minute he spotted me—he was all over me. Anytime he saw me outside of my developing room, he gave me hell about something. I couldn't understand it. I wasn't some recruit. What had I ever done to him? By this time, Marilyn had managed to get to Washington and fought the battle for an apartment. I would come home at night and pour out my tale of how Pennick was hassling me. In the morning at the Agricultural Building, we'd have what we laughingly called "reveille" up on the roof. None—I mean *none* of the other men in the outfit—had ever been to boot camp. They all had come straight off the studio lots into navy uniforms. They barely knew "right face." When they screwed it up, which was often, Pennick said not a word. I'd do it right, and he'd chew my ass out. He was always yelling, "Square that hat!" (Well, I did wear it on the back of my head). This went on for a few weeks. Finally one day I was in the camera shop, having coffee, and in comes Pennick. I thought, "Oh, my God!"

He looked me over real good. Finally, he said, "Hello, kid. How do you like the navy?"

I said, "It's a lot better than regular duty on a base, Chief."

He looked startled. "Hey, wait a minute. How long you been in, kid?"

I said, "Two-and-a-half years, Chief."

"Aw, my God. Oh, Sweet Jesus. Well, my God, kid, why didn't ya' tell me? The Old Man told me you were brand new an' to work ya' over real good." Well, from that day on, big tough Jack Pennick couldn't have been nicer.

Sometimes Marilyn would come down to where I was working and we'd go out to dinner. Pennick would always hunt me up and say, "Hey, Red. There's a mighty beautiful blond topside waiting for you. Go home and enjoy yourself."

Pennick had been in a lot of movies, but first and foremost in his heart, he was a topkick. He loved and respected that uniform. Years later, when we were shooting *Yellow Ribbon,* I wore the uniform of a second lieutenant in the cavalry. Pennick always snapped a salute any time he saw me. I said, "Jack, I'm in wardrobe, for God's sake. You still outrank me."

"No, Dobe," he said, "you're an officer in the United States Cavalry."

One day I rode back from location with Uncle Jack, and Pennick opened the car door and gave Jack a smart salute, as he always did. Ford said to me later, "There's one thing I'd love to see in my lifetime, but I'm going to miss it."

I asked him, "What's that, Uncle Jack?"

"Pennick at my funeral." But no one saw Pennick at Ford's funeral; Pennick died first.

April 12, 1945, Marilyn and I were in our tiny apartment when we became aware of the newsboy yelling in the street below. I ran down to get a paper and saw the huge headlines: ROOSEVELT DEAD.

Gradually the town seemed to grow quieter, and people everywhere were crying. The stores were all closed. Many had put his picture in their display windows. That weekend we took the train to New York City to see my grandmother, Banny, my father's mother. At every crossing signal, there were people standing with their hats off and their hands over their hearts. We couldn't understand it. When we got to Grand Central Station, we understood. There was a baggage car attached to our train, all decked out with the Colors and an Honor Guard. Franklin Delano Roosevelt's body was being transported to Hyde Park for burial, and we were on that train with him!

We were very close to history there in Washington D.C. VE Day was next—May 8th, 1945. The town went nuts. VJ Day was August 14, 1945, and we all went nuts again. Give-'em-Hell Harry had ended the war. Exactly four years after the attack on Pearl Harbor, I was honorably discharged from the navy, and six days later, our first son was born, Steven Harry Carey. Six weeks after that, we were on my folk's new ranch at the foot of Palomar Mountain in San Diego County, California.

They had sold the house at Corona del Mar while we were in Washington, D.C., and bought an 1,150-acre ranch—a truly magnificent piece of real estate. It had everything: rich soil, hundreds of old oak trees, and best of all, a whole mountain filled with water. It sprang out everywhere. My father named this place the Water Mountain Ranch. He tried hard to love it, but his heart was still up there in the old mesquite and sagebrush-covered canyons of Saugus.

When they drove down that long front road for the last time, I'll bet he never once looked back. I'm glad I was away in the navy—I never could have watched that. Well, my mom tried to make it up to him. In the middle of the war, she was able to build a 4,000-square-foot adobe ranch house for her old man, Harry Carey.

He did some horseback riding there, but he spent most of his time sitting by the fireplace in his new den. All kinds of people came from town, and it was nearly 200 miles, and no freeways. It just wasn't the same, though, and his cough was getting really bad. They finally moved up to Beverly Hills with the rest of the movie crowd. Pop made *Sea of Grass* for Elia Kazan, and his last film, *Red River,* but he was having a lot of trouble getting his air. He was very ill and had lost his confidence. No one could tell except my mom or me. He was the same old Harry Carey, because his film technique was so ingrained in him that his uncertainty didn't show. I can't see it on the screen, either, but Mom could see it on the set. Duke wasn't aware that Pop didn't feel well, because Pop still kidded with him and made him laugh. Had Duke known it, I'm sure he would have spoken to Howard Hawks about easing up on him a little. Mr. Hawks was wonderful to me when I worked on that same film later. He calmed me down before each take so I felt at ease with the character I was playing.

Admiral John Ford had been paid $300,000 by M-G-M to make *They Were Expendable.* He used all of that money to buy the Field Photo Farm out in the San Fernando Valley and set up a fund to keep it operating. It was for the members of the Field Photographic Unit of the OSS and their families. The house was a big colonial, quite lovely, but not used too much. There was a clubhouse, which was used for parties and Sunday barbeques, a tennis court, and a pool, which he had built especially to accommodate the needs of the paraplegics from nearby Birmingham Hospital. For the families of those who had made the supreme sacrifice, there was a tiny chapel just inside the front gate. When my father died in 1947, he lay in state in that beautiful little chapel with his horse, Sunny, tied to the railing out in front. The chapel now stands on the grounds of the Motion Picture and Television Country Home in Woodland Hills.

There was also a very nice stable area on the property, and so we moved Sunny and my horse, Mormon, there from Mandeville Canyon, where they had been boarded. Pop wasn't all that happy about the horses being out at the John Ford Farm. When I would ask him if he would like to go for a ride, he kept putting me off. I knew he wanted to, but he didn't want to run into Jack. He thought he'd have to sit and visit with him. Old wounds sometimes never heal. He and Jack had an abrasive yet loving relationship that made their infrequent meetings seem a lot like debates.

Uncle Jack had two really big events every year at the Farm. One was Memorial Day and the other was the Christmas party for all the kids and their parents. We would meet months in advance of either of these days to prepare. He gave every one of us on the board of directors special duties so that it would all go smoothly.

Memorial Day started about 9:00 in the morning with a solemn and moving ceremony. He wanted all the members to be in uniform, probably so he could have a reason to wear his admiral's uniform. Sometimes Duke would be there, but it wasn't a regular thing, like with the rest of us. Since I had been an enlisted man, I wore a "sailor suit" with the 13 buttons on the front of my pants and a little white hat. When I was young, I looked great in it and was proud to wear it, but I started getting too old for it.

Finally, I said to him, sometime in the early 1950s, "Uncle Jack, I've grown out of my uniform."

His comment was, "Rent one!" So for a few more years, my friend Bill Howard of the Western Costume Company would loan me one. At last, even the Old Man saw how ridiculous I looked, and from then on, I wore a blue blazer and gray slacks.

The festivity Uncle Jack enjoyed the most was the yearly Children's Christmas Party. It was usually held on the last Sunday before Christmas, and everything had to go like clockwork. The timing had to be perfect. I was put in charge—a *big* responsibility. The stagecoach had to be ordered, along with six saddle horses for the guest actors to ride. Every year, Fat Jones would send over not only the coach and horses, but all the harness and the tack and the wranglers to take care of them. Two full truckloads of horses and equipment—just like a Ford location—and it was all gratis. All I had to do was make one phone call to Fat to tell him the date and time, and they were there.

The next most important thing was to get a Santa Claus. Ford himself always appointed the Santa. Andy Devine had the job for two years or so, then Charlie Kemper, and then Alan Hale. Charlie and Alan each died the following year, and so the next year Jack got a "professional" to do the job, and he died too. It got very spooky. Finally the Santas stopped dying on us, but we had a different one every year. The last one was big, wonderful Mike Mazurki. Enough time had gone by so he didn't feel jinxed. The kids loved the Santa with the cauliflower ears.

On the big day around 9:30 in the morning, the huge trucks would arrive. They would unload at the rear entrance to the Farm on Erwin Street. Wingate Smith and his wife, Helen, lived next door, so Santa would be there, getting dressed. Santa's big chair and presents were already in the clubhouse, along with a Christmas tree that had been decorated a week or so earlier by the members of the farm. The parking lot would start to fill up, and everyone wandered around the grounds and into the house.

The stunt guys got out there early. They would gather at the stable with their horses. Nearly everyone had a bottle stashed in his pickup truck, and every time I'd pass, they'd offer the brown bag. Then I'd run back to the main gate and wait for the Old Man to arrive. Here he came, Mary went into the house, and I would escort Uncle Jack over to the barn so he could see how everything was progressing. It would make him smile. Here were his favorite people, his stuntmen. Here were the two Chucks, "good" Chuck Hayward and "bad" Chuck Roberson; Slim Hightower and Slim's best pal, Fred Kennedy; Terry Wilson, who also doubled Duke; Frankie McGrath, Billy Jones, and Ed Jauregui.

The main man this day was Post Parks. He was driving the stagecoach. Uncle Jack shook Cliff Lyons' hand. "Hi ya' Cliff. These boys behaving?"

"Yessir. But goddam—goddam—you know how stuntmen are, Mr. Ford—heh—heh—heh."

Then Uncle Jack would go out to where the stagecoach was parked to thank the wranglers and to check on Santa. Actually he was checking on me, to see if I had forgotten anything, but he was having a great time. It was a very special day for him. Then he would give me the word to get Danny Borzage and Jimmy Stewart up on top of the stagecoach. Every

Christmas party after *Liberty Valance*, Jimmy came to the farm. People often ask me, "Who's the nicest movie star you ever worked with?" I don't even have to think to answer: Jimmy Stewart.

After Uncle Jack saw that all was ready, he went back to the main house. I'd take one last run on my horse, and Jack would drop his famous handkerchief, which meant "Bring 'em on!" It was wonderful. Out we'd come—east on Erwin, south on Lindley, west onto Calvert Street, in through the gates of the farm, and down the pepper tree drive. Ford's cowboys escorting Santa in the stagecoach, with Jimmy Stewart and Danny Borzage on top, each playing "Jingle Bells" on their accordions.

It was something to see. Uncle Jack was as excited as the kids. The stagecoach stopped right in front of the big house. Santa got out with a big sack of presents on his back, and everyone followed him to the clubhouse. After cake and ice cream, Santa would leave, slip into his civvies, and come back to join the party. The kids were never the wiser. That was a Ford Christmas at the Field Photo Farm.

Late in the summer of 1946, I was standing on the corner of Ventura Boulevard and Laurel Canyon Boulevard in Studio City, near the old Republic Studio. I was holding my son, Steven, in my arms. He was only a year and a half, and didn't know what a movie cowboy was yet, but being a young father, I thought it my duty to give him a chance to see "The King of the Cowboys," Roy Rogers, the grand marshall of the parade coming down Ventura Boulevard. While we were waiting, I felt a tap on my shoulder. I turned to see who it was, and while the face looked familiar to me, I couldn't put a name to it. This pleasant-looking man didn't waste time jogging my memory, "Aren't you Dobe Carey?" he asked.

When I said I was, he said, "Well, I'm Bill Berke. I produced a few of your father's westerns." I replied, "Why sure, the ones that Harry Frazier directed!"

"That's right. You have a good memory."

He went on with a lot of enthusiasm. "Dobe, I'm in the middle of a little picture now, and there's a small part that you'd be very good for—a young cowboy. Do you think you'd be interested? What are you doing now?"

I told him that I hadn't been out of the navy for very long and that I was trying to have a career as a singer. (A totally futile idea that I didn't give up until I was fifty!) I was thrilled at the idea, but till that moment hadn't given movies a thought, because I didn't want to try and follow in my father's footsteps.

Now here was Bill Berke, throwing an offer at me. I was excited and confused by the prospect. Suddenly a thought came to mind. "Mister Berke, I don't belong to the Screen Actors Guild."

"That's no problem," he said. "I'll call them, and they'll give you a card. Do you want the part or not?"

I felt a big rush of blood to my cheeks and blurted out, "Yessir. Yessir, I'd like very much to do it."

He looked happy and told me someone would call me as to where and when to show up for the shooting. Three days later I did the scene. It didn't take long. There was no "coverage" (close-ups), but I wasn't aware of that. I thought I had just finished *Gone With the Wind.* Singing was secondary now. "I'm an actor," I said to myself. When I think back on it now, forty-six years later, I must have been nuts. The name of that little film was *Rolling Home,* and it starred Jean Parker and Russell Hayden.

That night, following my first day's work on a movie, my folks gave a big party for Elia Kazan. He and pop had just finished *Sea Of Grass.* I was tending bar when a hero of mine approached me with a wry smile on his handsome face. It was Fredric March.

He said to me, "I hear you played your first movie role today."

I was in total awe. I gulped, "Yessir, that's right."

He offered me his hand and said, "Welcome to the picture business."

It was like a blessing. I'll never forget that brief moment.

Wagonmaster

It was late summer 1949. I was at the Field Photo Farm, grooming my horse, Mormon. I had him tied up in front of the barn and was going to take him for a good ride. I was all alone there. Sunny was there, and some other horses, but I had not seen another person in the time I had been there. It was nice. I felt as though I had the whole farm to myself, and I was so lost in thought that I did not notice the man walking on the narrow footbridge that crossed the flood-control spillway that ran through the property.

Then I heard, "Is that Ol' Dobe?"

I looked up, surprised as hell, and sure enough, it was Uncle Jack. Had he planned this? Did he know I was going to be at the Farm? He did things like this all the time. It was part of his mystique, his aura, his genius for creating beautiful happenings.

I thought to myself, "It's a weekday. What's he up to? There's nothing special going on."

Then he said it again, as he got nearer, "Is that Ol' Dobe?"

"Yessir, it is," I answered.

He looked at my horse with great interest. "Is that your horse? I don't know that horse, do I?"

"No, sir," I replied, "I don't think so. We had him at the old ranch. He's a roping horse."

"What do you call him?" he asked.

"Mormon," I said.

"What?" There was disbelief in his voice as he repeated the name. "Mormon. That horse's name is *Mormon?*"

I thought I was in hot water somehow, that maybe his name ought to be "Pope" or something, but I said, "Yessir. Pop named him that because he was born and raised in Utah." Nothing ever seemed to surprise John Ford, but I could see he was surprised at that.

Then he asked, "That little horse comes from Utah? Moab, Utah?"

"No, sir," I said. "Saint George, Utah, Uncle Jack."

"Well, I'll be goddamned," he said. Then he stared at me for a few seconds. A small smile crossed his face, and he said some magic words. "How would you like to ride him in a western?"

I was flabbergasted, but I spurted out, "Boy, that would be great!"

"Okay, that's swell. You will," he said. He acted happy. He was happy because he was going to do something he loved to do more than any- thing—make a western. Then he said, as though he were letting me in on a secret, "I'm going to make a western in a month or so with you and ol' Ben."

"And Duke?" I asked. I know it seemed a dumb question, but I figured a movie didn't make any money without a big star. He straightened me out in a hurry.

"Christ no, not with Duke. I just told you. I'm making a western with you and ol' Ben Johnson. No Duke. You and Ben are the stars."

Well, I was totally speechless. I stood there looking off, with my mouth hanging open. Finally he said, "You don't want to do it? You don't want to make a picture without Duke?" Of course that was his Irish humor.

I couldn't help laughing, and then I tried to square it. "Oh my gosh— yessir—I didn't mean—well, that's the best news I ever had in my life, Uncle Jack, and—well, I just don't know how to thank you."

"You just did," he said.

Then I found out why he was so startled when he heard my horse's name.

"It's a pretty little story about some Mormon folks who came west after Brother Brigham had settled Salt Lake City. They journeyed further on to the southeast and stayed in the small valley where Moab, Utah, is today. Frank (Nugent) and Pat (his son, Patrick Ford) are writing the script, and I'm going to shoot it there in Moab."

Then he went on a little bit more about the story, "The wagon train comes upon a medicine-show troupe who are dying of thirst and drinking their own potions. You boys save them, and then along come the heav- ies—really bad bastards—and they take over the whole bunch. Then you and ol' Ben come to the rescue. It's a helluva nice story. We're going to make it cheap—not spend a lot of dough. Hell, you guys don't need much dough, do you?" He smiled, with a twinkle in his eye, and gave me a punch on the arm. Then he said in mock horror, "Oh shit! I guess I'll have to use Ward. Oh, I forgot—you like Ward."

I roomed with Ward many times on location. I always found him a good man to share a room with. He was a very upbeat, positive person. If there was something mental that was bothering you, he could usually fix it by bawling you out. If your problem was physical, he could fix that, too; he carried a small pharmacy with him. Ward Bond though, was one hell of an actor. He brought stability to every scene he was in.

"Well, take your ride, kid," said Uncle Jack, "and tell Mormon here that he's going back to Utah." And then, "Oh, by the way, there's a Mormon hymn called 'Come, Come Ye Saints.' I want you to learn it." With that parting remark, as if on cue, Bill Ramsey, Uncle Jack's butler-driver-friend, came across the larger bridge in the Buick station wagon to pick up his boss. The only time I ever saw John Ford break down completely was at Bill Ramsey's funeral, years later.

Ben Johnson was a fearless cowboy and stuntman, but he was deathly afraid of airplanes. We were sitting in one that was to take us to Moab. Ben had a window seat and was hanging onto my left arm as though I could do something if we got into trouble. The plane was a little DC-3. In those days, that was what you flew on short hops. For years, it was known as the safest plane ever built. When I told Ben that I had flown across the Pacific Ocean in one, he countered with, "Yeah, Dobe, but that there was over water where a fella' might have a chance, if he could swim. We're goin' over them big high mountains." To be honest, I was not feeling that secure, either.

We started over the mountains and that little plane started bucking and pitching like a bronc. "Dobe," Ben drawled, "this son-a-bitch is a-gonna fart and fall for sure."

He was gripping my arm so hard my hand was going numb. I said, "Ben, look at the Boss up there." Uncle Jack was sitting in the first righthand seat, reading a book and puffing on a cigar. His feet were crossed up on the partition in front of him.

Now that I think of it, I don't know why we didn't take the train to Grand Junction, Colorado, and drive from there to Moab.

We finally landed! Bumpity-bump—bump—bump—screech and stop. We bolted out of the plane and looked around. We had landed on an immense sort of mesa. The nose of that DC-3 was not more than 50 yards from a huge abyss.

"Ol' Dobe," Ben said, following a long look at where we had ended up, "you remember what I done told you about them Brahma bulls?"

"Yeah, I remember."

"Well," he said, "I'll ride one of them bastards any day before I'll take another plane ride like this one."

As soon as we had finished the first shot of the picture, I knew *Wagonmaster* was going to be a prize as far as work was concerned. I'll never forget that first shot. The Old Man never started very early, and when Ben and I arrived on the set that first day, we saw a long line of "dolly track."

"Dobe," Ben said, "he's a-gonna start us off with a lot of dialogue."

"Well, we know it," I said.

"Let's run through that sucker a few times before the old bird gets here," Ben replied. So we did, and we knew it good. I saw a good-looking team hitched to a little spring wagon up where the dolly track began, so I figured that Uncle Jack would have me drive the team. Ben would be riding his big sorrel horse, Steel, and be leading some other horses, since we played horse traders in the movie.

Pretty soon Uncle Jack showed up, greeted everyone, and said to Ben and me, "You guys ready to go to work? Do you know them words?"

"Yessir," we both answered at once.

"Let's hear 'em," he said. We ran the dialogue.

He changed a couple of minor things, as he always did, and then said, "I don't see any reason why we can't shoot this scene. Dobe, get in the wagon. You boys are old friends—probably grew up near each other. You're going to do some horse trading in town, and then go have a few drinks. Just play it relaxed. Have a good time with it. It's a nice scene. Okay kids. Here we go. Ben, you're riding beside Dobe's wagon. Stay back here so you don't turn too far away from the camera. Okay, here we go. This will be picture!"

One take! That was it! Not even one for protection. He yelled out good and loud, "Right!" and then, "Well, if you want to make better pictures, you have to get better actors." He *always* said that when he was really happy with a shot. I never quite figured out exactly what that meant, but I do know that it was a sign that things were very good.

The entire shooting was a piece of cake. He seemed very pleased with the way the shooting was going. It was right around this time that Uncle Jack wrote a note to my mother. My father and he were the only people who called my mother Goldie.

"Moab, Utah. Dear Goldie, In haste—the Kid is really hitting his stride in this picture—he is really swell. Well, we can stop worrying about him—he's in. Affectionately, Jack." Well, by God, he was treating me like Spencer Tracy! We were all having a good time. He used to tell me later that it was the best movie he ever made. Of course, that is not true.

The backbone of *Wagonmaster* was Ward Bond. Ward had a room to himself on this one, by the way. Ben and I were roommates at the Moab Motel. Moab was just a teeny town in 1949; uranium hadn't been discovered there yet. There were a lot of good people there; families who had been there since the days of Brother Brigham.

No movie company ever starts shooting without the equivalent of the legitimate theater's advance man. The movie advance man's job is much more complicated, however. Two or three months in advance of shooting, the studio takes over a lot of rooms at the local Holiday Inn or whatever. The main suite is the production office. Then there is accounting (where everyone goes once a week to collect their "per diem," the extra money given you to eat on), transportation, construction, costuming, and the casting office for casting local people. And that's only some of it. All those people are up there before the actors and are already tired of the place by the time actual shooting begins. Most of these jobs were filled by guys then, but now, there are more gals, except for construction. I like that; they are nicer and not so opinionated.

Boy, does the town make money when a movie crew comes to film! Movie crews today behave a lot less nutty than they did when I was young. Of course, on a Ford show you know the answer. It all begins with "The Man." If he doesn't have the leadership right from the start, nothing works. That causes unrest, boozing, and disruption. So Moab, Utah, went through the metamorphosis. The local folks were cast and dressed in period clothes.

Since this was a wagon-train picture, each wagon had a family in it. A few years later, the TV series "Wagon Train" starring Ward Bond was created because of our film. Every wagon had a family unit—Mom and Dad, sometimes Grandma and Grandpa, kids and, of course, dogs. Sometimes the families were related, but not necessarily. Moab was such a small town that everybody knew everybody, anyway. There were also people from the outlying towns who heard about the movie and drove over, "on spec," hoping to find work.

John Ford was wonderful to the townspeople who worked as extras. To him, there was no such person as an extra, and because of that, they all adored him. He knew most of them by name by the end of that first day. They'd do anything for him. He would talk to them before each shot about how he wanted them to react—sometimes he'd tease them.

One day, everyone was standing about, waiting to be told what to do—women, children, young, pretty women, middle-aged women, and some grandmas. Ford had been wandering among them, getting them relaxed, and then he returned to the camera area on a knoll. Ben and I were up there with him. Ford waited for the perfect moment. He didn't have to yell, "Quiet!" like he did in Hollywood.

Then he hollered out, "How many of you folks are Mormons?" Almost all of them raised their hands. Uncle Jack was happy to see this, and then he asked in a louder voice, "How many here know the Mormon Hymn? Don't be embarrassed. I mean, how many know it? The Mormon Hymn, 'Come, Come Ye Saints!' " They all just stood there and looked at him in a sort of stunned silence. So Uncle Jack announced to the crowd, "This young man here with the red hair," he put his hand on my shoulder, "is Harry Carey, Jr. He's one of the leads in the picture, but the important thing is, he knows the Mormon Hymn. So he's now going to show you how it goes."

Then he said to me in a normal voice, "Go ahead, kid, sing the hell out of it."

Little Danny was there with his accordion. He played the intro and I sang "Come, Come Ye Saints" for 50 people who had heard it all their lives but were just too shy to raise their hands and sing it. When I finished, there was a smattering of applause, nothing to bow over. Then Ford chided them.

Smiling, he said, "My goodness, I can't believe it. A young man from Hollywood has to come all the way up here to teach the Mormon people how to sing 'Come, Come Ye Saints.' That's amazing—just amazing." Then he went on about the business of filming *Wagonmaster.*

Uncle Jack didn't keep abreast of the current popular music or the current western music groups that were so abundant in those days, but he loved music. Western folk music was becoming very popular during the time of *Wagonmaster.*

One day just a few weeks before we began filming, I got a call from George O'Brien. We were living in Brentwood, and George's house was about a mile away. I am known as a pretty good talker, but George O'Brien made me seem like Silent Sam. George had attained stardom in *The Iron Horse,* directed by John Ford, back in 1924. So I'm talking about 25 years later now.

George was an Irish Catholic. He was born in San Francisco, the son of the chief of police. He was a natural father-confessor for us guys who thought we were so smart. George could set you straight in a hurry. George loved to recall the old days, but his stories were told in such rapid-fire fashion that it was hard to keep track of them. He was an arch conservative, and though I didn't agree with him politically, I was very fond of George. He had a good heart, like Duke, and Ward, and most of the rest of the Ford bunch. I have always found the political conservatives to be much warmer and friendlier people on the whole than the superserious political left of the movie business. I don't know why this seems to be, but it is.

Anyway, George was all excited about a guest he had at his house, and he couldn't wait for me to get there.

"My boy," he said, "drop everything, my friend, and get over here. There's a good man here, Dobe, my pal (that's the way George talked) who knows you, but you'll never guess who he is until you see him. Dobe, my pal, drop everything—and—well—you know where my place is, do you not?"

I did know, and immediately forgot the bamboo rake I had been using. I set off for O'Brien's house, a wonderful old Spanish-style home. George answered the door and led me into his huge, high-ceilinged, beamed living room. Big old Navajo rugs covered the tile floor. Rising from the sofa as I entered was none other than the park ranger from the deadly sands of Death Valley—the man who had the audacity to tell John Ford that you couldn't squeeze water out of a cactus during the filming of *3 Godfathers*, the year before. It was park ranger Stan Jones.

It flashed through my head, as I shook his hand, that I had seen his picture in *Time* magazine some weeks before. Stan had written a song called "Ghost Riders in the Sky." Burl Ives had recorded it first, but the big smash record had been done by bandleader and singer Vaughn Monroe. It's still sung today all over the world.

We had coffee and talked for about an hour, reminiscing about the Death Valley experience. Then George suggested that we do something that changed many people's lives. He said that perhaps Jack Ford would like Stan's songs. Stan didn't just write "Ghost Riders." He had been writing songs for years, using nothing more than his little Martin tenor guitar. He and his beautiful wife, Olive, had lived all over the West in the cabins of the National Park Service.

I said that, of course, Jack would love to hear Stan's songs, and besides that, he would get a kick out of seeing him again. So O'Brien called Uncle Jack and simply asked him if we could bring "a genius of Western music" down to play one song for him. Jack said for all of us to come down to his office at the old RKO Pathé Studio in Culver City, pronto.

George had a very breezy and charming manner, and he could kid Jack a lot and not have to pay the price. This afternoon, when we all marched in, Uncle Jack knew Stan right away. He didn't start up about the cactus, like I thought he would, but he never did what you thought he would do. He was really glad to see Stan, and right away, I knew they would get along.

He didn't play any of his "Ford" games, either. No long silences. He had a genuine interest in Stan and did what he liked to do with someone he didn't know well. He flooded Stan with questions about his background: how he happened to become a ranger, how he started to write songs. He was fascinated and impressed with the fact that Stan truly got his inspiration from the country he lived in—God's country—beautiful and majestic land of mountains, rivers, and lakes. The polluting had started even then, but the rest of us hadn't noticed. Stan had, though. He saw what was coming and wrote songs about that, too. Mostly, though, his songs were about pioneers, gunfighters, and the American cowboy.

After they had talked for awhile, I could tell that Jack had made up his mind. He was sold on Stan the man, and now he wanted to hear his music.

"What are you going to play for us?" he asked Stan.

"Well, Mr. Ford," Stan said as he took his guitar out of its case, "maybe you haven't heard 'Ghost Riders' yet, so I'll sing that first." So he did. It made the hair stand up on the back of my neck. I thought the walls were going to tumble down when he got to the end with the "Yippy, ay, yaaaah, yippy, ay, yooh." Ol' Stan made a believer of you in a hurry. I knew halfway through the song that Jones was in. He was one of us. When he finished singing, O'Brien said, "Welcome aboard!"

Then Stan said, "Mr. Ford, I wrote a sort of sequel to 'Ghost Riders' called 'Rollin' Dust.' I'd like to sing that, too, if it's okay. I really like it better, myself." So bam—bam—bam—he really got in high gear with that one. That did it for the man behind the desk. He was smiling before Stan even finished. When Stan brought the song to a close with the words, "They now hear ghostly laughter through a veil of heavy dust," Ford really flipped. Stan unhooked the guitar from around his neck and just stood in front of the Boss's desk and smiled. Stan wore a light suede jacket with fringe on the sleeves, his ranger hat, cowboy pants, cowboy boots, and a tropical flowered shirt. Uncle Jack wouldn't have cared if he'd been dressed like a pimp. He loved his music.

Marilyn summed him up: "Stan Jones was to western music what Charlie Russell was to western painting. There is Stan Jones, all by himself, and then there're the other guys."

Jack Ford knew that after he had heard one song. So did the rest of us. Stan was a poet, a name that Orson Welles was to use about Ford. They were going to make one hell of a combo.

John Ford took the pipe from his mouth, lifted his feet from off the desk, leaned forward toward Stan, and said, "Great. Great. Just great. But there's one problem."

We all looked worried.

"I need that song about the ghost town—the one you just sang—for my picture with Ben and Dobe. But I also need two or three more. Can you write three more before I finish the picture? They'll not be sung in the movie, they'll be used in the score after we finish shooting. Is that going to be a problem, Jones?"

Stan couldn't believe it. His songs in a John Ford film! His lips stretched from ear to ear in a big smile. His curly hair was spilling out from under his ranger hat in all different directions. It always looked like somebody had used an egg beater on it. He was a pioneer in scooping long hair from one side and plastering it across the bald part on top.

Stan exclaimed, "No, sir, Mr. Ford. That's not going to be a problem at all. Heck, I can write three songs by tomorrow night. No problem, sir. None at all."

Ford said, "Good boy. Good boy. Have Meta there in the outer office give you a script, and follow your own good judgment."

Stan then asked Uncle Jack, "Mister Ford, have you ever heard of the Sons of the Pioneers?"

"The Sons of the Pioneers?" He answered the question like "is that supposed to be a brilliant name for something?" It wasn't sarcastic, though, it was funny. He was being funny because he was happy with how things were going.

The Old Man said again, "The Sons of the Pioneers, eh? They sing, do they? Western songs, I presume."

"Oh, yes, sir" Stan replied. "Better than any others in the world. In fact, Roy Rogers used to be their lead singer." Uncle Jack got an amazed look on his face, "You want me to put Roy Rogers in my picture? What about poor Ben and Dobe?" He was in good mirth, all right.

"No, Mr. Ford, he doesn't sing with the group anymore.

"But if you ever heard the Pioneers sing—well, I sure wish you'd listen to them when you're ready to score the picture."

Uncle Jack smiled and said, "Okay, Stan, you write me three more songs after you read the story, and when we get back from Moab, you bring those guys over here. That's a good idea." He jumped up, put out his hand, and said, "You've got a hell of a start with that 'Rollin' Dust' thing. Make the others in the same vein. You know, western as hell. About a wagon train."

Then to all of us, "Thanks for coming over, boys!" When we got to the door, "Hey, Jones! For Christsakes, don't write anything about cactus. You don't know a goddamned thing about cactus!"

Stan came up to location after we'd been there about a week. He knew Utah well, of course, and he was out on the set, riding around on horseback much of the time.

Ward Bond was superb in the film. He really carried the picture, and of course Jack had his fun with him. The first thing I noticed was Ward's horse. That poor old pony had sure seen better days, and now he had to lug a 230-pound man around for three weeks. Most outsiders didn't know about Ward's physical handicap. Ward had never been in the service because of another serious disability, but this one happened during wartime, right on Hollywood Boulevard.

One night he was hit by a car, and his left leg was torn to shreds. The story is that one doctor wanted to amputate it because it was evidently hanging by a thread of flesh, but Duke Wayne threatened to annihilate the doc if he did that. Somehow, after months and months of treatment and skin grafts, the leg was saved. Ward wore a huge brace on it much of the time, but he covered it so well you could hardly tell. One part of his leg never did heal. He always had to wear some kind of dressing on it. Uncle Jack refused to recognize the fact that Ward had a bum leg, and there were times when he really put the poor man to the test. Ward never let it show.

One day we were shooting a scene where Ward and Ben are riding together along the edge of the river; the Colorado. They are looking for a place to bring the wagons across. Suddenly they hit some sand—kaboom—down went Ward and his old crow-bait horse. The poor old horse groaned as he fell. I could hear the sad sound from where I was by the camera with the Old Man. Ward struggled up, the camera still rolling, ad-libbed bawling the horse out, and never uttered a swear word. Of course today not swearing wouldn't mean a thing, but no one could say "damn" in those days, unless you were Clark Gable. The accident stayed in the movie, ad-libs and all.

That night Ford sent Duke a wire that read: "He fell off his horse." The big story, however, is that the horse fell to the side of Ward's bad leg. Somehow Ward managed to keep it from being crushed. I don't know how he did it. He wasn't even hurt! Had he injured that bad leg, he probably would have lost it. Uncle Jack and the luck of the Irish, and then some. Every time he made a movie, it seemed that nature and circumstances were always on his side. His incredible ability to believe in himself and believe in a Higher Power made these wonderful things happen for him.

Ward Bond never suffered from a lack of confidence in himself. *Wagonmaster* rolled along, just like "Old Man River." The film was such a happy experience, and the work so easy for Uncle Jack, that he got interested in a project that John Ireland had going. John had just married Joanne Dru, who was the leading lady on the film, and he was up there visiting. He took over the high school auditorium for a stage show to help out the needy people in Moab.

While John narrated the story of "The Shooting of Dan McGrew," the rest of us acted it out. We were all in it, including the character actress and old favorite of Ford's, Ruth Clifford. It was all a big spoof, and we hammed it up something awful. The audience loved it. Jack said he thought they took the whole thing seriously. He was there every night of rehearsals and for the two performances we gave each weekend.

Anyone who has been in a stage production of any kind knows that there is a stage right and a stage left. When you are on the stage *facing* the audience, stage left is on your own left side. If you have exited stage left and your next entrance is stage right, you have to get around backstage to the other side. You walk carefully behind the backdrop or even go down under the stage, where the Green Room is. Anyway, you must get there by hook-or-crook.

While we were rehearsing "Dan McGrew," I had to exit stage left and come back on stage right. During rehearsal, I simply walked across the back of the set itself and never gave it another thought. Opening night, I did my piece, casually exited stage left, visited back there a moment or two (whispering, of course, because of the "heavy drama" that was going on on stage), and then decided I had better get over to stage right. I *couldn't!* There was no walkway behind the backdrop. In a slight panic, I said to myself, "I'll just go outside and walk around the back of the theater." I zipped out the stage door under the starry night sky and boom—there was a high, slick, solid wooden fence there that Dillinger couldn't have gotten over in his best days. There was only one way for me to go—around the front of the theater and the whole block! That's what I did, running as fast as my legs would take me. All of the citizenry were in the audience, thank God, or they would have reported me to the sheriff. "There's a crazy guy running around the outside of the theater with six-guns on!" Fortunately, the stage door was open, and I made it on stage with my next line, just barely in time, and completely out of breath. I had to make this run every night of the performances. Uncle Jack got a laugh out of it when I told him.

Ben Johnson has been my dear friend for 45 years. As you get old, you realize that there are not too many people you can say that about. Our friendship has grown over the years, and we accept each other's shortcomings. That seems to make the bond between us even stronger. Ben Johnson was the only member of the Ford Stock Company who didn't have a screw loose somewhere. Ben's not a drunk, and he's not given to fits of temper or depression. Ben made it because of his incredible horsemanship, his humor, and then, Ford found out he could really act. You didn't last very long around Ford if you didn't have humor. Horsemanship was second, and acting was the least important. Ford himself would tell you that.

With profound apologies to the stuntmen, I have to say that Ford was guilty of lousing up what would have been a fine scene by giving important dialogue to stuntmen. He did that not because he was cheap, but because he thought in his dear, old Irish heart that anyone could act under his hand.

One day, Ben and I were on the set, just sitting and watching the Old Man—something we did most of the time, anyway. It was about the end of the second week of shooting. Uncle Jack was walking up and down with his hands on his hips, the big handkerchief hanging from his mouth. We could tell he was planning something, we were getting nervous. He had been gazing intently at a ridge of a mountain in the distance. He was dreaming up something, all right. He usually did this in his room at night, but evidently this ridge was giving him some problems.

Pretty soon he asked, to no one in particular, "Where's ol' Ben?"

Ben looked at me and winked. "Right here, Mr. Ford," and he went over to where Jack was standing.

"Oh, there's ol' Ben, by God." He put his hand on Ben's shoulder, "Now, Ben, I want you to get on your horse like a good boy and ride over to that ridge. Try to figure out for me how we can bring all of the wagons and all the people—including women and children—off that hill. I want it to look perilous and rough going, but I don't want to get anybody hurt. We'll be turning the wagons over in another shot with the stunt guys. Do that for me, will you? Sleep on it, and let me know tomorrow what your idea is. Okay?"

Ben did as he was told. He thought about the problem all night. He took his horse and rode all over that mountain ridge while Ford was shooting with Ward. He had formed a good plan to tell Uncle Jack. The following day, when Ford was relaxing between shots and seemed in the right mood, Ben went up to him.

"Mister Ford," Ben said.

The Old Man turned and play-acted looking surprised, "Ol' Ben. You don't want to say all them words. You want me to give you a wild ride to do instead, right?" Ford and Ben had this running routine about "all them words."

"Well, sir—no, I'm not worried about any dialogue right now anyway, but I think I've figured out a way for you to do that shot you were a-tellin' me about."

Then the Old Man said, "I asked you that?"

"Yes, sir, you sure did," Ben answered.

Jack Ford looked at Ben in amazement and exclaimed, "Jesus! So now you want to direct the picture!"

Ben came back to where I was sitting and grumbled some. He wasn't really mad, though.

I said, "Listen, if that's the worst thing that happens to you on this picture, you're one lucky cowboy!" Then we both laughed.

Ford did shoot the scene on the ridge (not Ben's way), and he realized right away it didn't look hazardous enough. He knew that without even having to look at the film. So he called Ray Kellogg (the same Ray Kellogg from my OSS days). Ray was in the middle of a multimillion-dollar production at Fox, but Jack talked him into doing a little miniature of the ridge with the wagons all crossing that mountain—a quick insert shot at Fox's expense. If you look carefully, you can see it's a fake, but it saves the whole sequence. Just another sample of the loyalty of his friend who loved him. Ray Kellogg hand carved all those little figures with his pocketknife, and then, God knows how, made them move across a miniature cliff.

Remember the dog in *Yellow Ribbon?* Well, there were dogs in *Wagonmaster,* too. More than one, though. There were a lot. A John Ford wagon train was not your typical movie version of a wagon train. Each wagon had all different kinds of props and different kinds of folks. Ford encouraged them to bring their dogs, but even if he hadn't, the dogs would have shown up anyway.

During the shooting of the movie, especially out-of-doors, there are many things that can screw up a shot. A scene can be going along splendidly and an airplane will fly overhead and mess up the sound. (Henry Hathaway once got so frustrated by this, he threw a rock at one.) On every set except John Ford's, the sound mixer will yell, "Cut please. Airplane!" On a Ford set nobody yells cut except Ford. Uncle Jack knew that many times, even though the sound may be impaired somewhat, there may be a piece of that scene that will never again be as good. Most of the time this is not the case, and he would yell, "cut!" himself. Sometimes if he felt that the noise was not detrimental, he would allow the scene to continue anyway.

The actor learns very quickly that, even if he hears some outside sound during his dialogue, for God's sake, don't stop talking or he might be silenced forever. Say, for example, a rooster crowed, Ford wouldn't stop the scene. A sound mixer would, though, and he'd tell you it wouldn't match in the close-up. You cannot tell a rooster to crow on cue. Ford would say to that, "I'm only going to use one of these takes, so what the hell difference does it make, for Chrissakes!" That ended that.

On *Wagonmaster,* because of the number of dogs around, there were a lot of dog fights—usually toward the end of a good take—and this would ruin it. Every day it sounded like the two same dogs were trying to kill each other; actually they were. These two despised each other and managed a fight or two every day.

The character I play, Sandy, has a huge crush on Prudence, a very pretty red-haired girl played by Kathleen O'Malley. But so does a big, handsome Mormon named Sam, played by an actor stuntman named Don Summers. Somewhere in the middle of the story, Sam and Sandy get into an argument about my using a swear word. One thing leads to another, and we start to fight. Ford didn't want it to be a John Wayne type of fight—neither of us are supposed to be good at it. It was to be more like ordinary guys really fight—a few punches and a lot of rolling around in the dirt, trying to gouge and hit each other. Don was much bigger than me, but that made it better. After a bit, Ward Bond, the Mormon elder, rushes in and grabs each of us (me by the hair, of course), and pulls us apart.

Uncle Jack told Ward to stand by the camera until he tapped him on the shoulder, so the fight could go on as long as Jack wanted it to. But then Uncle Jack got a hell of an idea. He turned to Wingate and said, "Wingate, see if someone can find those two dogs that keep screwing up my picture with their fighting. You know—those two damned dogs that are always in a fight. See if you can find their owners, and get them over here, will you?"

Everyone went on the hunt for the two mad dogs, so it didn't take long to locate them. Two Moab men in their period wardrobe showed up with their respective dogs, and Wingate motioned for them to stand in front of Uncle Jack. The guilty dogs turned out to be nice, peaceful-looking Australian shepherds, but as soon as they noticed each other, they began to growl and bare their fangs. This made Uncle Jack very happy. He greeted the two men and he also greeted the two dogs, but they didn't care, they wanted to fight.

"Okay. Okay. Hold them until I tell you to let them go. Now these two boys here, Dobe and Don," pointing, "that's Dobe and that's Don, are going to fight. They are not supposed to like each other—just like these dogs. Now prime the dogs!" So the two owners let the dogs get really close to each other, and boy, they could hardly hold them.

Then Ford said, "Now, when Dobe and Don have gotten to the point where they are rolling around on the ground—I'll let them fight for a few seconds—then, when I go like this with my handkerchief (he made a downward motion), you men throw these dogs at each other! I want to see them fighting each other at the same time the boys are fighting. I hope they fight in the same area. Then, when I cue Ward—" He looked around for Ward. "Where the hell is Bond?"

"Right here, right here, Boss," Ward yelled. He had wandered off.

"Ward, for Christ's sake, will you pay attention? We're *trying* to make a picture here. Why in the hell do I use you?"

"Cause Wayne can't play the part," was Ward's reply. Then he went into raucous laughter.

"Get your fat ass in here, Ward!" Then, to the rest of us, he said, "Then when I cue Ward—by kicking him in the ass—Mister Bond, I hope, comes in and separates the boys. And that is cut. Okay? Everybody got that?"

We all said, "Yes, sir."

"All right. Here we go. Ward, stand here by me off camera. When I send you in, really jerk those two boys off the ground."

Ward was all serious now and said, "Right, Jack."

Uncle Jack made one last check. "First there's going to be dialogue. They throw a few punches, and then they hit the ground. After they have fought on the ground for a bit, I'll bring my handkerchief down. When I do that, you men throw the dogs at each other. Prime them one more time."

Grrrrr-Grrr-Growl-Growl!

Ford yelled, "All right. This will be picture. We are rolling!"

Bobby Ray called the scene number and clacked the board—two seconds, and Pop Crane yelled, "Speed." Don and I said our dialogue, then bam—bam—bam—we began to fight like two crazy guys. Then—bam—we hit the ground, fighting and hitting and gouging—even biting. Ford swooped his famous handkerchief downward, and the men let the dogs go. The dogs lunged, then stopped dead and stared at each other for a second. Their eyes went wide as if they had seen a ghost. One dog turned around and ran like hell, and the other ran at Ward Bond and ripped the whole length of his pant leg wide open! I have never in my life seen Jack

Ford laugh so hard. Ward ran into the scene, torn pants and all, and separated the two of us.

Ford, still laughing, yelled, "Cut and print it! You can't get any better than that!" Don and I hugged each other. We had all made the Old Man very happy. After the dust had settled, Jack realized that the dog may have gotten his teeth into something more than just Ward's trousers, and asked Ward, with a concerned look on his face, "Ward, are you hurt?" Did the dog actually bite you?"

Ward replied, "No, no. Goddamnit, I'm all right" (no more laughing from Ward now).

Uncle Jack said, "Oh, that's too bad, Ward." Then, "Somebody get the vet out here and give that poor dog a shot, just in case he bit Ward."

"I do all of my own stunts," or "I used to do all my own stunts." I have read phrases such as these in many biographies and heard actors say them in interviews on TV. Now, the big question is: what makes a stunt a stunt? The first one that comes to mind is a saddle fall, as opposed to a horse fall. A saddle fall is simply falling off your horse. Of course you hit the hard ground. It's not especially difficult to do, but it's also not much fun. Cowboy actors are forever saying, "I used to do all my own saddle falls." Well, good for them! I never intentionally fell off my horse in my whole life, and the main reason is that I have been thrown off a lot, and I don't like it. Just like I don't like getting punched in the face. So why do stuff like that when very capable stuntmen can do it better? There have been many actors over the years (Bill Holden was one) with tremendous athletic ability, who were certainly capable of doing their own stunts, but it stands to reason that since even the best professional stuntmen get hurt occasionally, a director doesn't want to risk losing his star for a number of weeks. As we get older, we tend to embellish the stories about the movies we have made, particularly the action sequences, and hence the phrase, "I used to do all of my own stunts." After 40 years of telling it, he really believes it himself. Believe me, it seldom happened.

But—and this is a big but—Ben Johnson was an exception. With Uncle Jack, Ben did all of his own stunts. On *Wagonmaster,* there is a sequence in which Joanne Dru is taking a bath in her wagon. Today you would see the whole bath, but all you see in this scene is a big bucket of water being thrown out the back end of the covered wagon just as Ben is riding up to inform Joanne about the importance of conserving water. The bathwater hits Ben's horse in the head, and he starts to buck. After about ten jumps, he succeeds in throwing Ben off. That was the shot. Of course, Steel wouldn't buck if you put a firecracker under him and lit it. Ben didn't know that this scene was going to be shot on this particular day—another John Ford surprise. He didn't like you to think on things during the night.

As Ben and I approached the set, we saw the wagons still in a circle. The next thing we saw was the horse that Ben was to take his ride on. He was a real Andy Jauregui bucking horse, right off the rodeo circuit, and Andy had the meanest ones on the West Coast. He was made-up to look like Steel, who had a blaze face, a white streak running down the front of his head from his forehead to the tip of his muzzle.

The wranglers had a "twitch" on his nose, which gets the horse's attention and keeps him from stomping on them. There was a wrangler on each ear, too. If you hold a wild horse by the ears, he acts pretty much like a schoolboy under the same circumstances. He gets a lot quieter, but he doesn't like it. This horse was groaning, and his eyes were popping in anticipation of getting loose. The company was beginning to gather around, like jackals around a carcass, to watch the fun. No matter how basically nice most people are, there is a curious cruelty that makes them get fiendish delight from watching a man in a big jam or in some sort of mental or physical misery. They figured that Ben was going to get the hell knocked out of him, and they didn't want to miss it. The bucking horse was also blindfolded. That's another trick that is supposed to keep a horse quiet until he is turned loose.

I took one look and said to Ben, "Ben, today you're in trouble."

"Yeah," he replied, "Ah'm a-thinkin' that the Old Man is a-wantin' me to ride that son-of-a-buck, and I ain't sure ah can stay on him, Dobe."

Uncle Jack came up with a smile on his face, "Ol' Ben, do you think you could ride that bucking horse for me like a good boy?"

Ben smiled back and said, "Ah'll sure give 'er a good try, Mr. Ford."

This made Jack very happy "Ben, if you'll do that for me, you won't have to say any more lines of dialogue for the rest of the day. I'll make Ward do all the talking. Okay?"

"Ah'm ready, Mr. Ford."

The Old Man was in seventh heaven, but he still had more orders. "Now Ben, if you can, make him buck within the circle of the wagons, understand? Right around here." He walked the area where he wanted Ben to do it. Ben just nodded. The horse was still moaning and shivering and groaning. Ben cast a look in his direction and winked at the wranglers who were holding him. Ford reminded Ben that he had been nice enough to have the ground dug, so it would be softer. "But don't ride him outside the circle, because there are rocks, and also it's not in camera range."

"Yes, sir," again from Ben.

Everyone was ready. The camera was ready—and as Ben was reaching for the pommel of the saddle, Uncle Jack had his final word for Ben.

"Oh, by the way, Ben. After the horse bucks you offI mean, don't worry about it, but if you can think of it after you are bucked off, you might just start the dialogue with Joanne! Okay?"

Ben never took his eyes off the horse and replied, "You bet, Mr. Ford."

"All right, we're rolling," yelled Ford. As soon as Ben's behind hit the saddle, the horse started to rear up and down in one place, because the guys still had ahold of him.

"Speed!" yelled Pop Crane.

"Action!" yelled Ford.

"Let me have him," said Ben to the wranglers, and they let go! That horse went so high in the air on that first jump that he looked like he'd been shot out of a rocket. About four more jumps and some "sunfishing," and my friend was a goner. Ben's body left that saddle, he turned over, and came down on his back. I heard all of the air go out of him. It was a perfect shot. He'd stayed on just long enough for it to look good, but as soon as he hit the ground, an old-time wrangler named Alan Lee came running into camera range and cried, "Are you all right, Ben?"

Ford immediately called, "Cut!" After he was sure that Ben was okay, he took a look at Alan's clothes. He was hoping they would pass for the clothes of 1870, but after a quick look-over, he knew they would not. Ford didn't chew Alan out for running in, because he, too, could see how Ben landed, so he said, "Ben, I'm sorry. Goddamnit, do you think you can do it one more time? Are you up to it?"

Ben said, "Bring him on, Mr. Ford. Ah'll try to stay on longer this time."

Uncle Jack looked at him with real love in his eyes and said quietly, "Good boy."

So Ben rode that horse again. This time he didn't have so much buck in him, and Ben had to fall off on purpose. Just as Jack had wanted him to do, he got up, brushed himself off, and played the scene with the leading lady, Joanne Dru. A full day's work for a cowboy actor.

The bad guys in *Wagonmaster* were very nasty fellows. Charles Kemper played Uncle Shiloh and he was brilliant in the part. His nephews were played by Hank Worden, Fred Libby, Mickey Simpson, and James Arness. Of course, Hank had been a Ford-Wayne regular for years and is best remembered for his role in *The Searchers* as Ol' Mose. This was to come later in his career. Hank died in 1992 at the age of 91.

Fred Libby had been a pilot in World War II. He was a good actor, and Ford was very fond of him. Mickey Simpson was a huge man—bigger than Duke. When he wasn't working in a movie, he ran a hockshop. I bought a wristwatch from him, once. It was spectacular looking, but it ran for only two hours, and Marilyn made me take it back.

Then there was the other fellow, Jim Arness. He also was bigger than Duke. No need to go into what happened to him. I'll never forget Jim on that show, though. There is a sequence where the Cleggs get the drop on us and make Ben and me drop our gunbelts. After we rehearsed the scene, Uncle Jack said to me, "Dobe, after you drop your gunbelt and Jim reaches for it, stamp your foot on it really hard!" So I did what he had told me, and then Jack said, "Jim, this makes you madder than hell, so push him off of it. Give him a good shove." We started the scene again, and Jim gave me a pretty good shove, but I knew what was coming. Ford got Jim about half sore. He said, "Jesus, kid, you're a big strong guy! Shove him, for Christ's sake!" So we did it again, and this time Jim shoved me into the next area code.

"Don't shove him *that* hard. He went out of the shot!"

But Jack was happy. We got it right the next time.

Then Jim was to take the gun and throw it away—same routine, "Jesus, Jim, can't you throw any farther than that?" Well, they never found the gun. Don't get Jim mad.

One day toward the end of the second week, our professional Britisher, Alan Mowbray, came up to Ben and me and said, "I say, old chaps. I've been watching these stunt boys of Ford's. They're a brave lot, and I admire them. I would like to show my appreciation and admiration by giving a small cocktail party this coming Saturday night. What do you think, eh?"

Ben answered, "Well, Alan, they're not real used to cocktail parties, but ah' know they surely would enjoy it. Are me and Ol' Dobe invited too?"

Alan looked abashed. "Why, my God, of course you're invited. In fact, I was hoping you two chaps would spread the word. I don't know them except to nod good morning to." Then he added, "For God's sake, tell them not to bring anything. I have a well-stocked bar in my quarters."

As usual, Ford wrapped on that Saturday afternoon about 4:00, and by 5:30, the first knock was heard at Alan's door. Now Alan's room was no bigger than Ben's and mine—no sitting room—just twin beds, a table in between with a lamp, a small dresser, one chair, and a desk, that served as the bar. Alan had arranged for extra glasses and ice, because there were no Coke and ice machines in those days.

Eight tough hombres squeezed themselves into that room: Cliff Lyons, Post Parks, Frankie McGrath, Ed Jauregui, Slim Hightower, Ray Thomas, Billy Jones, and Freddie Kennedy. With the three of us—Alan, Ben and me—that made eleven of us on our way to getting stewed.

Freddie Kennedy was a rusty-haired, freckle-faced Irishman. He was a bull—an ex-fighter, five-feet-nine, and weighed around 200 pounds—all muscle, no fat on his blocklike frame. Fortunately, he was the sweetest-natured man I have ever met in my life. John Ford adored him. On the set, Freddie loved to run up to Ben and me really fast and go bap—bap—bap—with his huge middle finger on our chests. Then he'd giggle like hell and run off before we could catch him. We had black and blue marks on our breastbones through the whole picture.

We'd try to get even when we'd see him standing off by himself. "Let's get him," we'd shout, and we'd both jump on him at once, sort of bulldogging him, but we never could get him down. He'd just stagger around with the two of us riding him. While I'm talking about Freddie, I have to tell about his invention called his "safety wagon." It was his "safe" and "foolproof" wagon-wreck stunt. He designed the whole thing.

This is how it was to work. A covered wagon is flying along with many other wagons, like in an Oklahoma land-rush scene. Then all of a sudden one of the wagons (Freddie's), falls completely apart. The wheels come off, the doubletrees come away; the team gets loose and runs off. Whatever is left of the wagon turns over, end-over-end. Freddie always said there was no way he could get hurt because his safety feature, a box or coffin, was foolproof. He had control of the pin that held the entire wagon together, so when he pulled that pin, he had three seconds to get into the safety box. Once inside, he was okay—it was well-padded and had hand holds. But! Freddie *never* made it to his box! He'd almost make it, but the wagon would fly apart into 15 different pieces, and Freddie would be left with his head sticking out between the spokes of a wheel. He always got up and walked away from it, though. He was killed some years later, doing a simple saddle fall in Ford's *The Horse Soldiers*. I have to believe that this was one of the saddest moments of John Ford's life. It happened so suddenly. He closed down the set, and everyone came back home. When a stuntman is killed, many times it is while doing one of his easiest and most routine stunts.

Alan Mowbray had a *huge* capacity for drink, but he must have figured these simple cowboys would help themselves to one or two polite drinks and leave. No way, José. In no time, we ran out of booze. Alan, who was well along himself by this time, didn't even notice when a couple of the guys ran down the street for more supplies. After about an hour of story-telling and a lot of "out West" lies, I noticed Freddie giggling. He was wearing the 1890s policeman's uniform that Uncle Jack had ordered him to wear while patrolling the streets of Moab after work, looking for drunks. Of course, Jack did this to try to keep Freddie himself from getting drunk, and Freddie, thinking this was quite an honor, wore his uniform and policeman's hat every evening until he got tired, but this night, he wasn't patrolling.

Ben and I decided to get revenge and jumped on him. We knocked over the chair, breaking it in the process, but we were feeling terrific and didn't care. This made Ed Jauregui, who was on the prod anyway, think of something he hated about McGrath, so he threw Frankie out through the screen door into the courtyard. Frankie charged back in, ready to really have a go, but Cliff was already going at it with Ed. It was getting ready to be a real brawl, but Post Parks, bless him, somehow got them all quieted down. He had great leadership in emergencies like these.

Poor Alan plastered himself up against the headboard of one of the beds and watched his room become a shambles. Post finally got everyone herded out, but now Ben and I began worrying about what the Old Man would say about our drinking and being late to dinner.

"You two guys—grown men—afraid of that old man? That's downright shameful," said Post.

"But you don't have to act for him," we said.

Well, Post said he'd go up and have a word with the Boss. In a little while, he was back, and he was smiling. "He says all is forgiven, and you guys can come up and have your dinner. He's up there waiting for you."

That was it. Nothing ever came of it. He just teased us about having too much "Who-Hit-John."

A few weeks after we finished filming, Stan Jones called to tell me that the Sons of the Pioneers were coming into the studio to record for the scoring of the picture, and would I like to meet and hear them. Of course, I said I'd like nothing better, but I would have to check with Uncle Jack. Stan said he already had the go-ahead and for me not to worry.

When I got to RKO Pathé Studio, Jack's daughter, Barbara, was there. She was one of the most exceptional human beings I have ever known. She was small, pretty, and supersmart. Marilyn and I always thought of her as a relative. She used to say, "Water is thicker than blood." She was family. The Fords, the Careys, and the Waynes—we were all family. Unlike her brother, Pat, Barbara usually had her dad right where she wanted him. She had his wit, without his mean streak, and she made him laugh. She could make him mad as hell, though, but there was usually a good reason. To her dying day, she would fly into a rage if you said anything detrimental about him. It sure made you wish you'd kept your trap shut. Of course, Barbara was never on the set when her father was working, so she never saw any of the stuff he pulled. We used to fight like brother and sister, mostly about the merits of some actor or other. She worked as an assistant film editor at Fox for many years. If she were young in the business today, with the opportunities for women, she'd be right at the top—just like her dad. We lost Barbara to cancer in 1985, and we miss her deeply.

When I arrived at the recording stage on the old studio lot which was ancient even in 1949, Stan Jones was standing out in front with Uncle Jack. I said hello, and sheepishly asked if it was okay for me to be there.

Uncle Jack smiled and stared at me through those dark glasses, "Don't you want to hear the Sons of the Pioneers sing?"

I said I sure did, and he said, "Then it's all right for you to be here."

We went into what I guess was really a dubbing stage, probably a lot more primitive than what the Pioneers were used to, but they certainly didn't complain. It's pretty well known that Roy Rogers started his career as the lead singer with the Pioneers. Bob Nolan founded it, and they made those incredible recordings of "Tumbleweeds," "Cool Water," and dozens more.

We were all inside now. Pretty soon the door opened, letting some sunlight in. For Barbara Ford it shined on only one, a handsome baritone by the name of Ken Curtis! Her eyes opened wide, and she whispered loudly in my ear, "Oh, my God! That's for me!" She didn't point, but she didn't have to. Her eyes were zeroed in on Kenny. Almost as if he had heard her, he looked up toward us all and gave us that wonderful smile of his. Ken had taken over Roy Rogers' spot after Roy had become a western movie star. He had the most perfectly balanced voice for popular music I have ever heard. He could sing anything and sell it to the last row.

This group was sort of Pioneers II. I say that because only the fiddle player, Hugh Farr, and his younger brother, guitarist, Carl, were left from the original group. Bob Nolan had a very unique voice. He had an extremely throaty quality and was one of the main reasons that the Pioneers sounded different from any other western singing group. The manner in which they mixed their voices was their gift. It was like the formula for Coca Cola—a secret that could not be duplicated. A few years before, Bob Nolan had gotten tired of the plane and bus rides and had retired, but someone had found a young man in Nebraska who had taught himself to sing just like Bob. The only problem was that he was painfully shy and didn't want to sing in front of anybody. His name was Tommy Doss. By the time I met him, he had played shows all over the States, but he still acted very low-key. The sound was made up of Tommy and Kenny and Lloyd Perryman, who also played guitar. Lloyd died quite a few years ago. The Pioneers would never have been the perfect singing group they were without him. He was a first-rate musician and had a beautiful high tenor voice. He also was a first-rate human being. Marilyn and I loved him and his wife, Buddy. For years to come, these wonderful Pioneers would sing just for the fun of it at parties at John Ford's house and even at ours. What music! To sit in a living room right among them—the music lifted you to the sky. That's the only way I can describe it. It was an experience few people in this world are lucky enough to have had.

Uncle Jack always said *Wagonmaster* was his favorite picture. I think *The Searchers* was his best film, but *Wagonmaster* was the most joyful. The entire filming was done in a spirit of friendliness; every member of the company doing their best. One month of total unity and happiness—that was *Wagonmaster*.

Rio Grande

By the time Uncle Jack began preparing *Rio Grande* for Republic Pictures, Barbara Ford had made good her prediction and was engaged to marry Ken Curtis. That was sure okay with Jack, because he liked Ken, but what he was really tickled about was having a professional first-rate singer in the family to sing all those Irish songs for him whenever he got the notion. "The Young May Moon," "Down by the Glenside," "Danny Boy," "I'll Take You Home Again, Kathleen"; all he had to do was yell, "Ken!" If Borzage wasn't there, no matter; Ken sounded great without any accompaniment.

Stan Jones got himself in deep trouble with Uncle Jack over that engagement. I had wondered how long Stan would manage to go unscathed by the wrath of Ford. The engagement was his undoing. It was supposed to be a secret until the Ford family made the announcement, but poor Stan accidentally let the news slip out to someone, and it got back to Uncle Jack. His punishment was simple: Ford didn't speak to Stan during the entire filming of the movie. He'd notice Stan on the set, walk straight up to him, look him in the eye (you were never exactly sure about this, because of the patch and the dark glasses), and then call, "Dobe!"

Over I'd come. "Yes, Uncle Jack?"

Then Jack would say. "Ask *him* (he would not say his name) if he's rehearsed the songs with the Pioneers. The ones he wrote."

Now the three of us are standing in a tight group. So I would say to Stan, feeling very foolish, "Have you rehearsed the songs with the Pioneers? The ones you wrote?" And Stan would say, "Yes, I have, and they sound great."

Then Ford would say, "What did he say?"

And I would say, "He says, yes, he has, and they sound great." That's the way it went during the whole shooting of *Rio Grande*. The songs Stan wrote for the movie are fantastic, and the way the Pioneers sing "My Gal Is Purple," as Duke is wandering by the river takes your breath away. It's perfect for him and Maureen. Of course, Stan didn't write "I'll Take You Home Again, Kathleen," but no singer could do it as beautifully as Ken Curtis and the Pioneers did it in that movie.

Ken and Barbara were happily married for a number of years, and then things went haywire. It's none of my business why, and I just remember the happy times—the music and the laughter.

I heard that Uncle Jack wanted to go back to Moab, his miniature Monument Valley, and that he had moved over to Republic Studios. Then I heard that John Wayne, who still had a contract there with Yates, was going to be the star, and it was going to be another cavalry movie. That's when I decided that it was about time I paid the Old Man a visit. Before I had a chance to get there, though, Meta Stern called and said that Himself wanted to see Ben and me in his office that afternoon.

Republic was not a major studio like M-G-M, but it was a terrific lot to work on. It looked like a huge Spanish hacienda. I was over there not long ago, and there is nothing there now that reminds me of those days—towering ugly buildings mostly—and what little is left of the hacienda smells like B.O. inside. I hate going over there now, whatever they call the place. It always depresses the hell out of me.

Ben drove his brand-new cream-colored Studebaker right through the big front gate without a hitch. Just a friendly nod was all it took. I, on the other hand, drove up in my 1947 Plymouth coupe, without a big cowboy hat or fringed suede jacket and had a lot of trouble getting in, even though I had worked there before. The gate guard I knew wasn't on duty, and this one thought I was an extra in one of the serials or something. Anyway, I got him to call Meta, who really read him off, and I had no trouble after that.

As you came onto the lot, the long, low building on your right was the writers' and directors' building. There was a spacious lawn in front and a parking area for the big shots east of that. Ben drove right into the big shot area, while I went around looking for any spot I could find. I thought if I parked where Ben had, I would surely find a note on my windshield telling me, in no uncertain terms, what I could do with my car. When I finally got back to the entrance of the building, Ben was standing there waiting for me. There was safety in numbers, so we went in together.

Uncle Jack was glad to see us. "I'm going to make another cavalry picture," he said, "with Duke and Maureen. You two boys will be playing almost the same roles that you played in *Wagonmaster,* only this time, you're back in the Union cavalry. You've both been demoted. You're recruits—privates. Young Claude Jarman is going to be in it with you. He's the kid from Clarence's (Brown) picture (*The Yearling*), but he's grown like hell. I think he's taller than you guys. Ben, you can help him out with his riding. He's a nice kid—could steal the picture. He's a hell of an actor."

Neither Ben nor I could think of the right thing to say, so we lit up cigarettes. The room was already blue with smoke from Ford's cigars.

Then he blurted out, "Do you boys know how to Roman-ride?"

I said, "No sir, I don't."

Ben said, "We can sure learn, Mr. Ford."

I jumped right in because I remembered the Navajos on the ranch riding Roman, two horses at the same time, with one foot on each, in our weekend Wild West shows. I told Jack all about that, and he really liked the story. Said he remembered, now that I reminded him.

Then he said, "Well, kids, I've got a sequence in this story where Victor (McLaglen) ribs you guys about your horsemanship. You two show off—grab two teams of horses and do your stuff."

Then Ben explained that you couldn't just take two horses and hitch them together and Roman-ride them. They had to be trained to do that.

"Yeah, okay," said Jack. "Then get out there to Fat's (Ben's father-in-law) stable and assign someone to train two teams for you and Dobe. We don't have a lot of time, because we start shooting in a month."

Well, that was that! Ford bid us farewell, and when we got outside, Ben said, "Dobe, we're in a kind of a tight here. It'll take Kenny Lee at least two weeks to break them teams, even if he's lucky enough to find two pairs that run good together. Then you and me are going to have to get after it. Hell, I've done damned near everything there is to do with horses, but Roman-ridin' sure ain't one of 'em. Hell, that's trick ridin'."

I said, "I know I'll never make a trick rider in a thousand years."

Ben replied, "Dobe, you're gonna be one now, or you'll be damn sure out of a job."

Fat Jones was a remarkable man. He was an old-fashioned horse trader right out of another era. Andy Jauregui was another. He and Fat were partners in the horse-trading business until Andy went into supplying stock for the rodeos. Andy is the man who taught me whatever I do happen to know about roping. His teaching has sure helped me in all of my movie career, but there's one thing you can't teach even a willing student if he doesn't have the equipment, and that is to do vaults and jumps from on foot. I was a really good rider, much better than average, but I was never light on my feet, and the worst of it was that I was timid. I covered it up the best I could, but I was certainly not one of those guys who walks down to the water's edge on his hands.

About a week after our visit with Uncle Jack, I drove out to Fat's to see how the boys were progressing with the Roman-riding teams. Kenny Lee was working with a big team in a small arena. They were two nice sorrels, not too big, and they seemed to be going really well with Kenny on their backs. It was remarkable for the short time he had been working with them. They seemed almost ready. Every once in a while they would stage a small revolt, but Kenny would quickly sit down on the lefthand horse, gain control, grab ahold of their withers, and leap back up.

I watched Ben's reaction to all this. Of course, he was a professional stuntman, so he was anxious to try it. I, on the other hand, was really worried—especially about the getting up.

"See, Ben," Kenny said, "once you're up on them suckers, you can damned near jerk 'em over backwards."

Ben replied, "Hell, yeah. Ya' got yourself some leverage from way up there."

After Kenny dismounted, he walked over to the tie rail and undid the other team. They were pure thoroughbreds (beautiful conformation, but idiotic). They were hitched together, but neither seemed aware of that. One would leap in one direction, and the other would go in the opposite. Their eyes showed white and were rolled back. What they were actually doing was bucking, but Kenny managed to climb aboard the left horse.

"They're a little rough now (that had to be the understatement of all time), but they'll smooth out in a couple of days, Ben."

Boy, that team really took off! He lapped the arena a few times, but it was a rough go. Then he said, to my intense relief, "Ben, I think Dobe could handle the sorrel team a lot easier."

The following week, I got a call from Fat's secretary, Connie. I was to be out at the arena at 9:00 the next morning. When I got there, Kenny was loping my team around the small arena, and it seemed less hazardous then that first day. Before I knew it, I was astride the lefthand horse and loping around.

Then Kenny stopped me and took a hold of the team by their bridles. "Okay, Dobe," he said, "go ahead and stand up on them. We'll do it this way first, so's you can get the feel of them." He did the same with Ben and his team. We were each standing on the horses' backs, one foot on each horse.

"Put your feet kinda on an angle on the side just behind the withers. Okay, start 'em up. No big hurry now."

Because of the smallness of the arena, we were constantly in a kind of turn, making it impossible for either Ben or me to stand up straight. We couldn't get out of a squat. In a short time, our legs gave out, and we jumped off, our legs collapsing under us. This happened over and over.

Finally Ben said, "Dobe, ah know just the place that'll fix our legs up. I can hardly walk. It's one of them whirlpool places that a lot of the stunt guys go to over there on Vineland. If we don't get them loosened up, we won't be able to ride tomorrow." So that's what we did, and it helped some.

The next day, about mid-morning, John Ford showed up. Thank God, we were already up on our horses when he arrived. We were going around the arena in a baseball catcher's position; one foot on each horse, but having to hold the left horse back, so the outside horse could turn more easily. I thought we were learning fast. Lord, how my legs hurt! Of course there was to be no complaining—ever—even if the Old Man was not there. That was the Code of the West and the Stuntman's Code. You take the pain. I wasn't one of those guys, but I was trying my best to act like one. There were always a few cowhands around to rib us, especially Ben. "Ha-ha-ha—where you guys gonna take that act?"

Uncle Jack watched us for awhile, and when we jumped off to take a breather, he was very complimentary. He greeted us. "Ol' Ben, ol' Dobe, ya done good!" We thanked him, and we could tell that he'd seen enough to be happy with our progress. We had about twelve days to "graduation."

I wasn't too sure of my own progress. Ben had somehow managed to get into a semicrouched position on those two maniacs of his. He had a fabulous sense of balance, even though they leaped and flew off sideways. He fell off a few times. I never did because I didn't take the chances he did. In my heart, I didn't think I would ever be able to get to a standing position while they were running flat out.

About the sixth day of practice, a tough little bowlegged, old cowboy showed up at the Jones' stable. I had known him since I was six. His name was Hank Potts. He was one of the best-known horse wranglers in the movie business. He was the first man I ever saw do a "Running W." It's a very dangerous stunt, especially for the horse. While the horse is running full tilt, the rider pulls a rope that has been especially rigged, and the horses's front legs are jerked out from under him, making him turn a complete somersault. Many times the horse's neck is broken. The rider is seldom hurt because he knows when the wreck is going to happen. Because they use steel stirrups that look like steps, he can jump free. This stunt was outlawed years ago in the United States, but I still see it used today in films made in other countries. Now, in this country, they use "falling horses." There are some horses who can be easily trained to fall on cue. They don't get hurt and seem to enjoy doing it.

Hank had showed up on this particular day with a truckload of Fat's horses he was bringing back from location. He had been a great trick rider in rodeos in his younger days. He stood there staring at Ben and me in amazement. It wasn't long before he yelled out to Kenny Lee, "Kenny! You break these horses?"

Kenny replied, sheepishly, "Well, yeah, Hank."

Potts said, "Well, Goddamnit, what in the hell you got these guys in this goddamn arena for? They'll *never* learn in this here arena! Now get their asses outside there on that long stretch of road that runs along Sherman Way! Out where those goddamn horses can straighten out and do some running. The way they're ridin' now, they look like a cat fucking a baseball. They look like hell all hunched up that-a-way. Get 'um out there on that road pronto! I used to make my livin' doin' Roman-ridin' in a Wild West show! Did three goddamn shows a day, goddammit! These guys are riding like a couple of greenhorns!"

Boy, oh boy, did he get our attention! "Get offa' them goddamn horses." Then he said finally, "Hi, boys. Hello, Dobe. Hell, you'll never learn in there, kid. Ya' can't properly get up on those bastards until they're a-runnin' straight flat out. Then it's a cinch to get up and down on them because they're running smooth, not up and down like in that goddamned arena. Understand?"

"Uh, yeah, Hank. I sure see what you mean," I said. I saw too well what he meant.

Well, Hank led us out onto the stretch of dirt road outside the fence that enclosed the Jones' property. It was about 500 yards long and parallel to Sherman Way. "This is the only way you guys are gonna' learn to Roman-ride. These horses need some room to run. Now, get up there and aim 'um down that there road. When they're goin' real good, stand up on them like the men I think you are!"

A stab of fear went through me after that speech. I had known since I was a kid that when you rode your horse to a starting line, he knew it was post-time, and as soon as he was given his head, he would be flying somewhere in the neighborhood of 35 to 40 miles an hour! Today I would say to Hank, "Hank, for Christ's sake, I hope you realize this is scaring the living hell out of me!" Thus easing my tension and his natural combativeness. But this was more than forty years ago, and I was young and new at my trade. Ben, on the other hand, was no newcomer to stunt work. Up until *Yellow Ribbon,* he'd made his living that way. But that fact never crossed my mind. I wasn't so much afraid of falling and getting hurt as I was of making a jerk out of myself. You would think that after

Wagonmaster, I would be full of piss and vinegar, but I wasn't. Doomed—I was doomed. I put Roman-riding right in the class with all those athletic activities I was terrible at as a kid back at Black Foxe Military Institute. I was doomed, and Jack Ford would be sore as hell when he found out.

I was always fond of Hank, but I had never seen him this intimidating before. There really was humor in his gruff commands, but I couldn't tell it then. Ben went first. As soon as he reined his horses onto the starting line they went absolutely crazy and reared up on their hind legs. He gave them their head, and he flew down the road like a shot from a rocket launcher. After about 100 yards, or five seconds, Ben was standing up. His knees were slightly bent, but certainly he was not all hunched up like before. He was in total command of the team, and no matter how wild they got, he had good leverage from the higher position. Once up there, your whole body is pulling the reins, not just your arms and hands. This has to be done while they are "smoothed out," at, say, 30 or so miles an hour.

My turn! Ben came back toward us, his team at a canter now, and he was all smiles. I could tell he was greatly relieved that he had made good the very first time.

"By God, Hank, you're damned-sure right about gettin' above them. It's a whole lot easier when they're runnin' good." He was a little out of breath and one happy cowboy.

"Okay, Dobe," Hank said. "Let's see if you can do just what Ben did." "Okay," I said, underplaying it. I took them to the starting line. Kenny Lee was there. He reminded me, "Don't forget to let them get going good and fast, Dobe. That's when it's easier to stand up on them."

"Get after 'um, Dobe," Ben said. I let the little red team have their heads, and we roared down the road. I switched the reins to my left hand, put that hand on the horse's withers, leaned over and put my free hand on the withers of the righthand horse. Now I was able to push myself to a standing position. The trouble was, I was looking at the ground between the two horses, and it was flashing by like we were going a thousand miles an hour. I hesitated.

Then I heard voices, "Get up on 'um. Get up!" I did manage to get one foot on each back. Now all I had to do was stand! But I sat back down. Now we were at the end of the roadway. I sheepishly loped them back to the starting point. Ben didn't say anything. Neither did Kenny.

But Hank sure did! "Why in hell didn't you get up? You damned near did, but near ain't good enough, my friend. Go again."

I felt terrible. Why had I quit? The worst that could have happened would be to fall off. I could always slide down on that inside horse.

"Okay. Get with it, Dobe," I thought. "Don't give up. Don't quit!"

The jackals were starting to gather. Word gets around fast. The stable hands were closing in to see the wreck.

Ben had gone down the run again. He was having a good time with those nutty horses of his. Off I went! I tried something different this time. As soon as I got to the head of the road, I started my stand-up. Naturally, they started to run as soon as I put my hands on their withers. I got my feet under me once more, and looked at the ground once more. My ass was sticking up in the air, and I simply could not get the hell up! So—I sat back down. When I turned the team around to start back, Hank was walking down the road toward me. He had a big rock in his hand.

"See this?" he said to me. "I'm sure glad your old Daddy ain't here to see this! Now, I'm going down there at the finish line. If you ain't standin' up on them horses when they cross that line, I'm gonna' hit you with this 'ere big rock, so help me God!"

I didn't say anything. I turned the horses, loped down to the start, spun them around, and let them fly as fast as they wanted. Before I knew what happened, I was standing up with the wind in my face. When I flew by Hank, he had a big grin on his face. I was a goddamn Roman-rider after all!

About four days before we were to leave for location at Moab, I was again out at the Jones' stables and a call came over the loudspeaker that Ben had a phone call. In a few minutes, he came back with the news that it had been Wingate on the phone to say that Uncle Jack was sending Claude Jarman, Jr., out to learn to Roman-ride. Neither of us had ever heard that Claude could even ride a horse with a saddle, let alone learn this. We were apprehensive and afraid he'd get hurt.

It wasn't long before Claude and his father showed up on the scene. Right off, we liked both of them. Claude was a well-brought-up young man, but he was not timid. He seemed to have no fear about what he was about to do. In fact, just the opposite. He was eager to learn this Roman-riding business. Time was running short. He was 16 years old; six-feet-two, and still growing. He was long and lanky, as skinny as I was, but two inches taller and 13 years younger. He was wonderfully unspoiled, considering the success he had had in *The Yearling*. As soon as I met him, I knew he would be a joy to work with. That old-time director Clarence Brown had trained him well.

Hank Potts had gone on to other jobs, so it was up to Ben and Kenny Lee to teach this string bean of a kid who had no experience with horses. Kenny suggested that Claude go about halfway down the track so that he could get a good view of how Ben and I got up on the teams. We got mounted. Ben went first, then me. He saw a pretty good demonstration of the way the Romans used to do it. Kenny wanted Claude to use my team, so while I held their heads, Kenny got up on their backs. He showed Claude where to place his feet and other technicalities, while the team stood still. Claude was eager to get at it. I thought, "Is this kid nuts?" The kid was looking on calmly and nodding his head. Ben and I could not help exchanging ominous looks.

Finally Kenny said, "Claude, I'll hold them for you. You get on and just try to do what I did. Just do it in slow motion at first."

Claude thought a moment and then asked very politely, "Why can't I take the team down the road like Harry and Ben just did?" His dad was standing a little way off, smiling proudly. He didn't seem a bit worried, either.

Kenny and Ben exchanged a look and decided, "Okay, the kid asked for it."

Ben said, "Well kid, if you think you can do-er—well—just you jump up on them red horses and give 'er a try!"

With a "Thanks," Claude vaulted up on the lefthand horse with so little effort that we thought he would clear both of them and land on the ground on the other side. He walked them to the start and let them have their heads. They took off like two rockets! As soon as they hit their stride, that kid sprung up like a jumping-jack out of a box. Like magic, he was standing straight up, going as fast as we had! He did it better than we did!

"Hey, this is fun!" he yelled. He was a born athlete, totally devoid of fear.

Later Ben said, "The reason that kid did it so easy is that he ain't never been hurt. And besides his feet are so damned big they just wrapped around the horse's back!" Well, there might have been a little truth to that, but it was still amazing. Claude told me later that he had been first string on his high school basketball team. He was a natural.

I didn't even know what my role was in the picture, because I never found it in the script. For some reason or other, I wasn't a bit worried. After *Wagonmaster*, I knew that Old Man would take care of me, even if he had to make the part up as we went along. And that's exactly the way it happened. The part of Sandy was created on the first morning of shooting. Of course, that's not entirely true. Jack Ford had created the part in his head while still at home, sitting in his bed. That was the way of Uncle Jack.

Moab was just the same as the year before—peaceful and serene. The beer joint was still way down at the end of town by the river. Ben, Claude, and I were in the first shot, along with Victor McLaglen. We were down at the George White Ranch, where we would shoot most of the picture. The studio had built the entrance to the fort there, and out in the alfalfa field there were tents and tie rails, horses, and a lot of local "soldiers" standing around waiting to work. The Colorado River ran right by there. The Roman-riding track was a circle all around the outer edge of the alfalfa field. It wasn't much of a race track, but it was probably the way it would have been. That's what they would have had in those days to exercise their horses—nothing too fancy. We practiced on it every day.

That very first scene gave me the idea of the character I was going to play. He was more or less the kid from *Wagonmaster.* In fact, he was even called Sandy by the other men in the troop. His real name was Daniel Boone, like the legendary one. It was typical Ford humor.

The first shot was the roll call. Ben was Trooper Tyree, the same as in *Yellow Ribbon.* The three of us—Ben, Claude, and me—are all recruits. Ford had us all lined up—a whole platoon of new recruits with McLaglen shouting at us. Sound familiar? Ford loved that. He repeated the same gags in picture after picture and the critics be damned. Victor is calling out the roll, shouting out the names from a list in his hand. So far, all are present and accounted for. Then he gets to my name. "Boone," he yells. I keep answering wrong, saying, "Yeah," and "What's that?" until, in exasperation, Victor says, "Just say Yo!" That was the gag.

My part in *Rio Grande* was the easiest I ever played. The Old Man told me what to say before each scene—no lines to study on that one. *Rio Grande* was another one of Ford's "vacation" pictures. The filming was extremely easy for him—no strain on him at all. Only a cinematic genius is capable of achieving that day in and day out. He played a lot of his scenes in a master shot. He didn't go in for close-ups too much, unless he really wanted to punch up a scene. He used what is called a loose shot. That is to say, he left some room on either side of the frame of the lens so there was margin for error. When using livestock or horses, well, unexpected things happen. A horse might rear up or spin around. Ford liked to have that in the shot, and if you are too tight, like most directors today, the whole thing is lost, because the subjects are out of frame.

The British directors nearly all use what I call Ford's technique. They play the scene in a medium shot with all the principals in the camera at the same time. I believe the impact of the overall scene is much stronger that way, and the actors relate better to one another, too.

Uncle Jack didn't want you thinking about anything but the work at hand when you were a member of his cast. He wanted you to be there and on your toes, but he didn't want to discuss your specific role with you. You couldn't ask him a question about the movie, either. If you did, he'd insult you, bawl you out, and make you wish you had taken up a different profession. For instance, if you said to him, "Oh, I know you don't want me to talk faster, but you want more energy, right?" I can't even tell you what would happen if you said that. You didn't question; you did what you were told.

It was tough sometimes, because he'd have that damned handkerchief in his mouth, and you couldn't hear what he was telling you. And you'd better not ask him to repeat it! I was pretty young and stupid when all these classics were being filmed, but I could see that these rules also applied to the older and more mature actors.

One wonders how he made all those incredible movies with so many do's and don'ts. The answer is that there was only one way to do it—his. He said a surprising thing to me toward the end of his life. I had asked him what it was like directing Will Rogers, and he said, "Oh, you didn't direct Will. You let him do what he wanted."

If Uncle Jack happened to be over schedule, it was probably on purpose. Someone had aggravated him. He was always in total command. Some films he handled with a very firm hand, like *3 Godfathers*. That was blood, sweat, and tears. *Yellow Ribbon* was like that, too, but maybe not quite so bad. *Wagonmaster* was fun, and I could see that this one was going to be, too.

This was Ford's first film for Herbert J. Yates' Republic Pictures. Jack wanted to do it in color, but Yates won out, so it is in black and white. The Old Man must not have felt like fighting, or it didn't mean much to him, one way or the other. He did ride old man Yates about it every time he saw him, though. The love of Herbert Yates' life was a former professional ice skater named Vera Hruba Ralston, and she was his number-one leading lady at the studio. They finally did get married. I worked on a movie with her there at Republic a year or so after *Rio Grande,* and found her to be a very nice person. But she wasn't in *Rio Grande;* Maureen O'Hara was. I don't think Yates even tried. Uncle Jack wanted Duke and Maureen together. However, Vera had a brother named Rudy Ralston. He was a producer there at Republic.

After about ten days of shooting, word filtered down the ranks that Mr. Yates was coming up to location. You would have thought he would have had more sense, but evidently he didn't know Ford as well as he thought. Up he came with his producer and future brother-in-law, Rudy Ralston. Rudy was in his mid-thirties, and Yates probably thought it would be a learning experience for him to see Ford at work. He never got the chance—Ford wouldn't allow him on the set! Yates was allowed to come out one of the two days he was there.

At dinner that first evening, Ford made room for them at the head table. Now there was an actor who used to work a lot for Ford named Alberto Morin. I think the Old Man first got to know him through the OSS during the war. Alberto had a hell of a war record. He was an excellent actor and could play a variety of roles—a head waiter or a Mexican general. He spoke seven languages fluently. Jack also loved Alberto's great sense of humor. This night, Ford dressed Alberto up as a waiter in the mess hall and told him to speak with a French accent—throw in some real French phrases and be very clumsy at his job. Ford had Alberto make a big fuss over Yates and Rudy when they came in, speaking half-French, half-English, and lead them to the table. We were all watching and quite surprised; we had not been let in on the joke. But it didn't take long to see what Ford was up to. During the course of the meal, Alberto managed to break a few dishes, knock over their water, and spill the soup all over the poor guys. Alberto was so good that it was hard to tell he was not on the level. Neither Yates nor Rudy got mad. That's what made the whole thing sad and very unfunny. They went home soon after that.

Uncle Jack made *Rio Grande* in just 30 days, three weeks in Moab and one week back on Stage 11 at Republic. I was to work on that stage many times in the years to come. They are happy memories.

The Old Man enjoyed directing Duke in this role and of course Maureen was with us to make it all the more beautiful. She was so gorgeous it took your breath away to see her every morning. I wished I was a leading man and could do a love scene with her, like Duke did. Uncle Jack put that scene off until the last day of shooting.

Duke had said during the whole last week of shooting, to anyone who would listen (except Jack, of course) "Christ, we're right here on the set. We could shoot that scene easy now—where I have to take her in my arms and kiss her—he's duckin' it. He *hates* to direct a love scene. You watch—he'll put it off 'till the last goddamn day!"

Duke was right. That's exactly what happened.

Someone could write a whole book spanning a period of 50 years about John Ford getting mad at his actors and not using them for long periods of time, to punish them for whatever he thought they had done wrong. He did that all his motion-picture life, starting with my dad in 1921. Any little thing could trigger it and get you on his "you're a bad boy" list.

Ben did not work for Ford for 13 years after *Rio Grande*. Very few people realize that. An incident that took place one particular evening sure put a kink in their relationship, but I don't think it was the sole reason for the breakup. He had never jumped on Ben like he did Duke and Ward and Victor and me. He knew Ben wouldn't stand for it.

This day, we had been filming at a Spanish-like set with a big Catholic church that the studio had built there in Moab. The Indians were raiding it, and the cavalrymen were shooting at them from the tops of the buildings. Although there is a lot of shooting going on, none of the Indians were hitting the ground. Obviously that part of the action was to be shot later with stuntmen. Jack Ford's faithful gang of Navajos were very good horsemen and probably would have fallen off their horses for nothing, had Ford asked them, but Jack wouldn't do that.

Anyway, dinnertime at the mess hall had a set plan: Uncle Jack at the head of the table, Duke on his left, Maureen on his right, and then it graduated down. The further away you sat from the Old Man, the more relaxed the atmosphere and the freer the talk. But you still had to watch your step! This night, Ben and I were talking about the day's work when the rest of the table conversation subsided some. There just happened to be a very quiet moment when Ben said to me, "Well, there was a lot of shootin' goin' on today, but not too many Indians bit the dust." Then it stayed awful quiet.

After about five beats, from up at the head of the table came, "What did you say?"

Ben cleared his throat a bit and said, "I was just talkin' to Dobe, Mr. Ford."

Uncle Jack said, "I know. What did you say?"

Again, "I was just talkin' to Dobe."

Then Jack said, in his nastiest tone, "Hey stupid! I asked you a question. What did you say?"

With that, Ben got up from the table and stopped and said something to Ford that none of us could hear.

Ben says that when he stopped, he told Jack what he could do with his picture, in no uncertain terms. He must have. He sure left no doubt in anyone's mind that he was ready to kill! There was an embarrassed silence—an uncomfortable, deadly silence all around the table.

Then Jack said, "Oh, Jesus Christ, Dobe, go get him, for God's sake and bring him back." He knew he'd been wrong. He'd made a mistake and let his temper and vanity overcome him.

I got up from the table and went across the street to the telephone office. That was the only way you could call home in those days. Ben was there, and when he saw me, he said, "Dobe, I never thought I'd see the day when that Old Man could make me mad. Now I guess I'll be sent home."

"No, you won't," I said. "He knows he was in the wrong."

I've never seen Ben so unhappy before or since. He would not come back to the dinner table. I went back in and told Uncle Jack that Ben wasn't coming back, and that was that. The next day, it was as though nothing had happened. For the rest of the picture, it remained a relaxed Ford film. He'd joke with Ben about letting him go fishing if he'd do a good stunt, and things like that. I don't remember Ben brooding about it then, either. He does more now, I think. He says now that I stuck up for him and said, "Uncle Jack, Ben didn't say nothin'." But I'm afraid I didn't say anything in his defense. I wish I had. I'm sorry to have to admit that. However, I think the real reason Ben didn't work for Ford all those years was not that incident, but one that happened about two years later.

In 1952, Jack was going to shoot a remake of the old "Judge Priest" story and call it *The Sun Shines Bright*. He had made it with Will Rogers in the early 1930s. He wanted Ben for the young leading man. It was set in the South, and Ben had the looks and a built-in country accent. Wingate Smith told me this story some years later as to why Ben didn't get the part. Somehow, the unthinkable happened; Ben's agent managed to get Jack Ford on the phone. This agent let Ford know in no uncertain terms that if he wanted Ben Johnson in this picture, it would cost him X amount of dollars. Jack Ford pulled the telephone out of the wall and threw it across the room. Ben never knew that had happened. I think Uncle Jack missed Ben a lot, but the mean old bird had to mete out his punishment. It wasn't until 1963, 13 years later, that Ben worked for Jack again, in *Cheyenne Autumn*.

I had about a five-year stretch myself, but Walt Disney took up some of the slack in my case with the "Spin and Marty" series on the "Mickey Mouse Club," and I did many other TV episodics. In 1958, I heard that Uncle Jack was going to make another Cavalry picture for the Mirish Company, called *The Horse Soldiers* with Duke and William Holden. I figured I was a natural for that. I had not been to see him in his studio office for a long time. I'd seen him at home and out at the farm, but I'd started worrying about our working relationship. I knew something had been broken, and I wanted very much to repair the damage. I went over to see him at the old Goldwyn Studios. When I was called into his office, it seemed that nothing had changed—it was like old times. He was genuinely glad to see me and introduced me as Harry, Jr., to the producer, Marty Rackin, and writer, John Lee Mahin. He seemed proud of me—like he was showing me off. He was affable and kidded me about something or other, but then, all of a sudden, it was all over. He jumped up and said, "Good to see you, kid, but it's time for you to go. And we've already got an actor getting seven-fifty!"

I was totally confused and did not know what that crack meant. By the time I got to my car, I had it figured out. My agent (who shall remain anonymous) had called his office and stated that my salary was $750 a week, "on a four" (meaning a four-week guarantee). He did not like that, even though he must have known that that was an average salary for character actors at that time. On my last show for Uncle Jack, however, I had received $500 a week, "on a nothing." Bill Holden was to be paid $750,000 for his role in *The Horse Soldiers,* hence his "seven-fifty" remark. All of his old gang went on location to Louisiana and Mississippi for that cavalry picture, but not Harry Carey, Jr., and not Ben Johnson.

Anyway, back to the George White Ranch. Out in another part of the alfalfa field there were some "jumps" for the cavalrymen to show off their jumping ability to General Sheridan. I was hanging around between shots one day when Cliff Lyons approached me with a big grin on his face. Cliff had a strange habit, sort of a tic with grinning—grin, no grin; grin, no grin. It didn't mean he was happy or anything. Well, here he came, grinning, not grinning, saying, "Now goddamn—now goddamn, heh, heh, heh, the Old Man wants you to try riding some jumping horses. He's got some wild-ass idea he wants to shoot in a day or so. Told me to get you prepared—heh, heh, heh." That news shook me up a little. I thought I detected a trick of some sort. Well, I was an expert horseman, and it didn't sound as wild as the Roman-riding had a few weeks past. Anyway, up at our old ranch, Cappy and I used to rig up jumps of a sort, but I had never ridden an honest-to-God jumper. I didn't even know there were any up there on location. There were two. One was named Bracket and the other Tommy. Bracket had a hell of a rep. He could jump over a convertible automobile. No matter what kind of jump you aimed him at, low or high, he jumped the same height—very high!

She Wore a Yellow Ribbon – The day of the famous lightning storm. Photograph by Alexander Kahle.

She Wore a Yellow Ribbon – John Agar and me fighting over Joanne Dru. Photograph by Alexander Kahle.

She Wore a Yellow Ribbon – My horse's name was Uncle Sam. Photograph by Alexander Kahle.

She Wore a Yellow Ribbon – Lieutenant Ross Pennell. Photograph by Alexander Kahle.

She Wore a Yellow Ribbon – "I'll have a chaw if you don't mind, Sir." Duke thought up this piece of business. Photograph by Alexander Kahle.

She Wore a Yellow Ribbon – Looking for hostiles. Photograph by Alexander Kahle.

She Wore a Yellow Ribbon – Duke's favorite scene. Photograph by Alexander Kahle.

Board of Directors meeting at the Field Photo Farm. Left to right: Clarence Inman, John Ford, Ray Kellogg, Harry Martin, Harry Carey, Jr., Wingate Smith, Mark Armistead. Photograph by J.B. Allin.

A special day at the Field Photo Farm—Left to right: Patrick Ford, Kathleen O'Malley, Olive Carey, Mary Ford, Marilyn Fix Carey, Patrick Ford's mother-in-law, Barbara Ford, Harry Carey, Jr., with John Ford seated in front.

John Ford making Duke and me sing when we are obviously over the limit on booze. Hugh Farr and Lloyd Perryman of the *Sons of the Pioneers* in background. Taken at the Field Photo Farm. Photograph by Clarence Inman.

Christmas party at the Field Photo Farm – "Bad" Chuck Roberson on horseback. Danny Borzage with his accordion. Ed Jauregui driving, and Uncle Jack giving instructions to a hired Santa Claus. Photograph by Clarence Inman.

Wagonmaster – Two young sprouts.

Wagonmaster – Ben Johnson and me with Ward Bond, the actor who carried the picture.

Wagonmaster – Flirting scene with Kathleen O'Malley with me riding "Mormon".

Wagonmaster—Joanne Dru and me singing along with the great songwriter Stan Jones, with Danny Borzage playing his accordion.

Wagonmaster – The fight scene just after the dog bit Ward Bond.

Up came a wrangler named Bruce, a nice guy, leading the two jumpers. Both were saddled with English or flat saddles. I was no stranger to a flat saddle; I had ridden them playing polo and in the New York World's Fair in 1939 and 1940. I got on Bracket first, and under the expert hand of Bruce, was jumping around five feet with either horse. Neither Bruce nor Cliff seemed to care one way or the other about my being able to do this. I left the field sort of unfulfilled. A hell of a lot of actors I knew couldn't have done it without falling on their ass, and these guys didn't say a goddamned thing. As it ended up, I never even had to do it in the movie.

The day came when we were to film the Roman-riding sequence that people talk about so much today. "Did you guys actually do that?" "Yes, we sure as hell did." But there was one thing that I did not do. Cliff came up and informed Ben and Claude and me that the Roman-riding was coming up in about an hour and to get ready.

"Today is the day—heh—heh—heh," he said. "You guys are in for a busy afternoon—heh—heh—heh. But the Old Man just told me he doesn't want you guys already mounted when you start riding, 'cause it won't mean nothin' that way, see? He wants you boys to 'crupper' those goddamned horses—heh—heh—heh."

I didn't know what "crupper" meant, but I knew it had to be bad news. What we were being told to do was known in the stuntman's trade as a "crupper mount," and it is, indeed, beautiful to see when it is done properly. I remember the colorful and most famous western star, Tom Mix, doing it with ease and grace. You've seen it dozens of times in westerns. The cowboy runs up from behind his horse and leapfrogs into the saddle. You have to take a good jump at your horse's behind, then both hands hit his rump and you are propelled into the saddle. In our case, onto the horse's bare back.

It should be easier without a saddle, right? Wrong! Not for me. I could still be in Moab and not have mastered the crupper mount. It was just awful, and I felt like a first-class horse's ass. Cliff led us over to a nice, gentle, old horse tied to a rail out in back of George White's house—out of sight of the picture crew, thank God.

Cliff said, "Ben, I know you can do this. I've seen you do it doubling guys. But you might show Dobe and Claude here what it is."

Ben walked up behind the old horse and patted him on the rump so he would know something was coming. Then he walked back about 30 feet, made a short run, and did that leapfrog right on to the horse's back. It looked easy.

"Okay. Okay, now you boys try it." Cliff pointed to Claude. "Kid, give 'er a try. Just try to do what Ben did."

Claude did what Ben did, all right, only more. He almost leaped over the whole damned horse. He hit the horse's rump with those big hands of his, gave a push, and came within a few inches of a very painful landing, having lit in front of the horse's withers.

"Well, goddamn. Goddamn, kid, you almost cleared the horse! Well, that will make the Old Man happy. Just cut it down a little, that's all—heh—heh—heh." Then, he looked at me. Cliff's heart wasn't in it when he said, "Dobe, let's see how good you can crupper that horse there."

I am not an athlete. I didn't realize, until I was a much older man, that athletes are born, not made. One either has the reflexes, speed, and power in his legs, or he just doesn't. I have no spring in my legs and was never able to vault into a saddle. So now we're an hour before filming and Cliff is asking me to do the impossible. I made a hell of a run at that poor old horse's ass—the fly of my pants hit him right at the top of his tail. There I stood, behind him, with my arms on his rump and my head on my arms in total discouragement. Everyone there was full of helpful instructions. It went on and on. I wore that horse's hind-end out. I never was able to get any higher.

Finally Cliff said, "Well, shit! Can't say you didn't try. You just can't do it, that's all."

"Yeah," I said, "that's all right." What the hell was the Old Man going to say, I thought. But you never knew with that old bird. He might not say anything.

So we shot the scene where Victor McLaglen is giving us the business about how the Ancient Romans used to ride. When Ben and I make the run to our respective teams and crupper onto the horses, the "I" is Kenny Lee, and he made me look awfully good. In fact, it could have been Kenny all the way around the track, and I could have saved myself all that humiliation and hard work. Uncle Jack had seemed disappointed that I couldn't do the crupper, but I guess he figured I had kept my part of the bargain in learning to do the Roman-riding. I really only let myself off the hook about it when I started writing this chapter 45 years later!

After Kenny did the start for me, the rest went really well. My turns around the track are documented on film. It's so well cut, you can't tell Kenny had anything to do with it. Today they would use the telephoto lenses that brings the action up close. Back then, there would have had to have been an "insert road" alongside the track with the camera car going about 35 miles an hour. Jack preferred to shoot it with a stationary camera following the action.

Ben kept talking about going fishing, and word finally filtered down to the Old Man. The Colorado River was only a few hundred feet from where we were shooting, and Ben wanted to catch a mess of catfish, which he said were lazily feeding off the bottom, for "cook" to fry up for everyone for dinner. It got to be kind of a gag.

Uncle Jack kept kidding Ben and Claude and me about wanting to go fishing on company time. He'd say before each scene, "You boys do this good and I might let you go fishing." This went on for days. One day about 3:30 in the afternoon, he said to the three of us, "That is all! You kids are through for the day. Why don't you go fishing?" He was in a really good mood, and happy with our work. What a nice old bird. We thanked him profusely and scurried for the fishing poles we had stashed in the prop truck. We dug a mess of worms, baited up, and had those hooks waving along the bottom of the Colorado River before you could say "Maureen O'Hara." We must have been there about two hours and had caught 20 or so catfish. We had no idea what time it was, but figured we'd better be getting back to the set before they wrapped for the day. We had all the fish on a couple of stringers, and headed back to the shooting site. There was no set! There was not a sign of life or that there had ever been a film company there. It was eerie! We looked around. George White's place was off in the distance, but there was no one there, either—not even a pickup truck.

None of us said anything. Finally Ben said, "Well, that old bastard! He jes' done left us! That old bastard's got us again, fellas."

How did he do it? He got that whole company out of there without us hearing a thing. Catfish fishing isn't even that much sport. You pull the poor buggers up and take out the hook. He had really pulled one on us this time. There we were. There was the road to town, but not too much traffic goes either way on it. Very few folks lived out there.

The three of us started walking up the road. We walked until dark and still had a ways to go. Finally, there came some headlights. An old-timer in a beat-up pickup truck stopped and looked us over for a minute. What in the hell were three guys wearing 1872 cavalry uniforms and carrying fishing poles doing on the road at this time of night? Well, I guess he figured it out, and mercifully, he gave us a ride. We were tired! We asked him to let us off at the beer joint just outside of town. Ben and I each downed a 3.2 beer, and Claude had a Coke. The hell with being on-the-wagon this time. When we got to the mess hall, the company was still at dinner.

Ford looked up at us real peaceful-like and said, "How was the fishing?"

We held them up for him to see.

"Oh, good," he said. "How about some dinner? You boys eat yet?" Uncle Jack seemed to be the only one who thought his little game was funny. No one else was laughing. Nothing was ever mentioned about the beer, even though I'm sure he knew where we had stopped off. By that time, we wouldn't have cared anyway.

Rio Grande introduced two of the best stuntmen who ever fell off a horse for pay—Good Chuck and Bad Chuck—Hayward and Roberson. It was on that very first picture for the Old Man that they acquired their nicknames. The irony of their success is that they both got off to horrible starts. Hayward's was almost a tragedy, and although Roberson's was more on the humorous side, I'm sure he didn't think so at the time. Roberson got his nickname, Bad Chuck, from Uncle Jack because of his way with the ladies and his night life. That automatically made Hayward "Good" Chuck. Hayward didn't do too badly with the girlies, either, but Ford had them labeled, so that was that. Besides, their looks fit their labels. Roberson was almost as tall as Duke, and handsome enough to be a leading man. He had a devil-may-care way about him that Ford loved, and so did everybody else. Hayward was good-looking, too, but more reserved, and with a quiet humor. He was not as big as Bad Chuck. In those early days, they palled around together, but as the years went by, they became more independent, though they always remained good friends. I had an awful lot of fun with those two guys. Bad Chuck is gone now, but Hayward is still with us. He was extremely helpful to me throughout my western movie career.

It was on the first day of shooting that Good Chuck had his "wreck." He was made up as an Indian, and was supposed to do a stirrup drag. You see it in westerns all the time: it's when a stunt person falls off the horse, his foot gets caught in the left stirrup, the horse drags him for a spell, and then he comes loose. The stunt was rigged in a hurry by another stuntman while Chuck was changing his wardrobe. He didn't have time to check it out, because Cliff Lyons was yelling, "Hurry up, hurry up!" When he pulled his release after being dragged, the strap did not lengthen out, and he was whipped right under the horse's belly. There was a terrible blur of horse and rider, like they were glued together, and then the horse did a somersault. Chuck was very near death for a week in the local hospital.

He still has a steady ringing in his ears. Thank God, he survived to become one of the best stuntmen in the business.

Bad Chuck got off to a terrible start with Ford. Freddie Kennedy, as shy as he was, had highly recommended Chuck Roberson to Uncle Jack. That was the worst thing he could have done. To praise someone to Jack Ford was the kiss of death for the poor guy. Actually, Bad Chuck got off pretty easily. The first stunt he had to do in *Rio Grande* was his first horse fall in front of a camera; in fact, I think it was his first horse fall *ever*. Ford showed him where his mark was, and Bad Chuck, all nervous, had his borrowed falling horse going full out. He missed his mark by 15 feet, and by the time he got his horse to go down with him, he'd wiped out an entire row of chairs, along with some of the crew. Ford ignored him for weeks before he gave him a chance to redeem himself, and redeem himself he did. He had a great reputation later on in the picture business, especially because of his horse falls.

Not too many years after *Rio Grande*, he acquired the very best falling horse in the history of the business. He was only half-broke at the time he got him, and his name was Cocaine. (This was years before it became a national pastime.) Cocaine became more famous than Bad Chuck, who became a great stunt double for Duke, starting on *Rio Grande* and going all the way to the end of the line with Duke. Chuck Hayward also worked with Uncle Jack to the end of his movie making, and neither one of them ever got in the famous Ford dog house for some misdeed, like the rest of us did.

If you want to see the Chucks in action, just run *The Searchers,* one more time and concentrate on the big Indian fight with Chief Scar at Victory Cave in Monument Valley. Bad Chuck, on Cocaine, does a beautiful horse fall, doubling Henry Brandon. Then he and Chuck Hayward double Duke and Jeff Hunter in that fast-action stuff in their fight and flight with the Comanches. They make Duke and Jeff look so good it gives you goose bumps. Pick up any coffee-table movie book on Ford and Wayne, and you'll see them both.

With the public, *Rio Grande* continues today to be the favorite of the three cavalry pictures made by John Ford. Ford historians call *Fort Apache, She Wore A Yellow Ribbon,* and *Rio Grande,* the Cavalry Trilogy. He didn't start out with that in mind; it just happened. I'm very proud that I was in two of them.

The Long Gray Line

T*he Long Gray Line* was really a backdrop for a lot of wonderful "happenings." The picture is never talked about much, in spite of the fact that it starred Maureen O'Hara and Tyrone Power at the height of their careers. It went over great with me, though. I had a wonderful and adventurous time while filming it in the spring of 1954 at Highland Falls, or to be more specific, West Point.

I found out I was going to work in it earlier that year, while shooting another movie. The very best way for an actor to get hired is to be working on another picture when they want you for theirs—even Uncle Jack. He really must have wanted to use me, because he took a long walk, all the way from his office near the entrance of Republic Studio to the western street on the back lot, where I was working on a western called *The Outcast,* starring John Derek and Joan Evans.

Bill Witney was the director, and there were a lot of cowpokes and stunt guys in it whom I'd grown up with in the business: Jim Davis (many years later, head of the Ewing clan in "Dallas"), Slim Pickens (not yet the fine actor he turned out to be), and the Good and Bad Chucks. It was a good Republic B western. We were shooting the exterior of the saloon out on the boardwalk. I wasn't part of that sequence, so I was just standing there, watching rehearsal, when I heard the name John Ford. Then another voice said, "John Ford—there's John Ford," and another, "Hey, John Ford just came on the set."

Then I heard the Man, himself, say, "Hi! I'm looking for Dobe Carey. Is he here?"

Suddenly all of the milling around and general conversation that goes with a camera set-up came to a stop and everyone was making way for Uncle Jack. The Old Man was extremely polite and almost acted as if he were on his first movie set; looking around like it was all new to him. He said hello to Bill Witney, looked around some more, and said, "Is Dobe around?"

All the assistant directors and Bill, too, started calling my name. "Dobe! Dobe!" I was standing off to the side, watching this whole thing in a state of shock, wondering what could bring Uncle Jack all this way just to look for me.

Anyway, I walked up to Uncle Jack and stood in front of him. We looked at each other. He was checking out my wardrobe, I could tell. And then we shook hands. I hadn't seen him in quite awhile, but he was the same—gentle but fearsome. He was always a fearsome sight, but he wasn't always gentle. This day, he was.

He smiled and said, "That's a good outfit—a nice shirt. Isn't that your hat?"

"Yes, sir," I answered. He knew it was the same old hat I had worn in *3 Godfathers*, but neither of us said so. He steered me away from the crowd, over to one of the old sets where there was some shade. He took me by the shoulders and stared at me, like he was examining something he was going to purchase.

Then he said, "Take your hat off, kid." So off came the hat. He smiled and then held the back of my head with his left hand; with his right hand he pushed my hair back from my forehead. After a short inspection, he seemed satisfied, in fact, quite pleased. The idea was that he wanted me to look like I was getting bald; that was not a problem, because my hairline was already receding.

"How would you like to play Eisenhower for me in my next movie? Not like he is now (he was president then), but when he was a cadet up on the Hudson?"

I was flabbergasted. It was the best news I had had from him since the time he saw me grooming my horse at the farm. Finally I said, "Uncle Jack, nothing would make me more proud. Thank you." We shook hands and gave each other the Mexican hug of camaraderie.

He said, "Okay, kid. That's good. Go ahead and get back to work." And he was gone.

He moved his offices over to Harry Cohn's Columbia Studio on Gower Street in old Hollywood. Of all the studio lots I have worked on, there has never been a lot quite like Columbia, when it was run by the infamous Harry Cohn.

You felt his presence all over that little lot, with its winding rubber-carpeted, dark hallways. I mean, that place had character! It's been printed in movie books many times that Harry had the sound stages, and many of the dressing rooms bugged. I have always assumed that to be true, because I have heard it so many times. It seems that he wanted to know what was being said about him—or just what was being said, period. He also wanted to know who was romancing certain girls he had under contract. I've also heard that he had spies around. Well, so what else is new? All powerful men had spies. They didn't necessarily appoint them. There have always been natural-born stool pigeons who love to tell men of power who is sleeping with whom, who's on dope, who's a closet drinker or a closet gay. Nowadays, it's all right there at the market checkstand. But there were two directors who were absolutely and totally left alone. They called their own shots, and Mr. Cohn did not even walk on their set without being asked—no bugs, no bullshit, and a closed set, at all times. Those two were Frank Capra and John Ford. Frank Capra made many more movies there than did John Ford. Cohn was a smart man, and he knew he had the best in those two men.

The Long Gray Line was taken from a book called *Bringing up the Brass*. It is the story of an impulsive Irish immigrant by the name of Martin (Marty) Maher, who somehow made his way from Ellis Island up the Hudson to the United States Military Academy at West Point, in search of a job. He talked his way into being hired as a sort of Jack-of-all-trades, and failed at most of them. The one thing he did not fail at was winning the hearts of the young cadets. He finally found himself involved in the athletic program as a trainer, equipment manager, and general "pepper-upper" to those cadets who were worried about failing. Many of those cadets became famous, and they never forgot Marty Maher.

Two future generals who figured prominently in Marty's life at the Point were Cadets Dwight Eisenhower and Omar Bradley. Eisenhower, who was on the first-string football team, was present at the famous 1913 football game when Notre Dame defeated Army because of the first forward pass ever thrown—Gus Dorias to Knute Rockne. Eisenhower did not play in that game because he had a broken leg, but he was there on the bench, cheering his team on. More about that game later on.

We Ford veterans (this was my fifth movie for Uncle Jack) felt from the first day that we were working on an exceptional film. Perhaps it was the grounds of that famous school. The walls and buildings had a hallowed, ethereal quality. I thought we were making a wonderful movie. It had all the right ingredients: all of Ford's favorite flavors. There was the West Point military pomp and circumstance, the brass and the shining silver of the sabers; the buildings that looked as if they went back to medieval times; the accent on the physical—the virility of the place, the mental toughness and the dedication of the cadets; along with the light-heartedness and laughter of blooming healthy youths. The plebes didn't laugh too much, but they would next year, when they could "give it" to the new guys. Then there was the singing. Their choir was magnificent.

The Old Man was in a fine mood. He was having the time of his life. The brass treated him as if he were already an Admiral, which he would be later on. John Eisenhower, the president's son, was teaching there but was on leave the entire time we were shooting. Uncle Jack wanted very much to talk with him, but never got the chance.

I thought Tyrone Power might even win an Academy Award for his performance as Marty Maher, but it was not to be. The public did not accept the famous lover Tyrone Power as a comedic character actor. It never seems to work, or seldom does, when an actor who is established as playing one type of role puts on a whole new face, so to speak, and tries something different. The public wants him to stay what they made him.

Ty has an almost platonic relationship with Maureen O'Hara in the movie, even though she plays his wife, and the public didn't buy it. They wanted a steamy love story. Columbia even rigged the ads when it was released, to make them look more romantic. They didn't show Ty with his uncharacteristic mustache, either. It was a love story, but the love was between Marty and the Cadet Corps. The title was a problem, too. We all thought it conveyed just what was meant: the long gray line of America's greatest soldiers born out of that magnificent institution—the Black Knights of the Hudson. We, as actors, were proud to wear that uniform and march on those grounds, even if it was only make-believe.

I think Tyrone Power thought he was finally breaking new ground as a character actor. All of us younger actors felt that we were almost in the corps while we were there. I know those cadets who were there then and are probably retired generals by now, would laugh at that statement, but as an actor, you could not help but feel a part of it, even though we went back to the Thayer Hotel in Highland Falls after work.

Uncle Wingate was there, of course, doing the bed check every night and reporting his findings to the Old Man. The cadets of the Point didn't know that we were under command also, to Captain John Ford, U.S.N.R., a "four-striper."

My fellow "cadets" were Robert Francis (later killed in an airplane crash in the San Fernando Valley); Phil Carey—no relation; William Leslie; Peter Graves; Duke's son, Patrick Wayne; Martin Milner (later of "Adam-12"); Walter Ehlers (Congressional Medal of Honor winner); and Chuck Courtney. Along with Maureen, there was Betsy Palmer, Erin O'Brien-Moore, and those wonderful actors, Donald Crisp, Ward Bond, Milburn Stone (later Doc on "Gunsmoke"), and Willis Bouchey. Jack

Pennick was there, too, and went absolutely salute-happy. He saluted anyone with more than one stripe.

We did not go for any wardrobe fittings before we left home to start shooting, and I couldn't figure out the reason. I knew better than to ask, though. The answer came the day after we arrived at Highland Falls. The United States Military Academy tailor shop is on the grounds. What a place! We were fitted with everything from day-wear to dress-wear to full-dress-wear. We were outfitted as if we were entering the school. The only item that was different from when Eisenhower was a cadet was the hat. The hat of 1916 was slightly taller and had a smaller brim. The only other way you could tell the actors from the cadets was by our behavior. We did our best, but one day I really goofed. We had been shooting a scene in our full-dress uniforms. I went over to the big cannon overlooking the Hudson River, undid my blouse (exposing my white T-shirt), took off my hat, and lit a cigarette. Just picture that! A cadet slumped over, tired, on a rock, no hat, blouse open, and smoking! Then along came a Cadet Captain with more gold braid than the doorman at the Ritz. The expression on his face when he saw me was like he'd caught me giving military secrets to the Russians!

"Soldier! What the hell do you think you are doing!" That was the start. He corrected himself by saying he shouldn't even be addressing me as a soldier. I was a "turd-bird." God, did he give me a going-over. Finally I was able to tell him my story, and he calmed down.

But then, as an afterthought, he said, "You still ought to have more respect for that uniform you are wearing." I felt very small and awful.

After we'd been there about five days, the cadets invited the cast to dinner in their huge mess hall. Even the highest ranking cadet officers called us sir, but I'll tell you something, it was not a subservient sir. Then they would ask a question about Hollywood. I remember it as a friendly evening in spite of the spiked sirs. We all felt really old, though. We were in civilian clothes, of course, and I don't know which we looked the oldest in, the uniforms or the civvies.

The person they all liked the most was Ward Bond. They loved him, much to Ford's disgust. Bond stole the whole show that night in the mess hall. You could hear the cadets' laughter from one end of the mess hall to the other.

The Old Man walked over to our table and said to the boys, "That is Mister Bond who is causing the disturbance at that other table. Please do not judge the rest of the cast by his behavior."

"But we love him, sir!" they said in chorus.

Ward had been on the water wagon for about three years when I first worked with him in *3 Godfathers* in 1948, and it didn't seem to bother him one bit, even though, he hung out with a hard-drinking crowd! It was certainly no secret that Duke and the gang liked to drink. I'd learned from some of the older men in the Ford bunch that Ward couldn't handle his booze like Wayne could; that he couldn't control it and discipline himself. I was Ward's roommate a good many times, and he was always telling me that Wayne should learn to control his drinking.

"Look at the big bastard over there, for Christ's sake, making an ass of himself!" he'd say when we were at a party. Ward, cold sober, would sit at the piano and bore Jack and Duke with his imitation of Louis Armstrong. Nat Cole and Louie Armstrong were his favorites, and he really thought he was damned near as good as they were.

I used to think to myself, "My God, what was he like when he was drinking!" Then suddenly one night sometime in the early 1950s, I noticed Ward with a Rheingold beer in his hand. Rheingold over ice was his drink. It didn't seem to make too much difference in his behavior, so I wondered why he'd gone on the wagon in the first place. Of course, beer is not considered drinking by dedicated booze hounds. The Old Man didn't make a fuss over it. He always picked on Ward anyway. Sometimes Ward could wisecrack back, but sometimes Jack would get vicious. Not even Ward found humor at those times.

One Saturday we were shooting indoors at West Point's huge Olympic-size indoor swimming pool. We were scheduled to work there for three days. This was the second day, and we would be back there on Monday. The other "cadets" were suited up. They were on the swimming team, but Cadet Eisenhower was not. I wasn't in a bathing suit because Uncle Jack wanted me fully dressed when I jump in to save Marty Maher from drowning, the gag being that Marty is giving the boys swimming lessons from poolside, and he can't swim a lick himself.

The afternoon shooting was coming to an end when Phil Carey said to me, "Why don't you come down to New York with me tonight. We'll have some real fun!"

I said, astonished, "What?"

Phil said, "Dobe—you know—New York City? It's that really neat town down the road a piece. I'm hauling ass down there to have some drinks, maybe see a show. There's a lot going on. I'm going tonight and coming back on Monday morning. I don't work on Monday; I'm on hold, so I can sleep in."

I told him, "Phil, don't bet on it. I mean, not working. That shooting schedule doesn't mean a damned thing on a Ford show."

Well, my words of warning fell on deaf ears.

"That's a lot of baloney. All of you guys are scared shitless of that Old Man. I'm not on call for Monday, so I'm going to New York. If you're too scared to come with me, then stay here. Have two beers and play shuffle-board—live it up!"

We were at the far end of the pool, and I implored Phil to go up to the Old Man and tell him of his plans. Then I said, "He'll say, 'Go ahead, kid, and have a good time.' That's all you have to do."

Phil was flabbergasted, and he said, "I'm a grown man! I don't need his goddamn permission."

I was getting emotional now. "Phil, listen. John Ford really likes you! You're *in*. You've got everything he likes—you're handsome, you're six-four, 200 pounds, you're Irish Catholic, *and* you can act!"

Phil blinked a couple of times and replied, "No shit?"

"No shit," I answered, "he has plans for you. If you can ride a horse, you're in dreamland."

Well, he didn't believe me, because after Uncle Jack yelled, "Kids, I'm tired. Let's go home. I need my nap!" Phil took the next train to the Big Apple! I stayed on base with Peter Graves and Bob Francis. We raised a little hell in Highland Falls after we had dinner with Uncle Jack.

Monday morning, we were back at the pool again. Ty Power, with his Irish brogue, is giving the lads some complicated swimming techniques and falls into the water; real slapstick comedy stuff that Ford loved to do.

Around 10:30, Ford, sitting in his chair, cigar clenched in his teeth, asked, to no one in particular, "Where's Phil Carey? I need Phil Carey."

The assistants went nuts because he wasn't on the call sheet and ran crazily to the phone to call the hotel. Well, Phil was there; he'd gotten back an hour before. However, seeing as how it was daylight and he wanted a good sleep, he had just taken a sleeping pill!

The rest of us waited for Phil's arrival. Now I became one of the "jackals." I wanted to see what was going to happen to Phil. Of course, Ford knew where he'd been. He knew what everyone had done over the weekend. Phil didn't look too good when he made his entrance. He had on his civvies, a sweater, slacks, and loafers.

His eyes were half-shut, and he kept saying, "I didn't have a call and I took a sleeping pill. I didn't have a call and I took a sleeping pill." He looked like he wasn't sure where he was and didn't care.

Soon he knew, because Ford said, "Oh, hi! How was your trip?" No edge to it, though—as nice as he could be. But he figured out a way to keep Phil in the water for a very long time. After that, Phil was wide awake. No matter how painful it was, that Old Man had a way of making you feel better in the long run.

There is a scene in the movie where four of us cadets—Phil Carey, Robert Francis, Patrick Wayne, and I—go to rescue Marty Maher from getting drunk in his favorite saloon in Highland Falls. We are in uniform and are not supposed to be off the grounds without a pass, even though our intentions are very honorable. We are caught; get put on report; and have to walk extra duty for the offense.

Even under Uncle Jack's eagle eye, I knew I could pull this extra duty scene off better than the other three guys, because of all the practice I had had in military school years before. A distinction that I'm not too proud of, but I sure knew the routine backward and forward. You march from point A to point B with your rifle at right shoulder arms. At point B, you say to yourself, "Halt," and you execute an about-face. Then, starting with the left foot, you proceed back to point A. Another way to execute this is, at point A, you say to yourself, "Forward, march," and upon arriving at point B, you say, "To the rear, march." "March" is always on the left foot, or it won't work out. Then you pivot on the balls of your feet to your left, until you are facing point A. It's really quite simple.

I was prepared! It was late afternoon on a cool spring day, and we were shooting in a small courtyard. I had the feeling that after this sequence, it would be a wrap for the day. I couldn't think of another scene for us to do. The three of us were in a column and arrived at points A and B one after the other. If one of us screwed up by being out of step, there would be a small traffic jam, and you could feel like a real horse's ass. Well, it would not happen to me, the expert!

There were a few kinks in the rehearsal, but Jack Pennick straightened them out and whispered to me what a "good soldier" I was. I was really full of myself.

"Action!" yelled John Ford, and the marching started. We went up and back twice. On the third arrival at point B, I "to the rear, marched" with such a flourish, with such gusto and bravado, that my right foot slipped out from under me, and I almost fell. But I did not fall down!

"Cut it!" yelled the Old Man; he was delighted. He couldn't contain himself. He laughed and laughed, and then he yelled, "Cut it. Cut it. Dobe just fell down!"

Everyone on the set laughed, and he turned on them and shouted, "Shut the hell up!" Then, "Let's do it again, kids. And Dobe, for Christ's sake try not to fall down this time, will ya' kid?"

I was dying to say, "Uncle Jack, I did *not* fall down!" but he knew that, of course.

Weeks later, back in Los Angeles, we were at a big party, and Duke was there. He came up to me, laughing, and said, "Jesus! That must have been so bloody awful for you back there at West Point."

I, very surprised, asked, "What was that, Duke?"

"Well," he said, "when you fell down on the parade grounds in front of General MacArthur and the entire Cadet Corps walked over the top of you!"

Ward Bond thought himself irresistible to women. He thought that all the ladies in the world who had not been bedded by him had been deprived of heaven on earth. West Point had an abundance of attractive women. Not a lot in the "girl" category, but many in the early middle years—officers' wives, and such. Now, I want to make it clear that I'm not saying that Ward had his way with all those nice ladies, but that he was their "Entertainment Tonight" ambassador of goodwill, so to speak.

The Thayer Hotel had a cozy little bar just off the lobby. Right off, Ward became good buddies with the young bartender, who kept the fridge stocked with Rheingold beer. This bar was Ward's headquarters for the duration of the shooting. The ladies congregated there during the cocktail hour. Sometimes after hours the bartender would lock the door. God knows at what hour they all went to bed. Ward didn't act like he was a member of the cast; he acted like he was on a vacation. I would catch Wingate in there, sometimes, making mental notes to relay to the Old Man. The rest of us who liked to hoist a few mostly went elsewhere because of that, although, unlike the desert locations, Uncle Jack seemed to understand that it wasn't quite right to let the "new boys" hang out in the friendly pub and not let his "regulars" do the same thing; just so long as we didn't abuse the privilege. That meant showing up at the "Captain's Table" in the dining room every evening and getting to bed before midnight.

Peter Graves could never understand when I'd suddenly realize the time and say, "Jesus—I have to go!" Sometimes right in the middle of a shuffleboard game.

He didn't realize that I wasn't used to that kind of freedom on a Ford picture, and I'd simply panic. He'd say, "How the hell can that old bastard have that kind of power over you guys? What I do on my own time is my own damned business." I tried to explain that even John Wayne abided by these unwritten rules. He thought it was a bunch of bull and never did understand.

Ward didn't seem to care what Jack knew, but he didn't use common sense. He was creating a time bomb that was bound to explode in the near future, and it did. Ward had been up raising hell and waking me up to come down and sing for four or five nights in a row. One morning he went to bed about 4:00 A.M., and the phone in his room rang loudly about 5:30. It was Wingate.

"Ward, the Old Man wants you in the gym in the boxing ring by 8:00. You'll be working there all day with Ty and the stunt guys. You got that, Ward?"

Ward just muttered, "Yeah. That mean old bastard," and did what he was told.

Ford made him, bum leg and all, vault over the top rope of the ring—many, many times. He rode Ward unmercifully all day long, but that night, there was Ward, back in the bar at the Thayer!

The Thayer bar also had a television set; another reason Ward spent so much time there. In 1954, the Army-McCarthy hearings were going on on Capitol Hill, and by the time Joseph Welch got through with him, the senator from Wisconsin was finished. Ward was an admirer of "Tail Gunner Joe." Ward's political beliefs did not match his personality; you would not think him to be an extreme right-winger. He never brought up the subject, as Duke would. You wouldn't have to know Duke long before he set you straight about his political thinking. I can only speculate that it was Ward's way of getting attention, and a feeling of importance, that made him join that gang of reactionaries who organized the Hollywood "witch hunts" through a group called the Motion Picture Alliance.

Erin O'Brien Moore, the beautiful character actress who plays Ward's wife in the movie, was totally on the other side of the fence. She would join Ward in the bar on their days off. They would sit and watch the hearings together and cheer on their heroes. They liked each other and seemed to treat the whole thing as some sort of sporting match, never getting into any bitter arguing. Of course, it was anything but a sporting match, and thank God again, America's governmental process came to the fore and another villain was thrown out the door.

Shooting at Highland Falls was coming to an end. We had all had a good time, and I knew that Uncle Jack had had a good time, too. Like he said, directing a picture with the people he liked was a vacation to him. He knew his craft so well that directing a movie was easy for him. "It's just a job of work," he'd say.

There was one more thing I had to do before we went back to California to resume shooting. I had to go down to the Carey family mausoleum in Woodlawn Cemetery, in the Bronx. I had never been there before. This is what I wrote long ago on a rainy day in Sherman Oaks about that visit, when my kids were small and I was young:

> There is a granite mausoleum with an iron fence around it in Woodlawn Cemetery, New York. I went there for the first time in the Spring of 1954. I went with two friends and a hangover. I had some lilacs in my hand, and it looked like rain. Pop used to sing that to me "Giddy-yap Napoleon, it looks like rain." I saw CAREY over the door of that stone building. I had no idea it would be so big. It made me feel like I came from a family worth a lot of money. It made me feel like I should have arrived in a horse and carriage. My friends put their heads down to let me know that, for the next few moments, I was to be alone. I left them in the car and looked at the CAREY. It was 1890 again, and they were all there—Judge Carey, Ella J., Uncle Allen, his wife, Helen. I looked around at the names, almost forgetting why I was there.
>
> Two urns sat side-by-side on a stone shelf, apart from the rest. They looked so alone and separate. Harry Carey and Joe Harris, our own "man who came to dinner." Two men so different in nature, but so important to my being. Oh, Pop—dear Pop, why couldn't we have been young together? I laid the lilacs between them and cried, "Giddy-yup Napoleon, it looks like rain."

That's what I wrote about my visit way back then, and it still has a sort of spell about it, to me.

I must have done some pretty heavy celebrating the night before we left West Point, because I remember the long drive back to New York City and La Guardia Airport as a nightmare. Also the flight home. I gave up drinking many years ago, and it's a good thing, too, or I wouldn't be writing about it today. People do not drink as much today. The statistics on alcohol consumption bear this out, but back then, at least 50 percent of the young guys I worked with drank like I did. Of course, there wasn't that other stuff around then. Booze was what we used to boost the spirit, and I must say, I had a hell of a lot of fun. The trouble was, I had a built-in guilt complex that wouldn't quit. I envied Duke and Ward and my other friends who could drink gallons and then say, "I had one hell of a good time and I do my job, so the hell with it!" I never laughed off a hangover. I thought it was my punishment for being a bad boy, so I brought a lot more suffering upon myself. As a consequence, I was afflicted with many psychosomatic illnesses—chest pains, shortness of breath, pains down my arm—and I was only in my twenties and early thirties for God's sake! I later got all of these same symptoms cold sober. That's how whacko I was—or still am, I guess.

Actually, I had suffered all these feelings on the day I went to visit my father's final resting place. They had lifted while I was there, but returned twofold upon my return to West Point. I left a note in Uncle Jack's key box at the Thayer, thanking him for the work and telling him that I had taken lilacs to my Dad. He had said to me, "Take some lilacs. Harry loved lilacs."

Later I remember telling my mother this, and she replied, "Harry didn't give a damn about lilacs."

Everyone knows by now that there isn't any Hollywood. Yes, there is a town, and a pretty sleazy one it is these days, too. But there is no such place as a Hollywood with all the motion picture studios just a few blocks from each other. There never was such a place. Studios are scattered all over hell-and-gone. The four biggest are in the San Fernando Valley: Universal, Columbia, Warner Bros., and Disney. In fact, Columbia and Warners are on the same lot in the City of Burbank. Back in Hollywood's "golden years," Columbia, Paramount, and RKO were all either on or within spitting distance of Gower Street.

"Gower Gulch" was the corner of Gower and Sunset Boulevard. There was a drugstore there, and just east on Sunset was a bar called Brewers. It was a favorite hangout for those booze hounds who labored at Columbia. Film editors and others who were not confined to a movie set used to sneak over there all the time for a "quick one." Columbia's lot was so tiny that you had to park across the street. That parking lot was where two cowboys actually had a shootout back in the 30s—a guy called Johnny Tyke (my dad roomed with him once) and a bad hombre called Three-Fingered Jack. Three-Fingered Jack killed Johnny Tyke after being bullied into the fight by Tyke. Old Three-Fingers got off scot-free. So much for history.

Uncle Jack knew them both well. They were part of the "wild bunch" that was around in those days. There were only a few of that "wild bunch" of the early westerns left at the time we made *The Long Gray Line*.

Anyway, I made it home from New York, cuddled my wife, and gave the kids their "Daddy's-come-home" presents. We had added two more babies to the family by this time, Tom, born in 1951, and Patricia, born in 1953. I prepared to go to work at good "old" Columbia where, in 1943, Marilyn had been a messenger girl before she went off to college.

We had interiors to do at the studio and some exteriors at local locations. The studios had enormous soundstages for interior shooting. There was no traffic noise, no airplane noise, and few onlookers. The stages were soundproof, and unless a plane came directly overhead, you couldn't hear it. It was comfortable, practical, and very convenient.

Today, if they film a living room, it's not on a set, with the lights hanging from girders up out of your way; it's someone's real living room, in a strange town, with the lights, cables, camera, crew, and actors all crowded together and not a speck of air. Outside, behind ropes, with the local law enforcement pushing them, are hundreds of people trying to get a peek at, say, Burt Reynolds. It's different now, but I still love it. Going to new places around the country is fun, and I get to take Marilyn.

One evening after the Old Man had called a "wrap," I went to Wingate to get my call for the next day. Wingate dearly loved to dispense bad news—or what he thought might shake you up. I had gotten used to it.

He said, "Tomorrow you have to get up at dawn."

"Why?"

Then he said, smiling, "Your call is to be at the Columbia Ranch at 7:00 a.m., where a studio car will drive you to the location site."

Back then, most studios had a back lot where the western streets and the small-town streets with homey little houses were built. Columbia's back lot was out in the San Fernando Valley in Burbank. In those days, an actor was not allowed to drive to any location from his home. He had to drive to the main studio, and then be driven to location by a studio driver. The Columbia Ranch was classified a "main studio" because it had one soundstage. It was only a half-hour away from my house.

The following morning, after Wingate's grim message, I climbed out of bed at 5:30, took a shower, and went into the kitchen, where Marilyn had my breakfast waiting, as she always did. I got into my old Chevy station wagon and headed for the Columbia Ranch in Burbank. We had four kids, but the house was quiet when I left. I still have very early calls today, but it's not as hard to get up now, for some reason.

The Columbia Ranch is at the corner of Oak Street and Hollywood Way. There are two old, beat-up gates that you drive through after being cleared by a tired old gate guard, who sits in a little house built about 1928. He then tells you, in great detail, where to park your car. It turns out to be a patch of weeds. That was 35 years ago, and it still looks pretty much the same now.

Well, I parked my car and wandered over to where a few of the other "cadets" were standing around smoking. Then I noticed that there were many huge, very clean-cut young men standing around, too. They were not smoking. They were the better part of the Los Angeles Rams football team. There was Norm Van Brocklin, the future Hall of Fame quarterback who was playing the small but important role of Gus Dorias. And there was USC running back Jimmy Sears, who was to play Knute Rockne. Some very famous guys were there. They looked huge and powerful, but they were very shy. This was a new experience for them. This was the day we were shooting the Army-Notre Dame football game of 1913 that I mentioned earlier, in which the first-ever forward pass was thrown from Gus Dorias to Knute Rockne. They were on the Notre Dame team that defeated the favored Army team. It was played in the mud, of course. Ford wouldn't have had it any other way. Since I was playing Cadet Eisenhower, I didn't have to play with those bruisers. Phil Carey was out there with them, but he made sure they took it easy on him, which they would have anyway. On that memorable day, Cadet Eisenhower was on the sidelines, even though he was a first-string player. He had a broken leg. I had one hell of a good time sitting on the bench watching. I kept thinking Uncle Jack might have some trick up his sleeve, like having Cadet Eisenhower "accidentally" wiped out by an overzealous tackler, but it never happened.

Out there in the weed patch stood Uncle Jack's older brother, Eddie O'Fearna, or as my dad used to call him, Eddie Feeney—Feeney being the Americanization of O'Fearna. Eddie was a very pleasant man, and to this day, I do not know what he did for a living when Jack wasn't making a movie. He was always Jack's third assistant director and never seemed to want to go higher up the ladder.

This was Eddie's job; before every shot, he would yell out, "Quiet, children!" His old pipe never came out of his mouth. That was it! This morning, he said, "Let's go, children." We all got into "stretch-outs," and were on our way to our destination, which I assumed would be an old-fashioned football field out in the sticks somewhere. I was busy talking to the guys for the first 20 minutes, and as we ran out of conversation, I took a look out the window.

"We're heading right in the direction of my house," I thought. I said, "It's too bad I couldn't have been picked up on a corner somewhere out here. I don't live very far away." We drove a little further, and I couldn't believe what I was seeing! We slowed down at my street, but instead of turning right, we turned left into a gate off Riverside Drive and into what was then the McKinley Boys Home. We were filming 300 yards from my front door!

That turned out to be one of Uncle Jack's favorite stories. You can imagine what he did with that one. Marilyn getting up at daybreak to dress the kids for school, Marilyn getting my breakfast and packing the kids' lunch pails; Marilyn kissing me good bye, and then I wind up across the street. At noon, I walked home for lunch, much to her surprise. She loved the way I looked in my Army letterman's sweater.

I figured I was finished filming after the football sequence. I heard through the grapevine that the Old Man had only one more scene to shoot, and that it was with Maureen. I went home that night and told Marilyn and the kids that Daddy had finished his movie and we might have a little money left over for a summer vacation after all the bills were paid. There was no "plastic" in those "raising the kids" days. Everything was cash on the barrelhead, and I'm supremely grateful for that. What a mess we could have gotten into. We did have the Diners Club card, however, and I overdid that many a month. It's something I'm not too proud of.

It turned out I was right about being through in the picture. Wingate informed me of that fact. He knew I would show up on the set in Hollywood, anyway, just to say so long.

I drove into Columbia the next day. I parked across the street from the entrance to the studio in the "shootout" parking lot that I wrote about earlier. The guard nodded his head in recognition, and I went through the double doors that led to those funny old rubber-covered passageways.

As soon as I stepped through the soundproof door onto the set, I felt something was amiss. The first person I ran into was Wingate. He had an impish expression on his face as he nodded his head in the direction of the camera. He didn't say anything, deciding I could come to my own conclusions. It didn't take me long to do that. Uncle Jack was sitting in his chair with a Heineken's beer in his right hand. He took a big gulp out of the bottle and turned around to take note of my arrival. Danny Borzage had started playing "my song," "The Streets of Laredo." Each of Jack's actors had a song. It was a tradition with him, and it made me feel very proud and wonderful. Henry Fonda's was "Red River Valley," Duke's was "Marquita," Maureen's was "I'll Take You Home Again, Kathleen," and so on. I was about 50 years old before I realized what a very lucky young guy I had been. Jean Renoir, the French film director, said of Uncle Jack, "John Ford was a king; he knighted all those who had the immense luck to work with him."

This day, though, Uncle Jack was being a bad boy. He was drinking and directing at the same time—a very rare occurrence, indeed. He greeted me effusively, like he hadn't seen me in a long time, and then turned back to his work. He was shooting a scene that even I knew would probably end up on the cutting-room floor. This was rare for him, too, because mostly, if he shot it, he used it. He had Maureen shaking a small rug out the upstairs window of the Maher house. He was being nasty to her, and in fact, I remember that she was crying. Finally he said, "*Right!*" and yelled a very sincere "Thank you" to everyone on the set. He went over to Buddy Lawton, the cameraman, and gave him a big hug. Everyone applauded.

I don't know where Maureen went; she seemed to have disappeared. Uncle Jack then told me and some others to follow him up to his office for a drink. I thanked him for giving me the role of Eisenhower, and he told me I'd done a good job. That was almost as good as getting an Academy Award. He seldom said anything about an actor's performance, but of course he was in a particularly smashing mood right then.

There were a lot of us crowded into his office, and we all had a beer whether we wanted it or not. I was definitely drinking mine, but I noticed that Ty Power was just holding his. Uncle Jack had a fresh beer in his hand and his feet were propped up on his desk. He was regaling everyone with stories. Not movie stories, but war stories and stories of heroism and historical figures—the kind of people he liked to make movies about, the men and women in our nation's history. It was like being in a class at a great university when he was in one of these moods.

Then all of a sudden his mood changed. I saw him glance in the direction of a lady who was the wife of the technical director on the picture; a West Point graduate and a major in the regular Army. He was a nice, mild-mannered man, and Ford liked him very much. His wife was very striking, with her blond hair pulled back into an attractive bun. Uncle Jack got it into his head that she was a stuck-up, society-conscious snob. She was sitting in a chair to his right. I could see he was up to no good.

With great gusto, he announced, "I have a joke!" The first line of this "joke" is "This guy gets up in the morning to take a leak and looks at his cock. . . etc. . . etc."

That was the start, and it got much worse! He went on, relishing every word and nuance, until the bitter end. Then he looked around the room, proudly expecting great guffaws. Nothing happened. The poor major's wife turned beet red. Her husband sat there, stunned with embarrassment for his wife, and the rest of the people in the room looked at their feet or at the ceiling. There may have been a chuckle or two, but it was mostly from shock. But *me!* It seemed so bloody outrageous that I got a terrible case of the giggles and couldn't stop. It was like being in school when, in spite of all the teacher's warning, you cannot control yourself. I could not stop giggling. My eyes began to water, and it got so bad I had to sneak out into the outer office, where I fell on the floor in convulsions.

The next day, Jack headed out to Catalina on his beloved *Araner*. *The Long Gray Line* was in the can.

Mister Roberts

A job of work—that's what Ford called pictures he had fun on. "It's just a job of work," he'd tell interviewers. Directing came easy to him; he was really born for his profession. But on *Mr. Roberts,* he always seemed to feel the presence of Leland Hayward, who had produced and helped to cast the long-running production of the play, which Josh Logan directed. As we know, Jack had an aversion to producers being on the set, but Leland Hayward was not your run-of-the-mill producer. Mr. Hayward was a fine gentleman, and he and Henry Fonda were close friends, just as years before, Fonda and Ford had been close friends. Mr. Hayward always went to Henry if he had an idea, in the hope that Henry would bring it up to Ford, but Henry knew that Ford wouldn't accept that on this film any more than he would have on any other they had done together. Ford rehearsed a scene until the pace was right and everyone was comfortable with what they were doing, and then he shot it, nearly always in one take. Henry always wanted a lot more rehearsal, and he felt that Jack was taking too many liberties with the play he loved so much. There was tension building among Ford, Fonda, and Hayward right from the start.

Hayward stayed loose, but in spite of that, *Mister Roberts* was beset with problems. Some of them were Ford's fault. I think maybe he underestimated the job. It was cursed with a very bad case of "heart-lessness," and "heart" was one of Ford's trademarks. No other director could jerk tears from an audience like Uncle Jack. There was never the "Ford mood" on that set.

I had never before seen him compromise, and that's what he was being forced into doing. He seemed to treat *Mister Roberts* as a sort of half-vacation. Well, filming movies was always a vacation for him, but on *Mister Roberts,* he acted as though it was a working vacation for all of us. He unwrapped the wraps, you might say. It was okay to drink and raise a little hell at night. After all, we were in Honolulu, a paradise.

A nicer bunch of guys could never have been brought together than the cast and crew of that picture. Jack Lemmon was very excited to have landed the role of Pulver, which was to launch his film career. I think at first Henry Fonda was pleased to have Ford taking the helm and directing him in his favorite role. William Powell was perfect for Doc, and God knows, Cagney was a memorable Captain.

A few of us supporting players didn't even know what roles we were to play when we boarded the big Boeing airplane in the summer of 1954, on our way to Honolulu. We spent two riotous days there, and then we flew to Midway Island.

It was just 12 years since Midway had been taken back from the Japanese. Ford had shot his award-winning documentary there and had won his Purple Heart while hanging out of a plane to shoot the carnage below him. While we were there, Winton Hoch, the cinematographer, Uncle Jack, and I made a complete tour of the island. There were probably some others along, too—some of the local Navy brass—but I don't remember. I didn't realize the drama that must have accompanied us that day. I was 33, but still didn't realize how important that battle was for our country. It deprived the Japanese of an airbase only 1,300 miles from Honolulu. Oh well, ignorance is bliss. If I'd made any comments during the walk, I would have been shot down like one of the Japanese planes, anyway.

I have always felt that Leland Hayward should have brought out his original stage cast (with the possible exception of Jack Lemmon, although Murray Hamilton and David Wayne were both superb as Pulver), and simply filmed it right there on the lot at Warners. All of the wonders and panorama of the South Pacific were really unnecessary and didn't enhance the story at all. It wasn't *South Pacific*, it was the story of a young officer and the men who loved him.

There have been many stories about the conflicts during the filming. Warner Bros. wanted either William Holden or Marlon Brando for the title role. Henry Fonda had not made a movie in six years, so the Warners didn't feel that his name had the drawing power that Holden's or Brando's had. Holden said no for the simple reason that he thought the part belonged to Fonda and no one else. Marlon Brando accepted, but Ford was adamant about using Fonda. The sad thing is that when the sparks began to fly during the filming, it was Ford upon whom Fonda turned his wrath. It was evident from the first scene that he felt Jack was ruining his beloved play. It is very sad that Henry Fonda (one of America's finest actors) went to his grave resenting and criticizing Ford as he did in his book. He even knocks him for his direction of *The Grapes of Wrath,* as if Henry could have been better with some other director. Oh sure, years later they had a sort of reunion, when a documentary was done on Ford, but it was never the same between them.

Actually, the Navy Department didn't want *Mister Roberts* filmed at all. They felt that the role of the Captain was detrimental to the image of the navy. It took Captain John Ford and his influence with the top brass in Washington to get the matter cleared up.

The night before shooting began on Midway, everyone in the cast gathered in the big recreation hall. It was all very good-natured, and although Ford was present, the scene was very un-Fordian. He was there in body, but his greatness wasn't present. It was as though he were saying, "Oh, the hell with it!" Perhaps his thoughts were back on Odin Street in Hollywood, where the City of Los Angeles was getting ready to tear down the house he'd lived in for 30 years to make a parking lot for the Hollywood Bowl. I don't know—something was wrong. This was not the Uncle Jack I knew. No wisecracks about Jack Lemmon drinking a martini, for example; no "You sit here" and "you do this," and "there's not going to be any of this or that," etc. It was like Mervyn LeRoy was already waiting in the wings, and Ford was just filling in until he got there. I thought, "What the hell's going on? This isn't a Ford film."

Well, Ken Curtis was to play Dolan. Phil Carey was Mannion. The casting continued. It got all sorted out, but it seemed a haphazard way of doing it. I remembered a lot of the guys in the New York production, and I couldn't imagine myself as any of them. When I heard I was to play Stefanowski, I thought of the actor who had played the part in New York. He was a big, very muscular, blond Polish-American. I tried to put that out of my mind and rushed back to my room with the script, to see if I had any lines for the next day. I did, but not many. Nothing I couldn't handle. Besides, it didn't look like Uncle Jack was going to be too tough. I got the very definite feeling that Mr. Hayward resented Ford's choice of actors.

Ward Bond, who played Gowdy, was in his glory there on Midway. He appointed himself as the operations officer of the Midway Cocktail Hour. This took place downstairs (below decks) in the Bachelor Officers' Quarters. We were in "officers' country" on that two-square-mile island and had the good beach to swim at. We were given unlimited access to the Officers' Club, something I was unaccustomed to, having served in the navy for three years as an enlisted man. We all figured we'd better stick to beer, even though booze was only $1.50 a bottle at the navy store. We drank a lot of a great Philippine beer called San Miguel and were very happy that the Old Man didn't seem to mind, as long as we showed up at his table for dinner.

During the 1950s it was very common for those who felt they were overweight to take dexamyl. It was a real pepper-upper and made most people feel terrific, although they didn't necessarily lose any weight. Ward was famous for the "green pills" he always carried with him. Ken Curtis wrote a song about them. After that, Uncle Jack always had Ken and me sing it whenever Ward came on board. The tune was the old English folk song, "Greensleeves," and here are the words:

Alas, green pills you've done Ward wrong
To cast him out discourteously
When he's relied on you so long
To bring him comfort from misery.
Green pills are all his joy
Green pills are Ward's delight
Green pills will counteract
All the Rheingold he guzzled
The night before.

Of course, Ward thought it was great, and once in awhile, he shared some of those green pills with us.

Ace still photographer Slim Aarons was on the picture. I remember that he was the greatest ping-pong player I had ever seen. He'd give anyone 15 points to start and beat them 21-to-15. A Filipino steward's mate was the only player on the island in Slim's class. When they had a match, the recreation hall was filled to capacity.

On the first day of filming, Uncle Jack went up to Slim and said, "I don't mind you taking pictures as long as it doesn't interfere with the work. And do not take any pictures of me unless you ask me first. Do you understand that?"

Slim said that, yes, he understood and appreciated Jack's letting him be there. About halfway through the picture, Slim forgot his promise. "Click" went Slim's Nikon while Uncle Jack was in full throttle—the handkerchief dangling out of the corner of his mouth and the telltale cord on the right side of his neck going in and out. The Old Man caught him! He snatched Slim's camera and threw it over the side of the ship. Slim went into a total fit!

Ford just said, "I told you in plain English never to do that without asking," and walked off.

Nick Adams was still on active duty in the navy, but Uncle Jack got him a leave of absence to be in the movie after Nick barged into his office at Warner Bros. in his uniform. He was a truly upbeat and happy kid and hung out with Patrick Wayne while we were over there. He later became quite a well-known actor and had his own series called "The Rebel." I'll always remember him for this one day. We were on board ship—one of the first few days. Jimmy Cagney was sitting on deck in his canvas chair with his shirt off, sunning himself. He and I had been talking about how redheads can or cannot get tans. All of a sudden, up runs Nick, hitches up his trousers ala Cagney, and does his "You dirty rat" imitation right in front of the man himself. Jim was flabbergasted, but just for a moment. Then he looked up at me. "Jesus, is that the way I sound?" It was a funny moment, and Nick couldn't have been happier with his performance, in spite of what his hero thought. Nick committed suicide some years later. He should have hung around; there were still some laughs to be had.

There were two members of the *Mister Roberts* cast that Ford had aboard more for their aquatic ability than their acting talents. William Henry was actually a very accomplished actor whom I had seen since I was a kid. He had been a leading man in many B movies in the 30s. I'm not sure Uncle Jack was even aware of his acting talent. He did know that Bill was a superb swimmer and diver.

There was a sequence that called for Bill and another sailor to dive off the topmost part of the ship. The other sailor turned out to be Stubby Kruger. I'd seen him as a youngster, too, because my first job was in the "Railroads On Parade" show at the 1939 World's Fair in New York City. At the other end of the fairground was a marvelous spectacle called Billy Rose's "Aquacade," starring swimming champion Eleanor Holm and the great Johnny Weissmuller. The clown who worked on the high diving board with Weissmuller was Stubby Kruger. He did everything that could possibly be done on that high board to make you laugh. He was hilariously funny. My mom and dad and I went to see the show, and I'd never seen my dad laugh so hard. When the day arrived for the stunt, they both came through like the champions they were. They were well-paid for their dives, and they deserved it.

However, later, when we got to Kaneohe Bay on Oahu, there was a scene where the islanders swim out to meet the ship. Some of them were young Hawaiian boys about 11 or 12. They couldn't wait to climb up on our ship. Why? They wanted to dive off the top of it! Every one of those kids climbed to the top of the superstructure and executed beautiful and perfect swan dives, over and over again. They were having the time of their lives. Uncle Jack watched from his chair and laughed, "Are Bill and Stubby watching this?" They were not to be seen, and I don't blame them.

The swimming off the officers' beach was fantastic. You can scuba dive there for the lobster of the Pacific, the longusta. The water is very warm, so I don't think the meat is as tasty as the Maine lobster, and they do not have big claws.

Jack Lemmon is dark-haired, but he has fair skin. Henry was brown as a berry and always made a point of keeping a tan so he wouldn't have to wear makeup. One day, Henry and Jimmy Cagney decided to go diving for lobster, and they invited Jack to go along. Jack spent the entire afternoon floating along the top of that clear water, looking down toward the ocean floor. By that night, he wasn't just red, he was purple! I have never seen a burn as bad as that, except for my own a few years before when I fell asleep on the beach at Point Hueneme, California, where I was stationed for a few months. He should have been in the hospital. His whole body was shivering, but he refused to give in. He said it was sheer stupidity on his part, and he never missed one hour of work. He must have been in agony, but he never complained.

After four weeks, we finished filming on Midway, and flew back to Honolulu. John Ford's beautiful yacht *Araner* lay at anchor in the harbor there. It was a familiar place for her, as the Fords spent a lot of time there over many years.

They knew everyone in Honolulu society, and Mary Ford had no peer as a hostess. Pat and Barbara Ford both went to school there. Simply put, if you were "in" with the Fords, you were "in" on Oahu. I was having a marvelous time there, and I desperately wanted to share it with Marilyn, but we had four small children, and their grandmothers were definitely not the sitter types. Uncle Jack kept yelling for me to "Send for Marilyn!" and I wanted to say, "Okay, if you'll pay for the sitter and the plane ticket."

It was going to take a week for the navy vessel we were using as *Reluctant* to get to the island of Oahu. She was to anchor over in Kaneohe Bay, where we would finish the shooting. It was a beautiful drive over the Pali northeast of Honolulu to reach it. I seem to remember that there was a Marine base there at Kaneohe. There was only one shot left to be done while waiting for the ship to arrive. Uncle Jack knocked this off in about three hours and then had lunch with Leland Hayward and Harry Cohn, head of Columbia Studio. He said that luncheon gave him great joy because he managed to get the two of them into a fight. Of course, he might have been making that up.

One day during this waiting period, I was on the deck of the *Araner* with Barbara and Ken Curtis. She and Ken were on a sort of second honeymoon. We were relaxing with some huge glasses of iced tea. Ford's full crew was on board under the command of Captain Johnson. It was heaven. I couldn't believe I was getting paid for this.

Suddenly Barbara exclaimed, "Oh-Oh!" Ken and I followed her look toward the gangplank, and here came Uncle Jack. The "Oh-Oh" was for what he was carrying: a bottle of wine under each arm, and a sly smile on his Irish kisser that spelled trouble.

"Hi-Hi," he greeted us all. "Everybody having a good rest?" He set the raffia-covered Chianti wine on the hatch cover and reached into his pocket for his Swiss Army knife. He handed it to me and said, "Open one of these, will you, Ol' Dobe? I want you to be the taster and tell me if it is any good."

I felt about wine-tasting the same way I think he did—if it made you drunk, then it was good. Barbara and Ken were looking at me like they were sure I would botch it up, but I completed the task with surprising dexterity. In the meantime, Jack had yelled for Bill Ramsey to bring up some glasses. He complimented me on my performance, poured some of the wine into a beautiful goblet, and ordered, "Taste that!" I took a big gulp and told him it tasted good. He smiled like the cat who had just eaten the canary and replied, "Good. Good. I think I'll have a little taste, too." That was for starters.

I had never known Uncle Jack to drink while filming a movie, even if he had to wait for some reason in the middle of it. When he drank, you just had to let the bout run its course until he ran out of gas, and then it would be months before he would drink again. In this case, I think he got drunk *at* Mr. Fonda and Mr. Hayward. He was mad, and he just didn't give a damn, so he had some wine, I had some wine, and soon, everyone was having some wine. He sent for a Hawaiian band, and I knew this was going to be one hell of a party!

That party turned out to be famous because sometime during the festivities, he called Henry Fonda a traitor and bopped him on the chin. I didn't see that famous punch. I must have been up on deck.

Not too many days later, the ship arrived, and Ford was still on his toot. The biggest and most elaborate scene in the movie was next on the schedule. Ken and I were in a studio car with Henry Fonda, who was sitting up front beside the driver. We were still on the Honolulu side of Oahu, approaching the Pali. Henry was looking very grim. He was pissed off! Suddenly a fancy convertible with the top down pulled up even with us, the horn honking. It was the Old Man, and I had never seen him looking happier. He was waving frantically and yelling, "Henry! Henry!" His whole expression was one of joy and goodwill, like, "Isn't this great, Henry? Aren't we having a good time?"

Ford got Henry's attention. Henry turned, leaned way over in front of the driver to make sure Ford could see him, and yelled, "Fuck you, you drunken old son-of-a-bitch!"

Ford looked baffled. What the hell had gotten into Henry? The famous punch hadn't even stayed in his consciousness. They whizzed on past us.

When we arrived at the location and boarded the ship, Ford was nowhere to be seen, but there was a lot of activity going on among the film crew. Winnie Hoch was standing way up on the superstructure beside the number-one camera with the number-two camera a little lower down. Both were pointed at the shoreline. Along that shoreline was a hell of a sight. There were hundreds of natives in canoes, ready to head our way, and we could hear beautiful singing. Whenever groups of native Hawaiians get together, they start to sing. They all know the harmony, and it's as natural to them as breathing. It's the music of God. It sounded nothing like the commercial Hawaiian music I had heard while I was growing up. This was true native music wafting across the water toward the ship. Lots of laughter, too, just as it was written in the script, but they hadn't read the script. They had been told that when they heard the word "Action," they were to paddle out to our ship, climb up the cargo nets, and come on board. We guys, the crew, were supposed to go nuts with joy because of the pretty native girls. It was a major sequence, and there was no director in sight. He was acting like a spoiled kid. The preparations went on anyway. Henry had every right to tell him to go fuck himself. We needed him more this day than at any other time during the shooting, and he was drunk.

Ken and I were anxiously watching the proceedings. We could see the pier from where we were standing on the deck of the ship, and there was a lot of activity going on in front of one of the buildings—sort of like the outside of a beehive when the drones are preparing to transport the queen. Suddenly we saw Jack Pennick and Sam Kahanamoku carrying Jack Ford. He had one arm around each of their shoulders, like an injured football player being helped off the field. They managed to get him aboard the launch, and pretty soon he was being lifted onto the ship, a bottle of beer in his right hand. He made it to his director's chair pretty much on his own. A favorite trick of his was to act drunker than he really was. People took it for granted that he couldn't understand anything and said things they wished they hadn't, later on, when he got even with them.

I don't think this initial establishing shot at our long-awaited "liberty port" really came off. It was supposed to be a huge celebration on the deck of the "Old Bucket" with all the sex-starved sailors grabbing native girls and kissing them; but it wound up just a mishmash of confusion, with sailors and girls wandering around aimlessly. When we see the close shot of *Mister Roberts* smiling down on us, happy that what he fought so hard for with the psychotic captain was finally a reality, it doesn't really mean very much. Had Uncle Jack been sober, that scene would have brought tears to the eyes of the audience. The bond between an officer and his men was a Ford speciality.

By the way, the ship, besides having a hell of a nice skipper, also had a crew that had to stay down below decks until they heard the call "cut." Nine times out of ten, Ford printed the first take, however. Almost any other director would have kept that poor crew down there all day long; they all do at least two takes, the second one for "protection," then there is the "coverage," which means close-ups, etc. That takes many camera moves and repetitions of a scene. Ford hated to do that. He seldom shot many close-ups, unless he needed some emphasis. Then he'd hit you with a close shot when it had some meaning, to punch up the scene. Most movies you see today go from big head close-up to big head close-up. That comes from the director making too many TV movies for that small screen.

The hotel where we stayed in Honolulu is no longer there. It was called the Niamalu and was on the beach at Wakiki. Everyone had their own cottage, which was very unusual for those days in the picture business. Unless you were the star, you always roomed with another actor. That never bothered me in those days; today, it would drive me nuts. Even Jack and Mary stayed there, instead of on the *Araner.* However, they had a house with a kitchen, lanai, and lots of room. I was next door to Ken and Barbara. She and Mary had flown over a few days prior to our arrival from Midway. Along with the beautiful South Sea grounds surrounding the cottages, there was also a freshwater swimming pool, just in case you wanted to get your Hawaiian tan without lying in the sand. I was told most of the airline pilots and stewardesses stayed there between flights, and that was easy to believe, because the men were handsome and the girls too pretty to be the average overweight tourist.

On one particular day, while we were still waiting for the ship to arrive from Midway, I was sitting by the pool with Ken and Barbara and Betsy Palmer, on whom Jack had developed a huge crush. We all knew Uncle Jack was somewhere around and still on his toot, but none of us thought much about it. Then, all of a sudden, for some reason, we all looked in the same direction at once, toward the cottages.

Here he came! "My God," I thought, "he's not going for a swim, is he?" Well, he was. He had an enormous beach towel wrapped around his body and was holding it together with his left hand up near his left armpit. With a cigar between his teeth, he greeted us.

"Hi kids. Hi. Hi. Hi. Are you all getting a nice tan?"

He really seemed interested in whether we were or not. "Dobe, you're not. You're like me. You can't get tan, can you?"

"No, sir," I ventured. "I don't tan too well, Uncle Jack."

"Of course not" he said. "You're Irish like me—your Uncle Jack. We don't get tan. We belong in the fog. Ah, Betsy!" he said in mock surprise, as if he had just discovered that Betsy was there. "How about you, Betsy? Are you getting a tan?" He was ogling her chest lustfully with his good eye, and before she could reply, he reached down with his free right hand, pulled the front of her bathing suit away from her body, and had a damned good look at her breasts. Betsy just sat there smiling up at him, and after about the count of five, he let go and exclaimed, "Why, yes, you are. You're getting a *good* tan!"

With that, he bounded off like a man on a mission. Where was he going in such a hurry? This mega-pool had three diving boards at the far end—Oympic diving boards—one low, one medium, and one high board, for the very experienced. That's where he was headed. We watched, unbelieving. In a wink, he was on the ladder. How he managed to climb it and still hold onto his towel is a mystery. We wondered which board he would choose to show off his great diving ability. Little by little, he was getting everyone's attention. Up he went. He ignored the first board— screw that one—but when he bypassed the second one, Kenny and I knew we were in for a swim. Somehow he made it all the way to the top of the highest board. There he stood, in all his glory—glasses, eye patch, cigar in mouth, and still clutching the towel. By now, everyone was focused on John Ford. Since his left hand was feeling a little cramped and numb, he did the only logical thing. He relaxed it, thereby releasing the beach towel. Down, down, it wafted into its watery grave, and there stood John Ford, winner of four Academy Awards, bare-assed naked, a jillion feet above the water. After he heard the gasp from his spellbound audience, he spread his arms and launched into what I'm sure he pictured as a swan dive. In reality, it looked like that old film of the poor guy going off the Eiffel Tower. He dropped like a rock, legs and arms flailing, into the water, miles below. There was an enormous splash and what seemed like a very long wait. Then up popped his old bald head, a rather disgruntled look on his face that seemed to say, "That wasn't anything like I wanted, let's go for another take." The glasses were gone, but the cigar was still in place. Ken and I hit the water and in a flash had him in our grasp. Others were diving for the glasses and the patch. The man who found them said to me, as he brought them over, "That was a hell of a show!" and walked away in amazement.

Jack's binges got shorter as he got older. His body just didn't hold up like it did in the old days when he and Duke would tie one on. Duke was forever grateful for *Stagecoach.* All his life, he never forgot the break Jack had given him. He baby-sat Jack, and he would nurse him until Jack finally ran out of gas. Then they'd call the doctor, who'd knock him out with a shot, and he'd be carted off to a hospital to dry out. When I entered the group, that only happened about twice a year. Uncle Jack could easily have afforded a male nurse, but I think he liked to have Duke around him as much as possible.

There was another Duke there on Honolulu—Duke Kahanamoku, who had once been the world's fastest swimmer. He was a longtime friend of Uncle Jack's. It was his brother Sam, however, who did the dirty work when they were there on the island. Thank God for Sam—he knew the routine inside out. He took some of the weight off Bill Ramsey's shoulders.

In a few weeks, we were back at Warner Bros. in Burbank. That first day of shooting was very un-Fordian, because no shooting went on at all. No film was exposed that day. It was a day beset with problems. I can't remember why I arrived on the set late. It still confuses me, because when that old bird had his first look at the day's work ahead, I wanted to be damned sure I was one of the first of the troops he saw. It was better that way, otherwise, your ass would be in a sling all day. That had been my experience. I remember, later on, Dick Widmark and Lee Marvin referring to me, enviously, as an "old-timer."

The moment I stepped through the door of the soundstage, I felt an air of uneasiness. My first thought was, "Well, I guess it finally happened. They have started punching each other." Thank God, that wasn't it. I immediately headed for the director's chair. Uncle Jack was sitting there with his feet resting on another chair in front of him. He looked pretty much the same—bleached-out complexion, battered hat, dark glasses, cigar. He looked up at me with a look of amusement on his Irish kisser.

He pointed to his stomach and said, "Will you look at this! I can't even button my goddamned pants for Christsakes!" It was then that I saw the problem. His lower abdomen was swollen to more than twice its normal size. Naturally, his fly was unzipped—not that he gave a damn. The shirttail of his dark blue shirt covering most of that part of his anatomy—I'd never seen anything like it. "I guess they're going to haul my ass off to the hospital and take my gall bladder out," he told me. "Somebody called Maynard" (Dr. Maynard Brandsma, his physician). "Anyway, boys," he looked around him, "carry on. Good luck."

Then there was much fluster and the yelling of confusing orders because our commander-in-chief was ill, and then he was gone. Goddammit, I felt alone. I felt like I was in a room full of strangers. Who was going to direct the picture from here on into port? I knew one thing—it wouldn't be the same port Ford was headed for.

Mervyn LeRoy—and I use this term advisedly—took the helm. He had never seen or read the play. I don't think he had an inkling of who or what *Mister Roberts* was, but he took over. In fact, he shares directorial credit with Ford. For the life of me, I can't remember what Mr. LeRoy directed. He had a lot of little lenses (usually a bad sign) hanging around his neck, and he would peer through them, this-way-and-that, with Fonda at his shoulder, probably giving advice.

Anyway, some scenes were shot, and after a short period of time, all of the Ford gang was canned. Josh Logan, the original director of the stageplay and the man who should have been there from the start, came out. He patched up, or filmed—I don't know the correct term here—some more of the movie. As I said at the start of this South Pacific melodrama, it should have been Logan and Fonda and the New York cast right from the beginning. It would have been the *Mister Roberts* that Marilyn and I and Ward Bond saw on Broadway in 1949. That is the *Mister Roberts* America should have seen. Even Uncle Jack couldn't have done it better. Anyway, *Mister Roberts,* the movie, was a smashing box office success, and as a bonus, America got Jack Lemmon!

The Searchers

It was late spring 1955, and I was alone with John Ford in his office. He now had a big suite at Warner Bros. This was the same routine that I always went through prior to working on one of his films: I'd hear he was going to make a western, and I'd go out and visit him. Nine times out of ten, he'd tell me there was a part for me. I'd go home and tell Marilyn, and we'd leap all around from happiness. This time I got off to a very shaky start. I pulled one of those faux pas which nearly every member of the stock company had pulled at one time or another.

Everything was going along fine—a relaxed little chit-chat. He leaned back in his chair, cigar clenched between his brown teeth, feet on the desk, and told me about my forthcoming role in *The Searchers*. This made me extremely happy, because I had read Alan Le May's great novel a couple of years before and thought it was, perhaps, the best western I had read since *The Ox-Bow Incident*. I pulled out all the stops when expressing my gratitude and thanked him from the bottom of my heart. He nodded with a smile, recrossed his feet, took his chewed-up cigar out of his mouth, looked at it, decided it was good for another half-hour, jammed it back between his teeth, and then just sat there staring at me. It was one of those awful silences that used to happen in the inner sanctum. It was probably no longer than 60 seconds, but it seemed like hours to me.

Whatever the length of time, I could stand the pressure no longer and blurted out, "It's sure going to be good to see old Monument Valley again!"

His face took on a pained expression. Glaring at me, he said, "What?"

Of course there was nothing I could do but repeat that idiotic statement, so I said, "Ahem—ah—It's sure—ah—going to be—ah—good to see old Monument Valley again."

His reply was a terse, "Oh, for Christ's sake!"

I left there feeling like a horse's ass, but with a job.

My very good friend, British director and writer Lindsay Anderson and I argue endlessly when he is here in the States about where *The Searchers* should be placed on Uncle Jack's long list of credits. Lindsay, who wrote an excellent book entitled *About John Ford*, has it way toward the bottom. I have it right at the top. In fact, I have it not just at the top, but separated from the rest in a special place with gold letters. I believe it's the finest film John Ford ever directed. The fact I am most proud of in my professional life is that I had the good fortune to be in it—if only for a short period. I worked only three weeks in *The Searchers*, and because of that, I have fewer stories to tell about the filming of it than I do about the other eight I worked on.

So I am going to seize this opportunity to shift into reverse for a bit. I wish right here to take the year 1955, the year *The Searchers* was made, and resurrect, if you will, that period in the entertainment industry when the western ruled television.

These days the United States is absolutely overrun with vans. Vans, vans, vans, all the hell over the place, and Japanese pickup trucks that don't ever "pick up" anything because that will scratch the paint. In the movies nowadays (unless you are the star), if you are transported anywhere by car, that car is a van! They have a door on the side that you have to be Arnold Schwarzenegger to open, and they are bloody uncomfortable. They used to use station wagons. Ford and Chrysler made the best ones. They had real wood on the sides, and were very comfortable, very classy, and did a monumental job in Monument Valley.

Getting to location was a lot different in the 50s and 60s, whether it was a location around the L.A. area or out of town. Everyone had to leave for location from the studio and be driven there, no matter how close it was. The Teamsters union controlled how it was to be done, and the studios had to abide by those rules. Now, it's all changed around. Everyone must drive their own car to the location, if it's in the L.A. area, and then the studio pays you in cash according to the miles driven from the studio. It's very confusing.

A great number of westerns were being made then, both feature and television, and most of the location sites were way out in the San Fernando Valley. We certainly don't think of any of these spots as way out now, but they were then, before the Ventura Freeway and others. Sometimes we had to get to the studio by 5:00 A.M. so there would be time to get out to the desert or the Red Rock area. Lots of overtime that way—and also lots of fatigue. God only knows when the wranglers and the horse trucks had to start out, because the horses were always saddled and ready by the time we got there. But God, it was fun. I just loved it. I loved it because I knew all the wranglers, some even from my dad's time, and wranglers are great story tellers. They would tell some really "out West" tales about the old days, and all the "wrecks" they had. An accident was called a "wreck," and a "jam." Getting into some trouble was called a "tight." "I goddamn sure got myself into a real tight," they would recall. Of course, they had polished and embellished these stories over the years, so that by the time they were telling them to me, I wondered how they were still alive and kicking. Well, they were a rough bunch of guys. They had bodies like iron. Their wrists and hands and forearms were like few other men. When you shook hands with them, all you could feel was callous. I often wondered what women thought of those hands. All those young guys are old guys now, like me. Boy, those stories must be something by this time.

There is an intersection in the San Fernando Valley where Ventura Boulevard and Sepulveda Boulevard cross. There is a huge shopping Galleria there now on the northwest corner. That's where the studio vehicles stopped to pick up the actors and stuntmen. The most common transportation car was either a Cadillac or a Lincoln "stretch-out." I mean to tell you, those "stretch-outs" were really long—God knows how many doors on each side. Every studio had a fleet of them. One "stretch-out" could carry 14 to 16 people.

So, with eyes half-open, you'd park your old hack second car in an adjacent empty lot next to the Standard Station on the corner and wander over to where a group of guys were quietly standing, talking, and smoking. Yes, they all smoked. You'd join the group. "Hi, Al, whatcha' workin' on? Still doublin' Randy? I'll be damned!" That's the way it went—great camaraderie and mutual respect. Not too much laughter at that time in the morning—the laughter was during the ride back at night, when the prop man would have thoughtfully handed you a cold one prior to leaving the location, so you could wash the dust out of your throat. The young actors would only have a pack of cigarettes in their breast pocket and a comb on their hip, but the character men always had a small satchel or briefcase with them. I always wondered why. Now I know. You need a lot of stuff when you get old. Of course, the stuntmen always had their bulky stuntbags with the pads and other equipment to help them survive the falls and fights.

There were so many westerns shooting in those days that the "stretch-outs" would start arriving at the Standard Station by 6:00 in the morning. In the righthand corner of the windshield would be a sign—"Wells Fargo," "Wagontrain," "Gunsmoke," and so on. You'd look at the name of the show and hop in. One morning a cowboy named Chick Hannen hopped into the wrong car and rode in two chases before he found out he was in the wrong show. It was a great time for us cowboys.

"Boots and Stetsons and sixguns and the lilies grow high. They grow for a man with a gun-slingin' hand who before his time must die. . . . "

Those words are from a song called "The Lilies Grow High," written by my friend Stan Jones. I think those poetic words exemplify "prime time" of the 50s and early 60s. Stan was a dear friend and one of the many talented buddies I hung out with in those glory days. They were carefree, free-wheeling days, and thinking back, selfish days on the part of us married guys with little kids. Maybe we were the cause and inspiration for women's lib. We picked at our guitars and sang and drank with complete abandon. Our wives were present at a lot of those hoedowns, but they never had the freedom we did. They were worried about the baby-sitter and the 50 cents an hour.

When I was in my 30s, I had a good many buddies, all very talented. Stan wrote beautiful songs, and Ken Curtis and the Sons of the Pioneers sang them. I loved a guitar-playing composer-arranger named Jack Marshall; and Frank Miller, who cowrote "Memories Are Made Of This," the song Dean Martin made into such a big hit. Basically, I'm talking about the greatest western folk singers around at that time. I also had a really good buddy named Wendell Corey. I had to see Wendell separately, though. Occasionally, all of these crazies would be together at the same party. When all of the other guests would be screaming, "more, more, more," Wendell would yell out, about every ten minutes, "All you guys do is tune your fuckin' guitars!" He was using the "f" word long before it became the number-one word in the movies. He was my "spiritual advisor." He made screwing-up perfectly all right and normal. Drinking, to him, was a necessary part of life, on a par with eating, sleeping, and sex. Wendell had the power to give you a totally clear conscience. To him, no matter what you did, God forgave you. You were in the clear. But no *singing!* Wendell hated all that singing.

Then there was another group headed by Richard Boone, the star of "Have Gun Will Travel." Dick was one of the great all-time leaders. He and Wendell were cut from the same cloth. It's called volatile. I seemed to gravitate to those kinds of guys. "Have Gun" lasted many years, and I did well over a dozen of them. Andrew V. McLaglen was the principal director. He did well over a hundred of those shows, and sandwiched in between, the same number of "Gunsmoke." Both of these series began in 1955. Andy stands on your feet and gets you bruised up some, all that good stuff, but I love him—all six-foot-seven, 230 pounds of him. He's the best-natured man I know. He put a lot of bread on the Carey table. He is the son of the old-time Ford favorite Victor McLaglen and has had a first-rate career as a major motion picture director.

In the 50s and 60s, America was western crazy. Almost all of the shows on TV were westerns. Of course, the best and the granddaddy of them all was "Gunsmoke." Then, along with "Have Gun," there were "Bonanza," "Wyatt Earp," "The Virginian," "Laramie," "Wagontrain," "Wells Fargo," "Rawhide," and "Rifleman," just to mention a few. Marilyn's father, Paul Fix, was Sheriff Micah Torrance in "Rifleman." Warner Bros. had a bunch, too—"Maverick," "Cheyenne," and "Lawman." I worked in most of these shows over the years. We supporting actors didn't see much of the stars in the series socially, but it was like old home week when you were cast in one and arrived on the set. The going wage was always pretty much the same—$750 for six days. They were usually shot within 30 or 40 miles of Los Angeles, if not right on the studio lot.

The majority of those westerns were made at Universal, and I worked there a lot. The usual call was to be in make-up at 6:30 in the morning. The make-up department was on a rise in the middle of the huge lot. We'd park our cars down below, and as other actors arrived, you'd hear, "Jesus Christ, they're really scraping the bottom of the barrel these days! Look who's coming. How many lines do you have? I've got eight!" It would be the voice of an actor-friend who I grew up with in the business, someone I had competed against in a screen test or had had some screwy adventure with on location. All the guys you knew and liked, who you were always going to "get together" with so our wives could meet, but never did.

Then, of course, there were the stunt guys standing around. I knew them all because I rode a horse better than most actors, and we had been over some rough country together. And we'd been drunk together. The ride in the "stretch-out" to location in the hills of that big San Fernando Valley was full of talk of "broads," and sports, and "fuck-ups." "How's so-and-so? Is he still a fuck-up?" Sometimes the lead in the show was a real pain in the ass. It's amazing how those guys' heads blew up so big after a couple of years of big money. I always wanted to say, "Cary Grant stood off-camera and said his lines for my close-up." With these guys, you stood for their close-up, but they wouldn't stand there for yours. The script girl was there for you. Money was in short supply in those days, but we sure had fun.

There are acres and acres of houses now where we shot all those westerns. One beautiful area is called Thousand Oaks, and there were thousands of them before developers got to them. Out in the "West Valley," where we did all the chases and gunfights, there are golf courses, and malls, and condos. Smog lays out there like a dirty brown blanket. We drive by there often on our way to Santa Barbara to see our daughters and grandchildren, and I hate to see what has happened to the "Gunsmoke" country I loved. Farther north, near a town called Canoga Park, are huge elephant-sized outcroppings of rock. This was called Iverson's Ranch. Many people tried hard to save it, but it's just a memory now, too. All the low-budget westerns were made at Iverson's. Even my dad worked there. If you rent an old John Wayne tape, you'll see Iverson's for sure. Many times, you'd be in the middle of a dialogue scene and gunshots would ruin the take. They'd be coming from another company just over the hill. Sometimes there would be three shows shooting there on the same day.

The western series that was the most fun to work on was "Have Gun Will Travel." Dick Boone was a powerhouse physically, and he had extraordinary authority as to the casting and the scripts. It was a highly successful show. He even directed some of the episodes. I worked for him, and it was very easy. He probably had the best sense of humor of any star. He wanted the people he worked with to be happy, and after long, madhouse evenings with him, he made sure that there were pharmaceuticals available to get you through the day.

His favorite location away from Los Angeles was Lone Pine, California. It's a small town at the foot of Mount Whitney. Lone Pine has a long history where films are concerned. Many famous stars have made films in those Sierra Nevada Mountains. In those days, there was only one place to stay in Lone Pine, and that was the Dow Hotel. By the time the "Have Gun" company started going up there, the old Dow had expanded and added a motel and a pool. Lone Pine had two saloons; Boone's room made three. It was also headquarters. All the directives came from there. If he wanted your company, he rang your room and said, "Get your skinny ass down here!" He loved to take his followers out to a sort of ranch. They served terrific food and drink. He would take the whole place over for the night. He sat at the head of an enormously long table. If there was a guitar-picker in the cast, he was surely invited, and sometimes there were real professional actor-singers playing a role. There was always music at this restaurant in the sagebrush.

One night at dinner out there, I was sitting next to costumer Joe Dimmitt who, like all of us, was well smashed. I noticed he was looking far off with a reverent expression. He turned to me and said, "No wonder they come up here to make movies. Look at that beautiful goddamn view." I followed his gaze and saw he was staring at the Hamm's Beer poster with the waterfall. When Dick heard this, he was finished for the night. He laughed so hard I thought he would rupture himself.

My first "Have Gun" was with Charlie Bronson. He and I had the leading roles, and Andy McLaglen was directing. Boone always dragged Andy on those merry chases. Andy had it whipped, though. He didn't pass out from drink—he'd just go to sleep. The next day he would run our cowboy asses off. Every chase was an "over and under," meaning as fast as you can ride.

I was in Milburn Stone's living room when he closed the deal to appear as Doc on "Gunsmoke." He didn't seem too crazy about doing it. He had a short fuse, and I remember him wrangling over the phone about small details with Meyer Mishkin, his agent. He was simply taking it on as another western series, which he felt would be rather temporary. It was temporary, all right—it ran from 1955 to 1975 and became the longest-running show in TV history. Milburn was a marvelous character actor who was never out of work for long, which was why he didn't get too excited about this new show. I also heard that day that they had hired a great big guy named Jim Arness to play Matt Dillon. Jim and I had worked together six years before on *Wagonmaster,* where he played one of the bad Cleggs. Well, Milburn and Jim both became millionaires, but neither thought that would happen, at that time.

Jim Arness never changed. He was a really good guy and never got a big head. He was a very private person, though, and didn't hang around the set much. He was also war hero, but you'd never find that out from him. His favorite gag during a scene was to let loose with an enormous fart. He loved that, and you sort of waited for it. Jim's brother is Peter Graves, and we had many adventures together on location.

Matt Dillon's sidekick when "Gunsmoke" first started was Chester, played by Dennis Weaver. When Dennis left the show, my good friend, Ken Curtis was hired to play a character he created called Festus.

I'm not going to delve into all the TV shows running at that time, but "Rawhide" was an important one that had a lanky kid in it named Clint Eastwood. Clint was the sidekick to head man Eric Fleming. Eric was a classmate of Marilyn's at Hollywood High School. She dated him when his name was Edmont Heddy. Fate is strange, however. All TV series have a rest period called hiatus. It's a break in the shooting when the stars are free to do other projects. Most would love to do a feature picture, but it usually works out that the public won't pay to see someone they can see every week for free on their TV screen.

In Eric's case, he had no such delusions. He was a very private guy who liked to walk down Hollywood Boulevard barefoot. Eric and I had the same agent, Lew Sherrell. A producer in Rome called Lew, said his name was Sergio Leone, and that he was going to make an Italian western. He wanted Eric to star in it, and offered a goodly sum of money. Eric turned it down, so Leone asked about the other guy, that younger kid, "What's-his-name?" Lew answered that his name was Clint Eastwood, but that he didn't handle him. The rest is history. For some reason, Eric accepted a role in a film that took him to South America, and he was drowned while filming on the Amazon River. I didn't get to know either of them when I worked on "Rawhide." Today, of course, Clint has a wonderful reputation as a director. He knows what he is doing and doesn't waste money. However, if I ever get to work with him, I'm going to find out why he always wore his western hat tipped up in the back. He started that with "Rawhide" and continued it with Leone. It always drove me nuts. Clint's hat did.

The Walt Disney Studio was going great guns in 1955. It was also the year that Disneyland opened. One day, I got a phone call from my pal Freddie Hartsook. He had a very soft voice and was a great put-on artist, so I wasn't sure that he was serious when he said, "Listen, I'm in Pete Lyon's office (director Francis Lyon), and he's going to be doing a series here at Disney's called 'Spin and Marty' for the 'Mickey Mouse Club.' They're looking for a cowboy type to play the horse wrangler for the boys' camp. I told them you were good with horses but a lousy actor, but he wants to see you, anyway. Come over this afternoon about two."

I made a test and played the part of the counselor instead of the wrangler, with Tim Considine, who was to play Spin. That night Freddie called to tell me I got the part. We would start shooting on July 12. It is a date that was to be chiseled into my brain, a date I was to recite many times, and one of the things that kept me from working for Uncle Jack for five long years after *The Searchers*.

I asked Freddie how he knew I had the part, since they hadn't had time to develop the film, and he replied, "Don't worry about that. Disney himself was on the set." Walt (everyone called him Walt) had sneaked onto the set and stayed out of sight so I wouldn't be nervous. We shot it every summer for three years on the Disney Ranch in Placerita Canyon in Newhall, about seven miles from where I was born on the Carey Ranch. It was one of the biggest hits on the "Mickey Mouse Club." Kids everywhere wanted to go to the Triple R Ranch for the summer.

Back to the end of May 1955. Uncle Jack had just cast me in *The Searchers*. Memorial Day was coming up, and as always it was a big day at Ford's Field Photo Home. The services were heartwarming, reverent, and movingly patriotic. The glee club was there to sing, and there was a company of bagpipers. The names of the fallen from the war and others who had passed on were intoned to the beat of a snare drum played by my son, Steven. Then there was coffee and donuts and camaraderie.

I was assigned that year to one of the "grave details." Wreaths were placed on graves all over the city by different members of the Farm. I went out to Forest Lawn with three other comrades in arms, and then we found our way to the home of one of them, Al Lecknes. We had a few drinks and listened to the last of the Indianapolis 500, run on the *real* Memorial Day, and on radio only. After it was over, I said good-bye and headed home, except I felt so good and the afternoon was so young that I didn't want to go home. I thought, "Screw it!" and before you could say, "God Bless John Wayne!" I was at the gate of his home on Louise Avenue, Encino. I pushed the button, and from the speaker came a very familiar voice, "Yeah!"

I said, "It's Dobe," and the voice said, "Get your ass up here!"

B-zzz went the gate, and in I went.

Duke was half in the bag, as was his pal, writer Jimmy Hennigen. The afternoon wore into the evening, and to give you some idea how drunk we got, Duke asked me to read Lincoln's Gettysburg Address. When I finished it, Duke announced with great sincerity that he was going to make a movie about Lincoln, and I was to play him.

"I'll dye his hair or something," he shouted with glee, "But this asshole (a very big word in the Wayne vocabulary) is going to play Lincoln!"

At about 3:00 in the morning, Pilar and Duke began fighting over the intercom between the kitchen and the bedroom. I wisely decided it was time to get out of there, but when I got to the gate, I couldn't get it open, so I went to sleep in my station wagon and, at dawn, found the magic button and drove home. It probably saved my life, that gate.

I started *The Searchers* with a brand new ulcer. That night at Duke's must have blown a hole in my gut, because within a few days, the doctor informed me that I had a duodenal ulcer and should spend a few days in the hospital. He also told me that I should have been a milkman—have a full-time job, and that I was not cut out, emotionally, to be an actor. Well, I told him a trip to the hospital was totally impossible; that I had not one, but two jobs coming up, and that if my ulcer was to be cured, it would have to be in Monument Valley. I had a family to feed.

C. V. Whitney was the "money man" and producer of *The Searchers*. One evening we were sitting on the porch at Gouldings, looking out over Monument Valley. I mentioned my ulcer in the course of the conversation. He asked, "How old are you, Dobe?"

I said, "Thirty-four, Mr. Whitney."

He said, "Well Dobe, I'll tell you a story. One time when I was younger than even you are, I had one of those damned things. I was on vacation at a resort in upstate New York and was getting a massage from this big Swedish masseur. I told him I was on this very strict diet—you know, cottage cheese, milk, boiled eggs with dry toast—that sort of thing. He said, 'You want to get rid of your ulcer, Mr. Whitney?' and I said, 'God, yes!' Then he taught me a lesson I've never forgotten." I asked what that was, and with a slap on my butt, he said, "Forget it!"

With that, he got up and went to bed. I thought back to about a week before, when we were all in the club car on the train to Flagstaff. Uncle Jack had smiled benignly at me when I told him about the ulcer and promptly ordered me a Miller High Life beer. I hated Miller High Life (how did he know that), but I drank it anyway, risking what I thought at the time was certain internal hemorrhage. Nothing happened. So I decided there on the porch that Sonny Whitney's masseur knew what he was talking about, and my ulcer went away.

Then there was the hairpiece. I wasn't bald yet on the crown of my head, but the front was receding rapidly. I wanted more hair on my forehead to make me look younger, so I had Charlie Wright make me a beautiful "frontpiece." I was afraid to take it with me to show to Uncle Jack. That was dumb. I was thirty-four, and still playing a kid of 19. I was always a kid in Uncle Jack's eyes.

After the first shot, he sidled up to me and asked, "Don't you own a hairpiece?" How the hell did he know that?

"Yes, sir, I do."

"Well, go get it and put it on. It'll make you look younger."

"Well, Uncle Jack," I said, "it's in California."

"Christ! What good is it in California? Why didn't you bring it with you?"

I told him the truth. "I was afraid to tell you about it. I thought you'd be annoyed if I did."

He smiled mischievously and said, "Now Ol' Dobe, Have I ever been annoyed with you?"

He walked away very amused with himself and yelled back over his shoulder, "Send for it!"

When Duke saw me having it put on a few days later, he said, "Welcome to the club. I knew you were getting there, and now the day has arrived!"

Everything really eventful seemed to happen on the porch at Gouldings' Lodge. It's where Uncle Jack decided Ken Curtis should play the role of Charlie McCorry with a Colorado dryland accent. Jeff Hunter and Ken and I were sitting out there on the porch. The three of us hung out a lot together. Jeff and I both loved Kenny's singing, and he had taught us the harmony to "Tumblin' Tumbleweeds." We were doing a pretty good imitation of the Sons of the Pioneers, and Ford came out to listen. After he went back inside, Kenny started telling a hilarious story, using this "dryland" accent. Then Jeff told one with a "country hillbilly" accent, and back-and-forth it went.

All of a sudden, the Old Man emerged. "Do that again," he said to Kenny.

"What's that, Pop?" (Kenny, being his son-in-law, always called him Pop.)

"That routine you and Jeff were just doing. Do it again."

Kenny tried to explain, to no avail, that the accent only worked with certain words, etc. . . . etc., but Jack wouldn't take no for an answer. So Kenny told the story about a young hayseed explaining how he raised this gigantic squash from the "Eye-tal-yan squarsh side" (Italian squash seed) he'd ordered from a seed catalogue. Uncle Jack loved it. He had a way of showing great amusement without really laughing.

Kenny was embarrassed. Ford nodded his head and said, "Good. Good. I want you to use that accent in this picture. I want you to play Charlie McCorry that way."

And back he went inside to play cards.

Kenny was upset. He muttered in low tones, "I don't want to do that in the picture. I'll make an ass of myself!"

Jeff and I had no answer for him. We knew he was stuck with it.

The following day we worked over at Mexican Hat, shooting at the Indians who were charging across the San Juan River. Neither of us had any lines, but he brought up the subject of the damned accent. He said he'd already worked in a couple of shots without it and was trying to think of a way to talk the Old Man out of it.

Barbara Curtis and Pilar Wayne arrived during the day from Hollywood, and that night Duke broke the rules and got plastered. I was rooming with Ward Bond, and Ken was there, shooting the breeze with us.

Suddenly, Duke burst in. His first words were addressed to Ken.

"What in the hell is this crap I hear about you not wanting to do the accent that Pappy asked you to do!"

Kenny went through his routine about it only working with certain words. Duke, subtle as always, said, "Bullshit! Listen, you're a nice looking fella', but ya' ain't as good lookin' as this Jeff kid, an' on toppa' that, yer playing the second lead and there's nothin' more thankless than a second fuckin' lead! Dobe here can attest to that! Play it like the Old Man says, fer Christ's sake, an' you'll be noticed in the goddamned picture!"

So that was the end of that and Duke was certainly right. The part was a standout, and it led to a tremendous future for Ken. It was because of the accent that he wound up getting the part of Festus.

My mom was to play my screen mom, Mrs. Jorgensen. Ollie Carey and Uncle Jack had known each other since she was 18 and he was 19, and they argued like hell when they were not on the set. Not mean arguing—funny. I think they were always sort of in love. Mom certainly was not in awe of Jack, and she was very respectful on the set. But off! She'd give him hell. He'd be expounding about some daring feat he had done some years before, and Mom would listen for a bit and say, "That's a lot of bullshit, Jack. Why do you have to lie like that?"

And Jack would yell back to Mom, who liked to have a few drinks before dinner, "Goldie, you're drunk. Shut up, for Christ's sake!" Only my father and Jack called my mother Goldie. The rest of the cast would look on in shock when they heard her talk to him like that.

My relationship with Mom was different than at home. I was an actor and she was an actress, and we treated each other accordingly. Mom roomed with the beautiful Vera Miles, right next door to Ward and me. Ward was insane to molest Vera, and he'd parade around naked in front of the big picture window in the hope that Vera would look in and see him. Vera never looked in that window, so Ward, having failed at exposing himself, would try to catch Vera without her clothes on by rushing into her and Mom's room without knocking. He struck out there, too. He reminded me of that silly coyote in the roadrunner cartoons.

My mom was dearly loved by so many people. She was absolutely honest and said exactly what she thought. Usually she tempered it with her great sense of humor. John Wayne adored her, as did Barry Goldwater—and she was a lifelong Democrat! Before the 1964 elections, Barry asked her if she was going to vote for him. "Hell, no. We need you in the Senate more than we do in the White House!" Mom died in her little pink house in the hills above Carpinteria, California, at the age of 92.

On the Fourth of July, there was a big celebration down below Gouldings' Lodge on the little red-dirt airstrip. Once a day, a Cessna took off to fly the film to Flagstaff, Arizona, from where it was sent on to the lab in Hollywood. Also, the little plane always was in readiness to fly out anyone who was sick or injured. The film crew put on a huge barbecue for the cast, crew, and all the Navajos. The special effects men put on a spectacular show of fireworks, but one of the "powder men," nicknamed "Punky," set off a skyrocket and a piece of the wooden stick came loose from its mooring and lodged in his neck. The doc assigned to the company was actually a psychiatrist. I don't think he'd done any first aid work in 20 years, but he knew enough to leave the piece of wood alone. He gave Punky a shot for pain and shock and sent him off in the plane. He recovered, but not in time to come back to *The Searchers*.

The Navajos organized the races. There was the regular horse race which Chuck Roberson won, and then there was the Old Man's Horse Race—all Navajos. Then came the Old Man's Foot Race. That's the race Uncle Jack entered. He won easily, but he cheated. He won by such a great distance that he would not have had to cheat, but he wanted to make sure.

"On your mark! Get Set!" Uncle Jack took off. "Go!" The other racers took off. By that time, Uncle Jack was halfway to the finish line. He always reminded me of the football coach, Vince Lombardi, who said, "Winning isn't everything—it's the *only* thing."

That afternoon the Navajos made John Ford a member of the Navajo tribe and presented him with a sacred deerskin. They gave him the name Natani Nez, which means Tall Soldier, and on the deerskin was this message of goodwill:

In your travels may there be
Beauty behind you
Beauty on both sides of you
And beauty ahead of you.

In the years since Uncle Jack's death, I have been asked countless times, by students and writers, what John Ford's message was in the way he portrayed the Indians in his films. Did he really think Indians were evil? Did he think them inferior to the white man? Was *Cheyenne Autumn* his apology to them? They are never happy with my somewhat vague and indecisive answers. The truth is, I don't know! All I can remember him saying are these words: "It's a hell of a good story." He loved to make good stories into films, like those of James Warner Bellah. He loved to assign the original writer of the story, along with a screen writer like Dudley Nichols or Frank Nugent, to go to work on the screenplay. During the writing, Ford would hold story conferences. All of his writers accepted the fact that he took liberties with their work. It did not bother them. The stronger the screenplay, the fewer liberties he took: *The Grapes of Wrath*, for example. He did not make "message" movies, per se. He did not give any thought as to whether the Indians were "bad" or whether a black person was "smart" or "dumb." He portrayed them as they were in the story, in that particular period of history. He loved history, and he loved making movies about America's history. He loved to gather the people he enjoyed being with around him. Most of all, he loved going on location with them and making a picture he thought the American people would enjoy. He wanted them to feel better when they left the theater. The real world was overrun with greed, lust, and bloodshed, so why make movies about it?

Of all the John Ford pictures I worked on, the set of *The Searchers* was unlike any other. Uncle Jack was much more serious, and that was the tone, that pervaded the cast and crew. The first scene I was in with Duke was the one where I discover that my family's prize bull has been slaughtered. When I looked up at him in rehearsal, it was into the meanest, coldest eyes I had ever seen. I don't know how he molded that character. Perhaps he'd known someone like Ethan Edwards as a kid. Now I wish I'd asked him. He was even Ethan at dinner time. He didn't kid around on *The Searchers* like he had done on other shows. Ethan was always in his eyes.

Hank Worden had the greatest role of his life, playing Old Mose Harper to the hilt. I had known Hank since *Red River*. He had been riding broncs at Madison Square Garden in the 30s and somehow he snagged a role in Lynn Riggs' *Green Grow the Lilacs* on Broadway. And thus, began his acting career. That play later became the great musical hit, *Oklahoma*. Like Ethan says of *Old Mose*, Hank was "born old."

Every single day, he'd ask me the same question, "When do you have to be at Disney's?"

I always answered, "July twelfth, Uncle Jack." Technically, it was the right answer, but as far as my future with him was concerned, it was the wrong answer. Duke must have heard me. Why didn't he tip me off? The right answer was, "Whenever you're through with me, Uncle Jack."

One day we were shooting a scene in which Duke and a few of us were to come galloping over a sort of "sway-back" in a ridge, which ran down from one of the monuments. The wind was howling. We were over 400 yards away and unable to see Jack or any of the camera equipment. We waited and waited, and waited some more—very un-Fordian.

Finally Duke exclaimed, "Jesus! When's the old bastard goin' to call 'Action' ?"

He may as well have been talking into a high-tech loudspeaker, because the wind carried his every word clearly down to Uncle Jack. Soon the word "Action" drifted up to us, but the wind was blowing in the wrong direction and we barely heard it.

We did the run in one take, but when we arrived back, Ford looked at him a long time and then said, "You didn't have to call me 'an old bastard,' you know. You should have had the courtesy to say 'old gentleman.'"

Duke put his hands to his head. "Oh, Christ—the wind—that damned wind."

One of the best scenes I ever did for Uncle Jack was in this movie. Ford had motioned for Duke, Jeff, and me to sit on a mound of red sandstone. Then he said to me, "Kid, go back there about forty yards. When I yell, come running in here like hell, and sit down on Duke's left, and pull your boots on. You'll be pulling them on during the dialogue. You've taken them off so you could sneak up on the Indian camp and not be heard. Do you know your dialogue?"

I said, "Yessir."

He was starting to get a wee bit cranky, "Well, then, get your ass back up there and come running in. Let's hear the scene."

I thought to myself, "Oh, God, I have to cry in this scene and he's going to get all over me." This was a rehearsal, I thought, but one was never sure. "Dobe!"

Here I came, running like hell. I saw Duke looking at me—those eyes like an angry snake! I leaped into the sandy loam beside Duke and played the hell out of the scene. No chewing out from Uncle Jack.

"Good! Do it like that. That's the idea!" he clapped his hands together with satisfaction. Then he looked at me sternly and said, "Take your neckerchief off and wrap it around your right hand." Pause. "There's a reason for that." Period. Nothing for a minute. I looked at Duke. He just glared at me. Ford then said, "Yeah, just like that. Dobe!"

I jerked, "Yessir."

"Dobe, please don't leap into the shot. Just run in and sit down."

"Yessir."

We shot the scene, and Uncle Jack said those magic words, "Right! Print it!"

There was silence. Duke put his hand on my shoulder but didn't say a word. He didn't have to. Those are the great moments for an actor.

But wait a minute! There were murmurings and mumblings going on behind the camera. Ford was sitting in his chair, very satisfied, lighting his cigar for the tenth time. He became aware that something was afoot. He asked the camera operator, "What the hell's all the mumbling about?"

"The camera stopped, Mister Ford," said the operator, clearly in misery.

"What? The what?"

The poor operator repeated the report. "I don't know sir. It just stopped running."

Ford—typical of him not to lose his temper when you expect it—said mildly, "Well, Christ, fix it, whatever it is. Sorry kids. That was fine, but we're going to have to do it again. When we're ready, do it just the same way."

Later on, I found out the reason the camera quit. Ward Bond had come onto the set with his electric razor. During the highest point of the scene, he unplugged the camera, plugged in the razor, and proceeded to shave. John Ford went to his grave never knowing that. He would have dug Ward up!

When Duke died, it was that scene the networks showed most often when they reviewed his career. It makes me very proud.

The last shot I worked in was of the posse rushing out of the Jorgenson house, mounting up, and riding off. Ford had the camera way up on the top of a hill. Anyone could have been in my clothes at that distance, but the fact that Uncle Jack had kept me on salary as long as he could never entered my mind. However, it was my last scene, and he had to give me a good send-off! Out we came, and just started to ride off, when I hear "Cut! Dobe, for Christ's sake, can't you even get on the damned horse right! Let's do it again. Dobe screwed it up."

I had gotten my right foot hung up in Ward's blanket roll behind the cantle of his saddle, but from that distance, no one but the Old Man would have spotted it. Take number two! We come out of the house, mount up, ride off for about 50 yards, then "Cut! Dobe, all you have to do is walk out and get on. Try not to get behind somebody. I can't see you. Let's do it again."

Take number three. I tried my best to stay in the clear, but it was nearly impossible with so many in the shot.

"Cut! Dobe screwed it up again, but I can't waste any more film so we'll have to use it. That's a wrap!" I have never been so mad in my whole life! I wanted to kill him! I was literally boiling inside.

On all the other films I had done for him, on the last day, I would knock on his door where he was staying and thank him, or I'd leave him a note or give him a big hug and a lot of "Thank yous and good lucks." But *this*! I guessed he was sore that I was going to work for someone else, so I didn't say thanks. I didn't say good-bye. I didn't even go up to my room at Gouldings'. I didn't take my wardrobe off or take a shower. I got into a car with the stunt men, Frankie McGrath and the two Chucks, and went with them to their tent. They had booze. The next morning at 6:00 A.M. I took that little plane to Flagstaff, and then the train home. It was 1960—five long years—before I worked for him again.

After Duke passed away in 1979, everyone who had worked with him or had been close to him was in the public's eye. On the day of his passing, ironically enough, I was over visiting my father-in-law, Paul Fix. When I returned home, I had to turn right around and go back, because NBC's Jim Brown was on his way over to Paul's with a camera crew to interview us. Hank Worden also joined us, and we reminisced about Duke. Many more interviews followed from many countries. Then there were the book writers. I told them all my stories and then decided it was time to write them down for myself.

At any rate, one of the questions they invariably asked was, "Did you feel, while you were working on *The Searchers* that something special was happening? That it was a special movie?" my answer to that has always been yes. From day one, Duke was Ethan Edwards. That character seemed to be built into him, and no other actor, no matter how great his talent, could have played that part as well. It was not Duke's favorite role, however; Nathan Brittles of *Yellow Ribbon* was. I think his Oscar for *True Grit* should have been his second, after *The Searchers,* and he should have had a third for *The Shootist.*

There are moments and a certain feeling somewhere between your heart and your throat, that you rarely get on a movie set. It might be a moment while shooting a TV episode of little consequence, except for that moment. This was a day possessed of one of those moments. It didn't take Uncle Jack long to shoot it. One take, and boom, it was done. Had it been take five or ten, it would never have happened. It would not have been— well, one of the greatest endings of any picture ever made.

I wasn't in the scene, but I was behind the camera, able to see all of it—able to feel all of it. Duke was the only actor in front of the camera now. He was standing alone in the doorway. He had a hangover from the night before (that same night he had burst into our room and blasted Kenny). He had never showed up for dinner that night, much to Ward's delight, because he loved to see Duke's ass in a sling instead of his. There should be a sign put on the room in Gouldings' Lodge, "In this room John Wayne got drunk before he shot one of the most famous scenes in motion picture history."

There he was! The big man standing alone in the doorway, the red desert stretching out behind him. The other players in the scene, which included my mother, had passed by the camera, a joyous moment. Debbie was home at last, brought there in the arms of the man in the doorway.

He was to look and then walk away, but just before he turned, he saw Ollie Carey, the widow of his all-time hero, standing behind the camera. It was as natural as taking a breath. Duke raised his left hand, reached across his chest and grabbed his right arm at the elbow. Harry Carey did that a lot in the movies when Duke was a kid in Glendale, California. He'd spent many a dime just to see that.

He stared at my mother for a couple of beats, then turned, walking away into loneliness across red sand. The cabin door slowly closed. "What makes a man to wander—what makes a man to roam—what makes a man leave bed and board and turn his back on home."

Two Rode Together

Opening Shot: Early morning, late September 1960. A balding redheaded man in his late 30s is standing on the sidewalk across the street from Columbia Studio. He is slightly over six feet tall, weighs around 170 pounds, and at the time we pick up the action, it is evident that he isn't feeling too well as the result of excessive drinking the night before—and the night before—and the night before that! He is not aware that his aftersundown behavior is not normal. His wife, the mother of his four children, has driven him to this appointed spot, and the fact that she has given him a rather tepid kiss doesn't seem out of the ordinary, even though he is going to be gone for a rather long time.

This is the shape I was in when I left for location to work on John Ford's production of *Two Rode Together,* starring James Stewart and Richard Widmark. There I stood, hands in pockets, staring at the sidewalk, with a gigantic hangover. I was very nervous. Not so much from the hangover, but I was going to work for Uncle Jack again after five years. It was the unknown that scared me. I didn't know how he was going to be. Was I going to be "initiated" all over again?

Ken and Barbara Curtis were there, too. Kenny felt just fine and was anxious to get back to Bracketville, Texas. He had been there the year before on *The Alamo,* as had our star, Richard Widmark. Dick and Duke had not had a good working relationship on *The Alamo.* I was to learn quite a lot about that ordeal during our off hours on this forthcoming picture. This was to be Dick's first film for Uncle Jack, and I was a little skeptical about the personality mix. I knew them both very well, and it looked like a time bomb to me if Uncle Jack threw Dick one of his "high hard ones."

So, there we were at the famous intersection of Gower and Sunset. Ken was upset with Barbara because she was completely sloshed. Even in my condition, I wondered how she was going to drive home. In fact, there was a hint of superiority in my manner. After all, I didn't drink in the morning!

All of my thinking and reasoning and general outlook on people, places, and things had taken a very radical, negative turn during the five-year interval. My actions during the few hours after our arrival in the tiny town of Bracketville are unfathomable. It was night when we got there. I took a look around at those old buildings in the semidarkness and decided I was slumming. This was not a very nice place to be staying for four or more weeks! Kenny, however, had a large room in another compound and was delirious with anticipation. He kept telling me about all the fun we were going to have.

The place was loaded with history and was called Fort Clark. What I wanted was a drink and something to eat, but that was not to happen. I had just put my bags in my room and had trooped over to see Kenny, when in burst Uncle Jack. He wanted us to serenade Jimmy Stewart with the Ford version of "Bringing in the Sheaves," which Kenny had written some months before. Ford loved it, and we had to sing it for him every morning when he arrived on the set.

Here are the words:

Sowing in the morning
Sowing seeds of kindness
Spreading rays of sunshine
Through the dusty day
Courteous and kindly
Friendly and paternal
He shall come rejoicing
Bringing in the sheaves
Bringing in the sheaves, bringing in the sheaves
He will come rejoicing bringing in the sheaves
Now our lines are mastered...here comes that old gentleman
He shall come rejoicing...bringing in the sheaves!

I had never met Jimmy Stewart. I was really in awe of him, and I didn't want to sing that damned song to him without even knowing him. I was hoping for a better introduction. I had really become a horse's ass. But there we went, trailing Uncle Jack to Jimmy's cabin. Jack banged on his door, and after a moment, Jim peeked his head out (as only Jimmy can peek out).

"Go!" said Ford. Kenny and I sang. Jimmy listened politely, exchanged a few words with Uncle Jack, and closed the door. That was that!

Now, I thought, I can get loose. But Uncle Jack and Kenny followed me to my tiny room, which was in a compound way across an empty space the size of a soccer field. I had not unpacked, but I had put a bottle of whiskey on the dresser. As soon as we entered, Ford spotted the whiskey. He picked it up and examine the label.

"Partner's Choice Whiskey."

He looked at me with no sign of anger or hostility and exclaimed, "Partner's Choice? Are you kidding me? Partner's Choice?"

The word *partner* had great significance for Jack over many years. He used it when he was kidding around in western parlance, and one of his favorite people was Ed "Partner" Jones, a real sharpshooter and also a dear friend of my Dad's from way back.

"Are you going to drink on this picture?" he asked very politely.

"Yessir, I thought I would. If it's okay with you."

He looked at me with a twinkle in his eye and replied, "Sure kid. If that's the way you want it." Kenny looked at me quizzically and smiled. I didn't get a drink then, however. Ford dragged me along to the mess hall.

When I returned, I took a good look at my room with its tiny windows and decided it was like a prison cell. I'd had rooms like this one many times in the past, but I wasn't going to put up with it this time. Not me! I called Wingate and told him I wanted a bigger and better room. I cannot believe I did that.

I'd have been much better off to have stayed there, as it turned out. The phone rang. It was Uncle Jack.

"I hear you don't like your room," he said.

I replied that I thought it was a little small and didn't have enough air.

"Not enough air, huh?" Then he threw his "change up." Instead of being sarcastic and letting me know that I was not the star of this picture, he said, calmly, "I told Wingate you deserve a better room with more air," (was he going to put me out in a tent?) "so pack up your stuff and come on over and bunk with Kenny. Ken's got a great big room with lots of air. He said he'd enjoy having you room with him. You can talk over old times."

As I was leaving this small, airless cubicle, Andy Devine came out of his room and asked, "Where are you going, kid? Don't you like your room?"

I was downright embarrassed and mumbled something inane.

Andy, in his famous high-pitched, scratchy voice, said, "Well kid, I got the same kinda' room as you, and it suits me fine. I don't hafta' be around all that noise and bullshit."

Today I, too, would love that room—very private, with grass all around to practice chip shots. I didn't even see the grass then, or the birds, or the trees.

I moved in with Kenny.

"Let's see if there's a beer joint around here," I immediately said. There was one, but Ken suggested we have a drink in our room, instead.

We were just getting into it when the door flew open and in came Uncle Jack.

"Oh! You boys having a little drink?" Then he said, "*A* drink? Can you boys have *A* drink?"

He was smiling, but I was thinking, "Jesus, the Old Man's right across the goddamned hall! He's going to be barging in here every ten minutes!"

Had I thought back 12 years, to *3 Godfathers* and how horrible he had been to me, how inferior and unqualified he had made me feel then (even though he had a purpose), had I remembered those days, the thought should have entered my dumb skull, "You jerk! What has this man done to you, so far, but have you sing for Jimmy because he was trying to please him? He's being pleasant and friendly and trying to make you feel at home, you asshole! He's telling you that you are a free man on this movie. You are grown-up now."

But I wasn't. He might not have been aware of the turmoil going on inside of me. Maybe he was only aware of it if he created it, but he was an incredible judge of people's weaknesses. He was really a very lonely man. He wanted very much to be "one of the boys," but to do that, he would have to give up that mystique and authority he possessed. John Ford, the great motivator, the film genius, the man who enabled you to do things you never thought yourself capable of doing, who never gave you a good scene to do and then cut it from the final print, was there in our room, trying his best to be a "regular guy."

He said, upon leaving after a short visit, "Sure, sure. If you boys want to have a couple of drinks before dinner that's fine. A couple of drinks a night. Hell, I don't mind that."

I could tell he couldn't wait to see how Jimmy and Dick would work out together; or more to the point, how he and Dick would work out together. He'd already worked with Jimmy and loved him.

That night, after Ken and I had said our "Good nights," I lay there on my back, staring up at the ceiling into the darkness. I wanted another drink, but dismissed that as hopeless, and I began to wonder what fate awaited me. I was as healthy as a young colt at age 39, but I didn't feel that way. The only time I felt good was after a few drinks, but I hadn't figured out yet that I had a disease that was progressive. I knew some other guys who were terrible drunks—alcoholics, even. They drank all day long. I could stop anytime I wanted to. I just didn't want to, right now.

The drinks were wearing off, and I was beginning to get apprehensive. I thought, "Why do we have such an early call, when we're shooting on the western street? Ken and I don't work there; we're at the camp!" Didn't I remember? On a Ford show, everyone had a call! Didn't I remember that after seven movies with him? I finally worried myself into sleep.

Ken and I were both sound asleep when the door burst open again. Uncle Jack was back! There he stood in his silk pongee nightshirt.

"Hi. Hi. Couldn't sleep. Oh, were you boys asleep? Christ, I can't sleep!"

Then he wandered around the room, talking and asking us questions about our lives in general. He'd known me all my life, and Kenny long enough, but he had a way of digging up your thoughts, feelings, and opinions about things. Like all brilliant men I have met, he asked a lot of questions. He was an avid listener. That's one of the qualities that made him a great filmmaker: he learned what made people tick. Time was ticking away for me.

The next day I was driven out to location at the "Alamo Village," the one Duke had built for his movie *The Alamo*. I saw a lot of activity going on over in front of the saloon.

Jimmy Stewart was sitting on the boardwalk with his chair tipped back, his feet pushed up against the post, smoking a big cigar, exactly like Fonda in *Clementine*. I thought to myself, *When Ford falls in love with an image, he never lets go of it.*

He always repeated things from previous movies in every picture he made, all the way back to the silent days. When I was 18, I dragged my father into a theater to see *Stagecoach*. He hadn't watched for more than five minutes before he leaned over and whispered to me, "Christ, Dobe, I did the same goddamned thing in *Hellbent!*" And he kept that up until the end of the movie. "We did that in *Straight Shooting;* we did that in *Cheyenne's Pal*."

I went to see that movie again in New York some months later, alone, so I could enjoy it without interruption. Now I say the same thing to Marilyn. "They stole that from Jack. He had me do that in *Rio Grande*."

Two Rode Together seems to me to be a hodgepodge of incidents and pieces of business from every western Jack ever made. It was good old Irish stew. He threw everything in. If ever Ford was on a vacation, doing exactly what he damned-well pleased, and having one hell of a good time doing it, it was on *Two Rode Together.*

Jimmy Stewart and Dick Widmark were terrific together and gave Ford much joy. As it turned out, Jack and Dick got on marvelously; it was a mutual admiration society. Dick kept telling me how amazed he was at Ford's genius at simplifying a sequence, at the way he could get across so much drama with a minimum of camera moves. It knocked Dick out. Dick is, without a doubt, one of the brightest and most well-informed men I have ever met. He knows everything that's going on and doesn't miss a trick. He absolutely loathes incompetence, and he's really tough on most directors: "Most of them are idiots!" He loved Uncle Jack. He realized Jack was past his prime, but he said, "Even a gone-screwy Ford is a hundred times better than all these other idiots," and then he'd laugh his *Kiss of Death* laugh. If one wanted to get really blown away, he'd walk up to Dick and mention Tommy Udo.

Ken and I played two idiot brothers named Greeley and Ortho Clegg. That was Ford resinging an old song again. The Cleggs were Charlie Kemper and his bad boys in *Wagonmaster.* Greeley was an idiot, but Ortho (me) was a superidiot. Both were sadistic morons who had it in for Widmark. I didn't have much dialogue; Kenny did all the talking. I wore a complete wig, with hair hanging down over my forehead and eyes, which was good for the character. In spite of the fact that Uncle Jack was pleasant toward me; in spite of the fact that I had no pressure from dialogue, no big scenes, and not even any horsemanship to prove—in spite of all that—I was dying inside. I was so scared I was shaking. I peeked around a corner of a building and saw Ford working with Stewart. There was laughter coming from the set. I watched for a second. I didn't want to be seen. I didn't want to hear, "Hey, Dobe, come on over here."

I was scared that I would hear that familiar voice shout the familiar question, "Where's Dobe?" There was a knot in my chest that felt like a hand squeezing my heart. I lay down on a sort of loading platform with my head on a sack of grain, away from everything.

My actions on this day were directly opposite to what they had been five years before. Then I would not have been more than ten feet away from that Old Man's chair, waiting to go to work, waiting to see if he needed me.

"You're my Uncle Jack, and I'm here to please you."

I wanted to be in the middle of everything then and was jealous of others he was paying attention to.

The best remedy for what I was suffering from was back in my room at Fort Clark. If Valium had been invented then, I didn't know it.

"I wish Wingate would come and tell me I'm not needed today."

But he didn't, not for five hours. I didn't work that day or the next day, either. The knot in my chest was getting bigger. I'd drunk a lot after the first day's waiting, so the second day of waiting was even worse. I was going nuts! Did Ford know he was doing this to me? I don't know. He probably wasn't thinking of me at all. I was really nothing more than a glorified extra.

Shirley Jones was the leading lady in the picture, and she, too, was waiting back in her room to go to work. Uncle Jack had a big crush on her, like he had had on Betsy Palmer back on *Mister Roberts*. I'm sure she knew that, but she had never worked for Jack before and was probably nervous, too. There is nothing worse in the movie business than waiting to go to work on your first day. An actor never gets over that. Every new venture is like your first, and the smaller the role, the harder it is.

I imagine Dick was glad to get his first scene out of the way, too. No strain, no pain with Dick and Jack. Dick always asked Kenny and me to ride back to Fort Clark with him, and it was during those drives home that Dick expounded on the directorial gifts of Uncle Jack. I got the feeling he always knew that Jack was good, but not that good. And he found him tremendously funny.

He said to me, "Jesus, Dobe, you never told me how funny the Old Man is! He's the funniest old bird I've ever met!"

It was then I realized that over the years I had dwelt too much on stories of Ford harassing me. I had regaled him with dark tales of Ford's sadism. I knew one thing: when Dick did see the sadism, it would not be aimed at him. He had found these stories very amusing, but I had not revealed what a great sense of humor Uncle Jack had.

We finally worked on the third day, but Ford pulled one of his tricks during rehearsal. He remembered a gag he had seen Kenny and me do at some party or other (we were always doing imitations of situations we thought funny). The one he remembered was one where Kenny, playing a drama coach, was giving this total idiot—me—an improvisational scene to do. I didn't have a beard then, and could pull my very long upper lip down over my lower lip. Then I lowered my eyelids to half-mast and kept this same expression while Kenny told me that Marilyn Monroe was trying to seduce me. With this deadpan face, I would do little except blink at the coach's valiant attempt for a response. Ford loved it! He wanted me to do that! He wanted me to play my whole role with that expression! Well, I responded just the same as Kenny had five years earlier on *The Searchers*. I didn't want to look like such a jerk. The only thing is that it would have made a very minor role in the picture much more of a standout.

In the scene, Widmark is standing there, waiting to fight us. Ford had me jumping all around him like an 1890s boxer, and he wanted me to keep that dumb expression on my face all the time. I should have done it. I only half-did it.

Ford kept saying, "You know—like this, kid!"

Then he'd make a face and act it out for me. I wouldn't do it, not 100 percent. He never got sore at me; he finally gave up. I think a few years before he would have given me holy hell, but he knew. I was deeply unhappy. For the same reason he didn't bawl me out about the whiskey in my room, he said to himself, "The hell with it!"

He shot a lot of footage on us which was never in the movie. He did not supervise the editing. When he finished shooting, he just walked away from it. As I have said before, when you worked for Uncle Jack, 99 percent of what he shot was in the final cut. In recent years, I have found that only about 50 percent, if that, of what they shoot of you is in the movie. Today's directors are so unsure of themselves—that they may have forgotten an angle or something which the studio bigwigs may want—that they shoot a lot of footage they know they will never use. I still take the bait. I go to see the movie and go nuts! That adage still applies, "Stay with the money." If the film runs too long, the supporting cast is the first to go.

Well, the shooting went along very smoothly. Jack was having a lot of fun on this one. The weather is very changeable in Texas. Jack was causing the unit manager to have fits, because many mornings around 9:00 he'd ask Ken and me to just "hang around." Then he'd walk out onto his porch in his see-through pongee nightshirt, make an imaginary lens with his right hand, and look at the sky. To the rest of us the sky looked perfect, but if he didn't feel like going to work and just wanted sit around and visit with Jimmy, Dick, Kenny, and me, he'd say, "The damned light's not good. Let's wait awhile."

Then he'd say to me, "Kid, go get Widmark."

He could have called him on the phone, but he never did that; he didn't want to ruffle Dick's feathers. I was the liaison man.

I'd walk over to Dick's cabin and knock on his door. "Yeah! What?" he'd say, not knowing it was me. Then, "Oh! Hi, Dobe, Come on in." His tone would vary according to the time of day; the later the better. "The Old Man sent you, right?"

"Yeah."

"What's the old bastard want with me?"

"Nothing."

"That's what I thought." And that's the way it would go.

When my mother arrived there in Bracketville, I felt like I was ten again. Up to then, I had never been on an even keel. I went from despair to euphoria. I was never in neutral, but Mom's arrival seemed to smooth me out. I guess a guy always needs his mom at some time, no matter what his age.

The Old Man had an even better time after Mom got there. He'd say "Oh, Christ! Is Goldie here?" like it was a terrible thing and this happy location was now going to be torture. But he was as happy as a clam. He was always calling her to come over to his room. One time I went in, and she was darning his socks. Another time, she was digging a chigger out of his big toe. He called them "chiggrows."

"Christ, I picked up another bunch of those 'chiggrows,'" he'd exclaim.

There was to be a square dance in this movie, too, just like *Wagonmaster.* He had dance director Kenny Williams come down from L.A. to choreograph it. There is only a brief glimpse of it in the movie, but in reality, we worked like hell on it, practicing every day.

In *Wagonmaster* he had Don Summers and me go from a Russian Cossack squat to a high leap in the air about six times in a row, war-whooping as we went. That had been eleven years before, and I had been 28. Now I was 39, and hadn't exactly gone into physical training for this film, unless you call elbow-bending working-out. I should have been doing knee bends between drinks. Too late now. Now in 1960, it was Ken and me. Kenny was older than me, but he was as hard as a rock. No matter, legs are legs and years are years—ask any ball player. The first day of rehearsal, he had Kenny and me doing the leaps, but it wasn't the same.

Ford kept yelling, "Higher. Higher!" Finally, slightly disgusted, "Keep working on it."

The next morning, we felt fine until we stood up. We could barely walk. Kenny said, "Okay, down we go."

I exclaimed, "What?"

He replied, "The only way we're going to get over this is to do lots more."

So we started. It hurt so bad our eyes were watering. We started to laugh—up, down, up, down. It took two days of deep-knee bends before we could jump again. Uncle Jack didn't see that part.

One day Jack came over to the western street where we were practicing, and he had a new idea. Stuntman Dean Smith was just starting out in the business, and to say he was young and naive is an understatement. He had certainly never seen the likes of John Ford before. Dean was the coholder of the world 100-yard-dash record. He could run, jump over two horses, and land on the back of the third. He was a superb athlete, but Ford picked up on his shyness and inexperience. *3 Godfathers* came right back to my memory when he started in on poor Dean.

What Jack wanted Dean to do was jump over me every time I was in the squat position. Dean, of course, could do that easily, but leave it to Jack; he made up his mind that Dean would not be able to do that, and by God, somehow he got Dean so screwed up, he couldn't jump over an apple box. Once or twice Jack would wait until I was halfway up and then yell, "Jump." Dean would jump and hit me in the head.

Dean mumbled, "I don't know what I'm doing wrong." I told him he was not doing anything wrong, that Jack was deliberately trying to make him look bad.

"But why?"

I said, "Because he's putting you through your initiation."

"How long does it go on?"

I told him probably until the end of the picture. He said, sadly, "Well, I can't understand that."

"Nobody can," I replied.

The night to shoot the big dance arrived. Forget about Dean; I was nervous as hell. I had it in my nut that this was the time Uncle Jack was going to punish me for all my breaches of the Ford Rules. That was very neurotic of me, but that's the way I was in 1960. Riding out to the location at dusk, I was almost shaking. I needed a drink, but there wasn't one for miles around.

We could see the light from the huge bonfire way before we got there. It was a perfect setting for the Cleggs and their madness. I pulled myself together and decided that if the old bastard wanted jumping and hell-raising, he was going to get it. I was walking toward the set when I heard my mother's voice, "Where the hell are you going?"

I said, "Oh, hi, Mom. I'm going to the set."

Then she said, "You want a drink?"

"Mom! This is a John Ford picture. No drinking on the job!" I was forgetting my very own rule never to drink on the job.

"Screw him! Come on in here!"

I went into her dressing room. She had a dressing room! They were a rare thing on a Ford set. Duke never had one, that I remember. Mom had her own cures for things. Diet pills were in widespread use in those days, and she always kept a few in her purse for emergencies. She also never left home without her little silver flask of rum. She reached into her huge bag and pulled out the rum and the pills. I took a "Greenie" and washed it down with the rum. She knew I needed help to get through this.

Well, I danced and jumped like I was 16. One take, and we were on our way back to camp. I didn't sleep for about 18 hours! Uncle Jack was pleased with us, but I felt I had cheated.

One evening, I was unlocking the door to my room when the Old Man stuck his head out from across the hall and said, "Ol' Dobe, can you come in here for a minute?"

I entered, and he bade me sit down. I thought, "This must be serious stuff. Maybe a lecture on being more responsible. To be more like I used to be." Those thoughts flashed through my brain, but that wasn't it.

He asked the question again. "Where's Widmark?"

I replied as usual, "Over in his cabin, I guess, Uncle Jack."

"Yeah. He's a loner. Widmark is a loner. A damned good actor. But Widmark's a loner. People drive him nuts."

"Yeah, I know it. He's always been like that."

"He likes you, though."

I replied that I was glad that that was true, and that I had known him ever since he was under contract to Fox in 1948. The Old Man talked pleasantly for awhile about how happy he was working with Dick and Jimmy, and then he said, "Go get him, will ya?"

Off I went to Widmark's cabin. Same routine—very gruff, "Who is it?" When I told him it was me and the Old Man wanted him, he opened the door. He went into a minor rage. Not his mad rage, just his upset rage.

"I know what he wants. I know exactly what the old bastard wants! Wayne has called him, and he wants me to go to that goddamned premiere of *The Alamo* in San Antonio! Well, screw it! I'm not going to that goddamned terrible movie. It was enough grief working on it!"

I was just a messenger. I didn't know what to say. On the way over to Jack's room, Dick ranted about this being way above and beyond the call of duty, and he'd made up his mind that he wasn't going. He was fond of the Old Man, but this was asking too much.

"Damn it! I'm *not* going!"

Within the next half hour, Ken and I were called into Ford's room.

"Dick here has been kind enough to do this for Duke. He said he'd go to the premiere in San Antonio if he could take you boys with him. So, I'm giving you the whole weekend off. Have a good time. And Dick, thank you very much."

He patted Dick on the shoulder.

The three of us went. It was boring as hell, and we returned to Bracketville as soon as we could.

One weekend Dick decided he'd like to blow off a little steam. Jack was entertaining some navy brass (he was a rear admiral by that time) and Ken, being his son-in-law, was stuck with that assignment too. Now Dick knew the rules, and so he went to Jack and told him what he'd like to do, if it was okay. That way, Ford was almost sure to say, "Sure. Why not? Have a good time."

Dick came over to my place. "I fixed it up with the Old Man. We've got Saturday night all to ourselves and can go across the border to Mexico. We'll take Shirley (Jones) and Annelle (Hayes)."

Annelle played the sexy gal who owned the saloon. She was one of the most gorgeous gals I had ever known. She was married to actor Mark Stevens at that time.

Now I had never been on location with Dick before. *Two Rode Together* was the first film we had done together. I knew he didn't drink much, loved good food, and had a sweet tooth the likes of which I had never seen. I figured there wouldn't be much booze consumption on this trip, so I had about four big belts before we started off.

We had a hell of a good time on the way to Pedras Negras. Dick had been there many times while filming *The Alamo,* so we got the red carpet treatment from the maitre d' at the Casablanca restaurant. Dick liked Mexico because the other patrons left him alone. We were shown to a big table right by the dance floor. The waiter came to take our drink orders. I figured Shirley and I would get about one drink before dinner, but before I opened my mouth, Dick was ordering.

"Four double-Margueritas all the way around!"

"Doubles?" I nearly fainted.

Ten minutes later, "Waiter! Por favor—four Margueritas!" Annelle said she hadn't finished the one she had yet and didn't need another.

Dick barked, "Yes, you do, damn it! Cuatro mas Margueritas por favor!"

Then the orchestra started playing. We danced. More Margueritas. Dick never showed any effects from the drinks, except that he felt good, but hell, he had felt good when we arrived. He even sat in on a set with

Rio Grande – Ben Johnson, Maureen O'Hara, Claude Jarman, Jr., and me. Only Duke was allowed to kiss her.

Rio Grande – The hours spent learning Roman-riding pay off.

The Long Gray Line – Cadet Eisenhower.

The Long Gray Line – Tyrone Power, Donald Crisp, Harry Carey, Jr., Phil Carey (no relation), Ward Bond, Erin O'Brien Moore, Betsy Palmer.

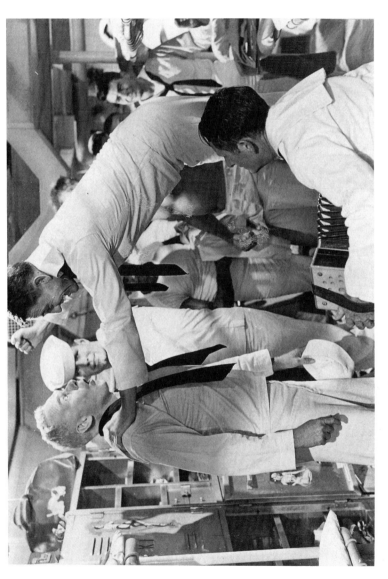

Mister Roberts – Ken Curtis and me just before "liberty".

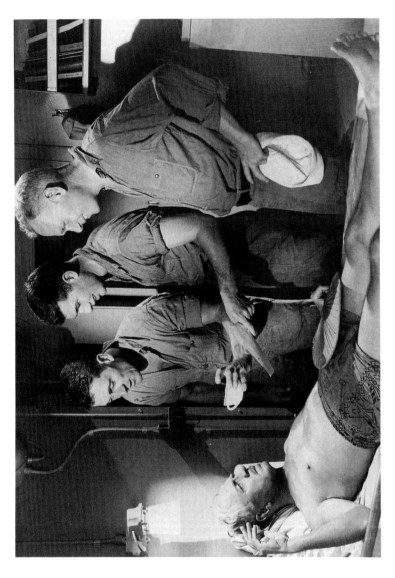

Mister Roberts – We were all in awe of William Powell.

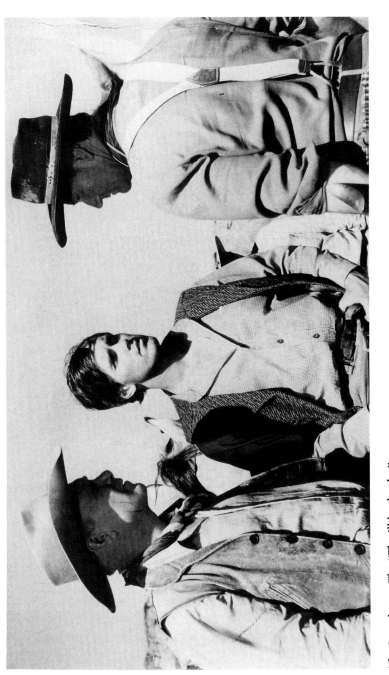

The Searchers – The "That'll be the day" scene.

The Searchers – Looking for Lucy.

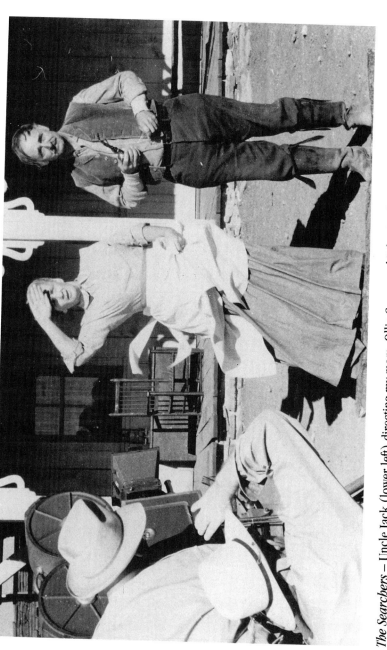

The Searchers – Uncle Jack (lower left) directing my mom, Ollie Carey, and John Qualen.

The Searchers – The best scene I ever did with Duke.

"The Adventures of Spin and Marty" for *The Mickey Mouse Club* television show. With Roy Barcroft and Walt Disney.

Two Rode Together – James Stewart, John Ford and Richard Widmark between takes.

Two Rode Together – Ken Curtis and me with our captive.

Two Rode Together – The only man who could touch Richard Widmark.

Tombstone (1993) – Still working. Photograph by James Pepper.

Tombstone (1993) – Working with director George P. Cosmatos.
Photograph by Ernie Bulow.

the orchestra and played drums. He's an expert drummer, and made a big hit. Wine with dinner, and B&B after, and then Dick yelled, "Let's go! I know another great joint!"

So off we went to a place with the greatest mariachi music I have ever heard. Dick knew everybody there, too, and they favored him with anything he wanted to hear.

We got back home pretty close to dawn. It was one of the best times I have ever had. Later that Sunday, I ran into him and asked how he felt.

"I feel great. But listen, don't tell Jean (Dick's wife) about this."

"You mean because we took Annelle and Shirley?"

And Dick said, "Hell no! Not that! Don't mention to Jean that I drank."

I said, "Why not? You practically never take a drink."

"That's just it. She's always after me to have a drink when we have a party."

One day Ken and I were surprised when we looked at the call sheet because we had a very late call, which was weird. When we arrived, we saw everyone assembled around a clearing close to the river. The second weird thing was that nobody seemed to be doing anything. They were just standing around, like people waiting for something to happen. A Ford set was usually quiet, but this was even more so. It flashed through my mind that perhaps someone had just been chewed out and this was the lull after the storm. It was not unlike the period prior to my death scene years before in Death Valley.

I began to tense up. As far as I knew, the scene we were to shoot was an amusing one—a comedy fight in which Ortho and Greeley gang up on Lieutenant Gary (Widmark). I had thought the Old Man would have fun with this, but I started noticing that people were glancing sideways at me. I was becoming the focal point. Uncle Jack knew I was there, but he did not acknowledge my presence. I began to feel very uncomfortable. There were bad vibes. Kenny had walked off, and Dick was sitting off by himself.

Then I figured it out. I saw Chuck Hayward dressed in Ken's wardrobe and Billy Williams dressed in Dick's, but no one was dressed in mine. That explained the late call and the silence. Ford was a master at this.

Finally, he yelled, "Where's Good Chuck and Billy Williams?" Pause. Then, "Dobe, get over here!"

I thought, "Oh boy, here it comes. You're going 'on duty,' eh? Time to pay the piper."

We all gathered in the middle of the clearing. Uncle Jack looked at me with a glint in his eye. "You do not have a stuntman. Do you?"

"No sir. I guess not."

He said, "Take it from me. You don't."

All movie fights are choreographed by the head stuntman. You go through every move and every punch, no matter how long the fight goes on. It's worked out punch-for-punch, miss-for-miss, fall-for-fall. The stunt guys and the actors go over it time and again, so no one gets hurt. Not with Ford! He puts you out there and then yells, "All right, go at it! Make it goddamned rough. Action!"

That's the way he always did it. Years before, he had made a movie with Victor McLaglen and George O'Brien. McLaglen had been a heavy-weight champion of the British Empire, and O'Brien the middleweight champion of the United States Navy. There was a prizefight scene, and Jack employed the same tactics—only he added a little something.

He went to Victor and said, "Listen, O'Brien said he's going to try to knock you cold."

Then he went to George and said that Victor was going to try to knock him out. Neither did anything; they were each anticipating the other's Sunday punch. They just danced around. No matter how much Ford insulted them, nothing happened. I never heard how the Old Man got even, but you can bet he did, somewhere down the road.

He hit me with the worst thing he could think of to say. "Now listen. Don't quit on me." He started back to his chair. While his back was turned, Billy whispered, "I'll tell you what I'm going to throw—right hand, left hand—so keep your ears open."

There was a lot of wrestling around on the ground with Ford yelling for me to hit Chuck (as Kenny) because we were too dumb to know any better. We went all out for him, but he had us do the whole thing a couple more times. I was pooped. I was out of air. I was shot. Chuck put ice packs on the back of my neck; I was getting heat prostration.

Then he called for Dick and Kenny. We go roundy, roundy, and boom, boom, boom, all over the clearing, doing the fight all over again. Suddenly, the Old Man noticed that Dick's foot was over my shoulder.

"Bite him. Bite him!"

So I bit him on the ankle. With all that adrenaline going, I overdid it and bit him really hard, even through his sweat socks.

"Ow!" he screamed, making Ford very happy.

Finally he yelled, "Cut," and Dick said, "Jesus, Dobe, you could have faked it."

Between one of the takes, Uncle Jack came over to the three of us while we were lying on the ground. I was lying on my stomach, head-to-toe beside Dick, trying to catch my breath. Uncle Jack made out he wanted to adjust Dick's neckerchief. He came up beside me and fell to his knees. One knee buried itself in my back between my ribs. He leaned as hard as he could on that knee while he reached over and fiddled with Dick's neckerchief. Then I heard a sound like a dry stick of wood breaking in half.

Andy Devine, who was a considerable distance away, said, "There goes Dobe's ribs!"

I was so exhausted, I hardly gave them much attention and did the fight again. By that time, I didn't care if I died. By the time I got back to L.A., it hurt so much every time I took a breath that I went to my doctor, who told me I had two broken ribs.

I was sitting in the dining hall having a cup of coffee one afternoon after I'd been there about three weeks. We had about another week to go on the location, and I was looking out the window, thinking about home. Wingate Smith and Kenny were stopped outside. I couldn't hear what they were saying, but I suddenly realized Kenny was crying. My God, what the hell had happened? Tears were rolling down his cheeks. I rushed outside.

Ken looked at me, "Dobe, Ward's gone."

He had died of a heart attack, sitting on the toilet in a motel in Dallas.

"They had to take the door off the bathroom to get to him. Poor Maisie was there with him."

I asked the big question. "Does the Old Man know?"

Kenny said, "No, we have to go tell him now."

I remembered that the last time I'd seen Ward on the *Wagontrain* set, he'd been drinking heavily and seemed very tired.

There was a driver standing by who took us out to the location. It was flat country, sagebrush and tumbleweeds. As luck would have it, Uncle Jack was sitting there alone, looking off, away from the center of action— sitting there as though waiting for the news we were about to give him.

"Pop," Ken said, "I have some awful news."

"What? What's happened now?"

"Ward's dead."

Uncle Jack said nothing for a long time. We stood there waiting.

Finally, he said, "Son of a bitch!"

He paused a long time and then, "The doctor told him! The doctor told him over and over again! For months and months, he's been warned." Then, more softly, "Heart attack wasn't it? Huh?"

Kenny told him, "Yes, sir, it was, Pappy. I guess it was a big one, too."

Then he told the rest he knew.

Andy Devine had come up beside us. Uncle Jack looked up at him and said, "Now you're my favorite shit. Ward just died."

Of course, that was meant to be a compliment to Andy. He knew full well how much Jack loved Ward. He was his most reliable actor. He never let him down. Ward could drive Jack mad with his flamboyant mannerisms and ego, but he knew he would miss Ward terribly as a friend.

After the McCarthy fiasco, it was said that Ward had trouble getting work. Then he got the series "Wagontrain," which became a tremendous hit. Ward loved every minute of it. He loved the public's adulation of him as Major Adams. He made TV stars out of two wonderful Ford stuntmen, Frankie McGrath and Terry Wilson. Frankie used to be kidded unmercifully on Ford films because he couldn't say a line of dialogue. Ward taught him how to play the role of Wooster, and Frankie didn't have to hit that hard ground anymore. Frankie and Terry went on tour with Ward to rodeos and fairs. Ward drank everything that was offered him, chain smoked, and got very little sleep on these junkets. Then he would return home, physically worn out, to start a new episode of the show. He fell in with a crowd in Dallas that just loved him to death, literally. Ward would fly back as an honored guest for all the Cowboys' home games, and they partied and raised holy hell all weekend. The Dallas people would rest up, but Ward would go back to Hollywood to shoot his series—dialogue, dialogue, horsebacking, and dialogue. No human body can take that kind of punishment, not even a well one. So the Grim Reaper called Ward Bond's name, and Uncle Jack lost his dear friend and favorite actor.

Ward liked the power of fame. He loved people, no matter what their beliefs, even though he hurt some with his McCarthyism. He didn't know better. I think Duke did, but not Ward. If looking for commies made him important, then he embraced the cause. Many people believed that my politics were similar to Ward's and Duke's because I worked with them so many times. That was never true. I wouldn't join the Motion Picture Alliance. Many of the ones listed as so-called "commies" were friends of mine, and I knew that they were, as I was, good, caring Americans who wanted only the best for their country.

Uncle Jack called to Wingate, "Charter a plane for me to go to Dallas. I'm taking Ken and Dobe with me. Oh yeah. Better get me a thousand in cash. Do it now, will ya'?"

Then he turned his attention back to us, "Poor Maisie is back there in Dallas. She needs family with her. You'll fly with me to Dallas. I want to visit Ward's remains, and then I'll come back here to wrap it up. I'm sending you on the plane back to L.A. with Ward's body and Maisie. I don't need you boys here anymore, anyway."

Kenny and I were surprised and honored to be given this assignment. We both loved Maisie and would try to help her any way we could. We flew in a great little plane on that trip to Dallas. I can't remember what make, but it wasn't so small you didn't feel safe. Uncle Jack sat up front with the pilot, with Kenny and me right behind. He was anything but solemn. After we had been in the air about ten minutes, he turned around and looked at me with a big smile (very rare, a big smile) and said, "Is that old Dobe?" There was more love and affection in his silly question than I had felt in our whole relationship. Under those sad circumstances, he was saying to me, "I love you, Dobe." He looked at me a long time, smiling.

"Sure is, Uncle Jack." He patted me on the knee and turned back toward the front. He talked cheerfully for most of the trip. It was as though he was saying, "Ward! You big dumb bastard. You had to go and do it, didn't you? You're in heaven now, with Harry and all the rest. Damned if I'm going to cry, Ward, but I'll miss you like hell."

Gordon MacLendon, a very nice and gentle man who owned many radio stations, picked us up at the Dallas airport. He used to recreate the major league baseball games over the air in the 1940s and 1950s. Old Joe Harris (our man who came to dinner) listened to them regularly.

We went to a fancy private club for dinner. Ken knew the whole Texas gang really well. He'd produced some movies for them. They were high livers, and I didn't mind that at all. The liquor started flowing, and it didn't stop for a long time, I'm sorry to say. Gordon then drove us to Bob Thompson's, home where Maisie was staying. He was one of the Clint Murchison crowd. He personified the rich and famous of Texas.

He'd yell at Ford, "Listen, Jack, you may scare the hell out of those actors of yours, but I know it's all bullshit!" Stuff like that. Ford didn't acknowledge any of it.

He seemed to say, "I guess I'm forced to listen to this man for a day or so, out of respect for Ward and Maisie."

I am very ashamed to say that I stayed smashed from that day until we brought Ward's body back to L.A. There was a funeral service out at the Field Photo Home. Ken sang Bob Nolan's beautiful religious song, "And He Was There," and I groaned out "The Mormon Hymn." Duke, bless him, stayed sober through that whole time. Then they took Ward back to the Midwest for burial. Whenever I want to, I can slip *Wagonmaster,* or *The Searchers,* or *The Quiet Man* into my VCR and watch Ward walk off with the show. He was always there for me, and he was always there for Uncle Jack.

The next time I worked for Uncle Jack was in 1962, after I quite the booze. He was shooting a baseball story for television called "Flashing Spikes." It starred Jimmy Stewart and Patrick Wayne, and he wanted me to come over to the set to work on it. No mention of a script, money, or any other stuff like that. He just wanted to give me a job. I have since realized that there was something rather poetic about it all. He was giving me a payday because I was trying to turn my life around.

So I went over there to our old home, the old Republic studios which had another name by now. As soon as I walked in, I could hear Danny Borzage's squeeze box, so I knew I was in the right place. The set was very quiet, and when Uncle Jack saw me he greeted me very warmly, which made everybody stare. I noticed that there was a baseball dugout and Ford told me to go sit in it and when Jimmy Stewart walked by, to stare in awe at him. That was a cinch because Stewart was always one of my idols. I still felt pretty silly because I was playing a rookie and I was forty-one years old! I would always be a kid in the mind of John Ford. A few weeks earlier, over the phone, he had gone into an elaborate discourse on the past and present drinking habits of the Ford and Carey families, claiming in a most warm and charming way that the whole bunch were alcoholics. And that last but not least, so was Himself and yours truly. Then, after I said I was in total agreement, he threw in Duke for good measure. At one point, John Wayne didn't speak to me for eight long years. I never found out why. My friend, Bob Totten, recently offered a pretty reasonable explanation, "You were not a man if you didn't drink."

In 1968, we were in Durango, Mexico, making *The Undefeated,* with Duke and Rock Hudson. Andy McLaglen was directing. Duke was fond of "Big A," as we called him. It was late one Sunday afternoon at a party at Andy's cabana. The whole cast was there, and Duke looked at me like he had looked at me on *The Searchers.*

"What the hell were you mad at me for, for all those years?"

I couldn't believe my ears! I answered, aghast, "Duke, I was never mad at you. For some goddamned reason, you got sore at me!"

"Bullshit!" he replied. But we were friends again.

Cheyenne Autumn

I have read more than once that *Cheyenne Autumn* was Ford's "apology" to the Indians. Uncle Jack never apologized for anything in his life. He made *Cheyenne Autumn* because he thought it was a good story. The fact that the Indians were not the enemy in this picture might have given him some comfort, but no more than a fleeting thought. Also, he had enjoyed working with Dick Widmark and wanted to do another film with him.

The original script was well written, but terribly long. There were many good supporting roles in it. Ben Johnson and I were wondering what parts we were going to play, but as Uncle Jack did in *Mister Roberts,* we were already on location in Monument Valley, waiting to go to work, before we were told. We needn't have concerned ourselves. I don't think we spoke more than ten lines between us in the whole movie. Ben was worried, though. Well, as worried as Ben can get. He has always said, and maybe it's true, that it takes him a long time to learn dialogue; that he has to have a script at least a month in advance for a leading role. He holes up with his wife, Carol, and studies and studies. The funny thing is, though, Ford could throw him new lines during rehearsal, as he often did, and it never bothered Ben one bit. I'm sort of that way myself. I see young actors today learning all their lines on the set before a take and then pulling it off! I can't imagine what Ford would have done with those guys. All the big stars learned their whole part before filming began, in those days. Those old-time directors were too tough for an actor to take a chance. Ford wasn't the only one. With Wellman, Hathaway, or Wyler, you had better be prepared, no matter what your name was.

Ben and I were quartered along with an electrician and actor named Bing Russell (his son is Kurt Russell) in a mobile home about a mile down the road from Gouldings' Lodge.

In 1963, Ben and I were well past 40, but not in Uncle Jack's eyes. In his mind, we were still in our mid-twenties and we were still expected to do the same things on a horse that we had done 20 years before. And we did! Ben played Plumtree, and I played Smith. Uncle Jack had thrown most of those smaller parts out the window, and we wound up playing two people who were not even in the original script. By the time *Cheyenne Autumn* came around, I was in terrific shape both mentally and physically and it was a happy experience.

Uncle Jack was having a very jolly time shooting this film, but each scene seemed to be a tiny movie in itself. For example, people wondered why he stuck a "mini-movie," with Jimmy Stewart as Wyatt Earp playing cards with Arthur Kennedy and John Carradine, in the middle of the picture. That's easy—he wanted to direct these guys once more before saying "Adios." Victor Jory, beautiful (even in 1963) Dolores del Rio, Gilbert Roland, and Ricardo Montalban marched and marched across the red sand of Monument Valley. Every so often, one of them would say something as though it were a world-shattering statement, and then they would continue to march, stop, make another announcement, and march, march. It was all very grim. I never knew what was going on, but I chalked it up to my being just plain dumb. I was to discover, however, that no one else did either. They did what the Old Man told them. Naturally, they trusted him—he was John Ford—so there must be *some* reason for what they were doing.

He was having a great time with all his actors. Sal Mineo played a young Indian brave. Uncle Jack kept calling him Sol, instead of Sal. He was very grim, too. After our first day's work, Ben and I knew we should just relax and have a good time. I was in my seventh month of sobriety and boring the hell out of everyone about my new life. They didn't know I'd had any other kind of life, so they could have cared less about what I drank or didn't drink. Uncle Jack knew, though, and he treated me like his dearest friend.

Cheyenne Autumn had a really super cast. Along with Richard Widmark and the others I've already mentioned there were Jimmy Stewart, Carroll Baker, Edward G. Robinson, Karl Malden, Arthur Kennedy, John Carradine, George O'Brien, and Patrick Wayne. You can see that Jack forgot very few of his old stalwarts. Bing Russell's name is dead last on the cast list, and he had more to say than Ben and I put together. He was the one I bored the most with the tale of my miraculous recovery from alcoholism. The young electrician who shared the mobile home with us must have found the BS of three actors unendurable, because he was out most of the time.

Ben and Bing and I would swap tales on into the night. Well, Bing and I would. Ben would fall asleep. We were both pretty low on the totem pole at that time in our careers, but were happy to be working.

What Ben and I did most in the picture was ride like hell. It seemed to us that while Uncle Jack was thinking of what else he could do to Mister Webb's script, he'd set the camera in position and have us ride as fast as we could over some hill or come dashing hell bent for leather past the camera as close as we could without running over it. Most of those rides were not used, but it made us feel wanted—sort of like the old days.

Ben's own steer-roping horse was injured on the first day of shooting. He'd torn a muscle completely loose in his hindquarters and had to be put down, so Ben was forced to ride an inferior one because it matched the color of his original horse. So now I had a faster horse than Ben—a first in our history of making movies together. Ben doesn't like to be second to anybody, and he knew that with that poor little horse they'd given him as a replacement, this was sure to be a frustrating reality. In truth, it bothered me, too. I was not used to seeing Ben on a second-rate horse. We were shooting this day at a place called Mexican Hat in Utah, just north of Monument Valley. The San Juan River flows right by the little town. Uncle Jack shot there a lot when he had river crossings, because the water is the perfect depth and there's good footing for the charging horses to come across without having to struggle or swim too much. It looks great on film, water splashing in all directions as the horses come racing by. This day, even though there were scenes Uncle Jack should have been shooting with the principals, he couldn't resist the temptation of having Ben and me charge across the San Juan. Where we were supposed to be charging to, I have no idea, and neither did Uncle Jack.

Ford had the camera set up on the opposite side of the river from where we were. He yelled across on the bullhorn, "I want you boys to make this really western. Come past on the right of the camera! All right. Get back out of sight until you hear me yell, 'Action,' and then ride like hell!"

Now, Ol' Ben *knew* he was going to get beat crossing the river, but he has always been a foxy guy under duress. We had our horses near the bank and were dismounted to adjust our cinches. You want them a little on the loose side when riding through water so the horse can move with more freedom. Ben, with a very concerned expression on his face, gave me some instructions prior to mounting. Naturally, I took note of what he said, because of his tremendous horsemanship.

"Now Dobe," he said, while looking at the ground at the river's edge, "see that mud right there in front of you?" He pointed to some bluish mud right at the water's edge.

"Yes, Ben," I said, very concerned, "I see it. It's kinda blue."

"Yeah—yeah. Well, when ya' git to that there muddy place, kinda' take a good hold of your horse, because if he's a-goin' fast an' hits that mud there he could sure as hell fall with you, 'cause he can't get his feet under him fast enough."

I looked at the slimy stuff and bought the whole package, no questions asked.

"Yeah," I said, "that does look kind of dangerous. Thanks Ben. I'll sure do that."

We mounted up and rode back to the willows to await the order from Uncle Jack. It wasn't long before we heard, "Come ahead...Come ahead...Ride like hell!"

We were side by side when we started, but in no time, I was a good two lengths in front. In no time at all, I came to the "mud spot." I did as I'd been told—I pulled Jimmy in a little so he wouldn't get caught up in that thick slime and when I did, Mr. Johnson went by me so fast he was just a blur. Before I could even take a breath, he was in the middle of the river, and I was chasing him. He'd gone through that "dangerous" mud like it was the Santa Anita race track and was heading for the other bank.

Thank God, my horse Jimmy was so fast that I was nearly neck-and-neck as we passed by the camera.

Uncle Jack shouted, "Right! That was great!" And that was our work for the day on the "Sunny San Juan." Ben had beaten me on that old Navajo horse. I'm glad it worked out that way.

Out of the dozens and dozens of horses I have ridden in pictures, there are only a couple that I would have liked to own because of their behavior and speed. Jimmy, the horse I was riding that day, was one. Even though he was hot blooded, he had good sense. He was very manageable, even after you'd done a lot of running with him, and he would always stand still when you wanted him to. That's very uncommon in thoroughbred horses. Sadly, he too, had to be put down a few years later, having injured himself by stepping through some grillwork on the Universal Studios back lot.

Dick was upset by the fact that Uncle Jack was shooting the film in such an off-hand manner, but he never lost sight of the fact that he was working with a movie genius, because every day he saw flashes of it. Dick loved him.

Dick had driven from his ranch in the San Fernando Valley to Monument Valley in a well-used pickup truck with a camper on the back of it that he'd borrowed from his foreman. He was always driving like mad from up the hill at Gouldings' down to where I was in my quarters. Most of the time, it was because the Old Man wanted me. I felt like saying to Uncle Jack, "If you'd given me a larger role, I'd be up there with you." It's hard to recall what all those trips were for. Sometimes, Uncle Jack wanted me to sing "The Mormon Hymn." Of course, he made everyone else listen, too. It must have been a painful experience, because I was really lousy. Uncle Jack didn't seem to care. I had had a benign node taken off my vocal chord the year before. It made my voice quaver.

Every time Dick came to pick me up to take me to Gouldings', I felt I was deserting my old saddlemate, Ben Johnson. Was Uncle Jack still "getting even" with Ben because of those misunderstandings? My guess is affirmative—as though forgetting him for 13 years wasn't enough. But it didn't matter to Ben. He is a special person, and he was on to the Old Man's games.

Sometimes I would be invited up there for dinner with the "A" team. It was just like *Yellow Ribbon* and all the others—Uncle Jack at the head of the table, and on down the line. Dick sat wherever he pleased. It was fun to be up there and be a part of it, knowing that I would be set free in a little while.

The cast included two real characters. One was great, big, ex-wrestler Mike Mazurki. Mike was a wonderful guy, and Ford was very fond of him. He had a kisser not unlike old Victor McLaglen. That's why he was there. Ford was resurrecting old characters and images. Well, Mike could never replace Vic, but he did one hell of a Mike Mazurki, and that was good enough for Ford, even though he picked on him a lot.

The other character was Victor Jory. I had always loved Victor Jory. He was one tough hombre. He once fought an even brawl against the renowned Guinn "Big Boy" Williams. It was over a girl, of course. Victor was at an advanced age by this time, but he still had an eye for the ladies. John Ford scared him not one teensy bit. Ford would see him coming into the dining hall and yell, "Don't let him sit near me!"

Victor would reply, "Why the hell would I want to sit next to you? I've had three double-bourbons and feel good, so why should I ruin my evening!"

Ford would mutter another insult. On the set, it was a different story. Victor did exactly as he was told, without argument.

One day Uncle Jack was shooting a scene he had shot dozens of times in the past. Widmark, an officer, and Mazurki, the sergeant, were riding along at the head of a column. Ben and I were right behind them. Widmark discovers a whiskey bottle in Mazurki's saddlebag. It was a moving or "tracking" shot. Ford was picking on Mazurki something awful, even when he did it right. We all knew the routine. Finally Widmark got fed up with the Old Man browbeating poor Mike.

When Jack told Dick to hold the whiskey bottle, "Up higher, so the camera can see it," Dick, in a white rage, yelled at Jack, "You mean like this?" And with that, he smashed the whiskey bottle against a big rock. The contents splattered all over the place, scared all the horses, and even made Jack jump with surprise.

It was Dick's way of telling Jack to let up on Mazurki. After this outburst, Dick got off his horse, stomped over to his chair, picked it up, took it halfway across the desert, and sat in it. There was a period of deadly silence. Everyone was looking at Ford to see what he would do. There was more silence. Finally, Ford said, in a very soft voice filled with mock awe, "What a *terrible* temper."

Then he let about five minutes elapse. Dick was still sitting in his chair, his back to all of us. Uncle Jack rose to his feet, walked over to Dick, leaned over him, and with his hand, tickled Dick under the chin. "Kootchie...Kootchie...koo." Widmark laughed like Widmark, and came back to work. But Ford left Mazurki alone!

Four of us—Ben, Bing, Jimmy Fitzsimons (Maureen O'Hara's brother) and me—were playing a game with rocks and stones we had dreamed up, when Ben noticed something strange out on the range. Two tiny dots were moving toward us on the horizon, little puffs of red dust following them as they approached us. When they got closer, we saw a young couple in their 20s, and they were making a beeline for Ford.

In no time at all, three assistant directors started to wave them away, making all kinds of hand signals—Vamanos! Ben went out to meet them. They said they had come a long way, from New York, just to see John Ford. They were Peter Bogdanovich and his wife, Polly Platt. Peter wanted to do an article on Ford for *Esquire* magazine. When Ben saw that Jack wasn't too busy, he took them over and introduced them. When they told Jack they didn't, as yet, have a place to stay, Jack said to Wingate, "Find them a place, even if you have to kick that rude son-of-bitch out of his room." (One of the assistants had been particularly nasty to Peter and Polly, and it had not gone unnoticed by Ford.)

Here stood a young man who would be famous in the business in a few short years. And more amazing, here stood Ben Johnson, who was to win an Oscar under Bogdanovich's direction. This was the young man who would give Ben his greatest role as Sam the Lion in *The Last Picture Show,* and Polly went on to be production designer and Oscar-winner herself, with movies like *Terms of Endearment.*

Polly and Peter stayed for quite a few days. I was present on a few occasions at dinner, and was amazed at what Peter could get away with. The rest of us usually thought a thing through before we'd say something to Jack, so as to avoid the "What!" routine. Not Peter. He went on his merry way, throwing questions at Jack with complete abandon, and he got away with it, too. He asked all kinds of questions about Jack's least-favorite subject, movies. Peter would hurl them at him, and by God, he got a sensible and polite answer. We were all astounded when Peter didn't get his head chopped off. In fact, we all learned a lot about the Old Man that we hadn't known. The only nutty answer I ever heard him give was when Peter asked him what he thought his greatest film was. "*Arrowsmith,*" he said emphatically.

There is an action scene, improvised, of course, in which Widmark yells back to the ranks at Ben and me, "Plumtree! Jones!" I don't answer because my name is Smith, so I look around for Jones. This was the running gag Uncle Jack had thought of for this film, Dick was never supposed to be able to remember my name. He yells, "Jones" again, and I finally figure it out and answer, "Name's *Smith, sir.*" Had this been *Yellow Ribbon,* I would have gotten a rock thrown at my head, because I kept saying "The name's *Smith,* sir."

Ford would then tell me again, "Name's *Smith,* sir." I never figured out how I could be so stupid.

Then he said, "Quit padding your part. Just say 'Name's *Smith* sir,' not 'The name's *Smith* sir!' " And, honest to God, I did it again. I finally got it right, but Ford never got angry. What a mystery he was. In another scene, Ben and I are sent up a canyon to see if there are any hostiles up there, and Ben gets his horse shot out from under him. Then in another set-up, Dean Smith, doubling Ben, leaps on behind me, as I fly by him. It was a tough stunt for Dean, and he did it the first take. The point I am making is that it's Ben's horse which gets shot out from under him, not mine.

Now, later in the day, we're all lined up holding our horses. Everyone has a horse except me. That's the way Ford arranged the shot. I figured he must have a reason for this. You never second-guessed Uncle Jack. Bill

Clothier is a tough, Jimmy Cagney-type director of photography, and without even thinking twice, he said "Where's Dobe's horse?"

Jack replied sharply, but sort of amused, "What?"

Bill wasn't put off by this, so he said again, "Where's Dobe's horse?"

Ford, hands on hips, replied, "Dobe doesn't *have* a horse! Remember?"

"No. *Ben's* horse was shot, not Dobe's. Ben should be the one without the horse."

Now I knew that Uncle Jack had painted himself into a corner and was really on the spot, but he used his old standby. "Jesus Christ! Are you trying to direct my picture?"

It didn't bother Bill one bit. "No, Jack, but Dobe should have a horse!"

Ford looked at him, looked at us, and tried to act nonchalant. Dick was standing in front of all of us, holding the reins of his fancy-looking sorrel horse with the blue and yellow saddle blanket of a Cavalry officer. Jack kept acting as if there was nothing wrong. Finally, he reached a decision. He came up to me on the pretext of fixing my neckerchief and whispered in my ear, "Kid, when I yell 'Action,' break ranks and run and grab Widmark's horse, jump on him, and ride off back that way (pointing behind all of us) as fast as you can. It'll make a funny gag."

Of course, Widmark knew nothing about this. Ford was off the hook he'd hung himself on. He wasn't about to admit to Clothier that he'd made a mistake. So, that's exactly what happened. The shot was already set up, the sound mixer yelled, "Speed!" and Ford yelled, "Action!" All of the men mounted their horses except Richard Widmark, who didn't have a horse to mount. I had grabbed it from him and ridden off into the sunset. Widmark looked confused, and Ford was happy. I don't know what the final comments were after Ford yelled "Cut!" but I can guess he probably said to Clothier, "See! *That's* why Dobe didn't have a horse." Of course the shot was never in the picture.

When Widmark came down to pick me up one evening, he said the Old Man had something up his sleeve he wanted to talk to us about. I expected the worst, of course. Well, we waited all through dinner and finally he asked Dick, "Have you ever been to Canyon de Chelley?"

When Dick replied that he never had, Jack said, "You oughta' go! You really should go!"

Then, including me in on the conversation, he said, "You and Dobe and Pat (Wayne) should all go to Canyon de Chelley."

He went on a bit about this fabulous canyon. "I want you boys to see it before we go home. I made a picture there once with Harry and Ollie.

Can't remember the name of it, but we shot a picture there. You boys will enjoy it very much. Dick! Haven't you got your truck here?"

Dick answered that he had it. Uncle Jack surely knew this, as it was Dick's taxi service that brought me up to Gouldings' on his orders.

"I'll give you boys Friday off so's you can make a whole weekend out of it. I'll shoot Victor, God help me, and the rest of the Indians."

So that's what we did. Captain's orders. We wore old work clothes, took our shaving gear, and were on our way early Friday morning. Dick had already found out that there was a nice motel there, practically on the edge of the canyon. He knew exactly what roads to take and how long it would take to get there. Whenever I brought up this ability of his to him, he would simply say, "I read maps!" There was no stopping to see which highway to take or which turnoff. He went right to it!

We checked into the motel about the middle of the afternoon, and Dick said, "Now listen, I don't want any arguments. This is my treat."

That was a relief to me, anyway. I don't know about Pat, but I had about ten bucks.

We were in our rooms about five minutes when Dick collected us. "Let's get something to eat, and tomorrow we can spend the day in the canyon."

We followed him into a little cafe. Dick went up to the counter, and after grumpily admitting he was Richard Widmark, asked with great relish for a "big, thick chocolate shake, please."

"I'm sorry," the waitress informed him. "We don't have milkshakes."

Dick went pale, "What! What do you mean? Everybody has milkshakes!"

She said she was very sorry, but that they didn't serve them.

Dick said, "Well, do you have ice cream and a blender? I'll make it myself."

Now the poor girl was all flustered, and said, "No, we don't have anything like that here."

Dick was beside himself. "Where's the nearest place around here that has a malted milk or shake of any kind?"

It didn't take her a second to answer, "Gallup."

"That's in New Mexico, for God's sake. How far is Gallup?"

"Seventy miles," she replied.

Dick didn't hesitate. "Let's go. I have to have a milkshake."

It was startling news to both of us. All I wanted was a cup of coffee, a smoke, and a nap. But off we went to Gallup. In about an hour-and-half, we were in a Walgreen's drugstore on the outskirts of town. We had a not-too-good milkshake, turned around, and drove back just in time for dinner. The following morning, we went down into the canyon.

The Pueblo people built apartment-style homes in the red sandstone walls that rise from 30 to 1,000 feet. It took the three of us one hell of a long time to wind our way down to see the "White House" and the other buildings carved out of the huge canyon walls. The Hopi lived there too, and today the Navajos graze their sheep among the cottonwood trees.

We all were in damned good shape because it didn't tire us out too badly. When we got back to Monument Valley on Sunday evening, Uncle Jack wanted to hear all about our trip. He talked as though he had some future plans for the canyon. Then he launched into a romantic version of his adventures while making a movie there with Mom and Dad.

When I got back to town, I told Mom this story, and her reply was to snort, "He's full of baloney. We never made a picture there!"

One day we were shooting out on a ridge. I was just standing there wondering what the day held in store for me, when Dick ran up to me in a hell of a hurry.

"Let's get the hell out of here! We're going to Moab!"

"Wait a minute, Dick," I said, "I can't just take off. I don't know if the Old Man needs me."

Dick almost shouted, "Christ, I know that! It's all fixed! He's letting you and me and Ricardo haul ass out of here! Go get your stuff together. I'll pick you up in half an hour."

That was that. He had the Old Man in his hip pocket.

Dick and Ricardo Montalban and I squeezed into the front seat of the pickup. Ricardo is a very friendly man, and he and I talked nonstop for the entire day's drive to Moab, Utah. Dick looked at the road straight ahead the whole way with a very grim look on his face. The next day he asked me, with an expression of complete astonishment, "How in the name of God could you two assholes think of so much crap to talk about?" I didn't know how to answer him. We must have driven him nuts.

I have always felt Uncle Jack could have completed his location shooting right there in Monument Valley, but that he wanted to see Moab once more. All of us Ford "old-timers" were amazed at how much the town had changed in 13 years. The reason was uranium had been discovered there. Ben and I couldn't even find where our old hangouts had been. We stayed there only about a week.

The interior shooting at Warner Bros. was interrupted for a short location visit to Gunnison, Colorado, to film the snow sequences. That trip would have been a pretty routine trip in subfreezing weather, except that Uncle Jack managed to make things interesting for the frazzled production department.

He had injured himself somehow in Gunnison. I believe it was an ankle sprain, and I know it was very painful for him. But he took care of that! On about the third day's shooting, Ben and I realized there was trouble when, on arriving at the location site, we saw that Dick was directing the picture. We stood around in the cold for about half an hour, when, all of a sudden, Uncle Jack's station wagon pulled up, with him sitting in the front seat. It didn't take us long to figure out why Widmark was directing! One look told the story.

Uncle Jack was stewed to the gills, but not on alcohol. He looked like a circus clown. It was a horrible sight. He was all white around his lips. His tongue was coated white too, and was darting in and out of his mouth.

Ben said, "Jesus Christ!" He had never seen him that way before.

Ray Kellogg was sitting in the backseat, waiting for Jack to make the first move. Finally he did. It was snowing, and the ground was hard and icy.

I thought, "He's going to fall flat on his face."

And that's exactly what he did as he stepped out of the car. He had on galoshes at least four sizes too big. He took a step, but the galoshes didn't move. Then we saw that his pants were on backwards. The same old spotted white flannel trousers were back-side front. The unzipped fly was at his ass, and his shirttail was sticking out of it like a rooster that had just had the shit kicked out of it.

Then he spotted Dick behind the camera. This didn't annoy him; it made him quite happy.

"Thatta' boy, Dick," he yelled. "Good work! These goddamned galoshes."

He gave up trying to make it up the small hill to where Dick was, mumbled something more, got back into the car, and drove back into town.

Not long after, I found out from Wingate what had happened. The local doctor had given Jack a bottle of codeine pills the day before. He immediately took a handful of them. Ray Kellogg managed to get the bottle and tried to substitute some sort of placebo for the real thing, figuring Jack was so out of it, he wouldn't know the difference. No way! Jack chewed up every pill he was given to make sure it was the real thing. How he could do that without throwing up, I'll never know.

Wingate told me that the doc had told him that if he didn't know it was John Ford, he'd say there was an old guy who was really hooked. Big deal. To my knowledge, Uncle Jack never took them again.

Cheyenne Autumn reminded me of Woody Guthrie's great song, "So Long, It's Been Good to Know You." That was what John Ford was saying to Monument Valley. The happiest times of his life had been spent there.

President John F. Kennedy was assassinated while we were finishing filming at Warner Bros. studio in California. I was not actually working on that terrible day, but when I heard the news, I rushed over to the set. Uncle Jack had called for a period of silent prayer and then sent everyone home. When shooting resumed, Lyndon B. Johnson was the President of the United States.

But for me, *Cheyenne Autumn* was really finished in Monument Valley. It was the last time I would work for the man I loved and, at times, tried very hard to hate.

So Long, But Not Good-bye

Andrew Sinclair, in his book about John Ford, wrote such a beautiful tribute about the last days of Uncle Jack's life that I will not attempt another here. I could never paint the picture that he did. I can, however, tell you what I remember most.

I was down in Durango, Mexico, around 1971. We were shooting *Cahill, US Marshall,* for Andrew McLaglen. I hadn't seen Duke for about a year, not since *Big Jake.*

I had been visiting Uncle Jack quite a lot because I knew he was ailing, although he never complained or mentioned it. They had sold their plush house in Bel Air and moved to a more simple one in Palm Desert, on Old Prospectors Trail. I was sitting in the cafe at the Mexico Courts in Durango when in came Duke with all his entourage. I went over to him and asked if I could talk to him privately. This seemed to make him sore. Maybe he thought I was going to ask for an advance or something. He pointed to a table far away and said, very harshly, "Does this suit your fancy?"

What the hell was he sore about? I thought we'd gotten all that bullshit behind us. I stated that the table would be fine and it would only take a minute.

"Okay, shoot!" he said, looking like he was going to shoot me.

I told him that I had been visiting Uncle Jack quite often lately because I thought his days were numbered, that he was quite ill, and I thought it was cancer.

"Bullshit!" Duke yelled, when I had finished. "Bullshit! All he has to do is get out of that goddamned bed, and move around, and stop feeling sorry for himself because no one will hire him."

I don't think Duke really meant that. His words were untrue and too nasty. Probably he'd heard some bad news about the production when I had accosted him.

I said, "No, Duke, you don't understand. I know he's always liked to sit all day in bed and read, but I'm certain that, this time, he's really ill."

This made the big man stop and think, and then he said something about "checking into it" or some other nonsense to get rid of me. It pissed me off.

Anyway, to his everlasting credit, John Wayne must have made one of his infrequent phone calls to Palm Desert, because he was on a plane the next day. He was gone only long enough to have a visit with his old "coach," and then he returned to Durango to get on with the movie.

I think Duke really believed in the line Nathan Brittles says a lot on *Yellow Ribbon* "Never apologize, soldier. It's a sign of weakness."

He did come over to me after he got back. He'd been on the saloon set, and he wasn't in a very good mood, but he saw me, came over, and said, "Wasn't it great when we didn't have to think?"

"Yeah," I replied. "You sure didn't have to worry when Uncle Jack was running things. If he shot it, you knew it was your best."

He looked off, sadly, and after a few seconds, he exclaimed, "You were right, Dobe, he's down there in that goddamned Palm Desert, dying, Dobe! And we need him! We need him real bad!"

He said that just like he had said a line in *3 Godfathers*. It had all the futility that Ford had made him feel in that scene back in Death Valley. Duke was very much the same man he usually portrayed on the screen.

I have a scarf—a bandana. It's light blue with some white mixed in. It's all tattered and frayed and faded now, but it's a bandana John Ford tied around my neck the day we started *The Searchers*. It's my Medal of Honor, that scarf, because it was his. He asked me to fetch it from his room there at Gouldings' Lodge.

If you remember your feelings when you were sixteen and asked the prettiest girl to a dance, and she said, yes.

If you remember your feelings when you were looking for a job and someone said, yes.

If you remember your feelings the first time you broke 90 in golf...

That's how it was with this man in the slouch hat, rumpled clothes, and unlaced shoes, with a cigar in his mouth—whose eyes you could not see. This strange figure, so stingy with his praise, so caustic with his words. He was a human slot-machine who kept you gamely hoping for three cherries. Then one more pull of the lever, and you hit the jackpot. You went to work every morning hoping for that.

When I sit out on the deck of my home here in Durango, Colorado, I can see the white, billowy clouds that John Ford loved so much, drifting southwest toward Monument Valley. I know everything that's under those clouds. I watched and heard things only a handful of other actors have experienced. I know film history was made under clouds like those, and I was a part of it.

Harry Carey, Jr.'s Appearances in John Ford Films

The following filmography lists only the films Harry Carey, Jr., made with John Ford. In addition, Carey has appeared to date in over 100 motion pictures and dozens of television shows. Among the other distinguished directors he has worked with are Howard Hawks, Raoul Walsh, William Wellman, Henry Hathaway, Lindsay Anderson, Walter Hill, Peter Boganovich, and Robert Zemeckis.

James Pepper

3 GODFATHERS (1948)

Producers: John Ford, Merian C. Cooper. *Director:* John Ford. *Screenplay:* Laurence Stallings and Frank S. Nugent (based on the story by Peter B. Kyne). *Cinematographer:* Winton C. Hoch. *Editor:* Jack Murray. *Music:* Richard Hagemen. *Art Direction:* James Basevi. *Assistant Directors:* Wingate Smith, Edward O'Fearna. *Production and Distribution:* Argosy Pictures - Metro-Goldwyn-Mayer. Filmed in Technicolor. *Release Date:* December 1, 1948. 106 minutes. *Cast:* John Wayne, Pedro Armendariz, Harry Carey, Jr., Ward Bond, Mildred Natwick, Charles Halton, Jane Darwell, Mae Marsh, Guy Kibbee, Dorothy Ford, Ben Johnson, Michael Dugan, Don Summers, Fred Libby, Hank Worden, Jack Pennick, Francis Ford, Ruth Clifford.

SHE WORE A YELLOW RIBBON (1949)

Producers: John Ford, Merian C. Cooper. *Director:* John Ford. *Screenplay:* Frank S. Nugent and Laurence Stallings (based on the story "War Party" by James Warner Bellah). *Cinematographer:* Winton C. Hoch,

Charles P. Boyle (second unit). *Editor:* Jack Murray. *Music:* Richard Hageman. *Art Direction:* James Basevi. *Costumes:* Michael Meyers and Ann Peck. *Production and Distribution:* Argosy Pictures - RKO Radio Pictures. Filmed in Technicolor. *Release Date:* October 22, 1949. 103 minutes. *Cast:* John Wayne, Joanne Dru, John Ager, Ben Johnson, Harry Carey, Jr., Victor McLaglen, Mildred Natwick, George O'Brien, Arthur Shields, Francis Ford, Harry Woods, Chief Big Tree, Noble Johnson, Cliff Lyons, Michael Dugan, Mickey Simpson, Fred Graham, Frank McGrath, Don Summers, Fred Libby, Jack Pennick, Billy Jones, Bill Gettinger, Fred Kennedy, Rudy Bowman, Post Park, Ray Hyke, Lee Bradley, Chief Sky Eagle, Dan White, Frank Baker.

WAGONMASTER (1950)

Producers: John Ford and Merian C. Cooper. *Director:* John Ford. *Screenplay:* Frank S. Nugent and Patrick Ford. *Cinematographers:* Bert Glennon, Archie Stout (second unit). *Editors:* Jack Murray and Barbara Ford. *Assistant Director:* Wingate Smith. *Music:* Richard Hageman. *Art Direction:* James Basevi. *Production and Distribution:* Argosy Pictures - RKO Radio Pictures. Filmed in black and white. *Release Date:* April 19, 1950. 86 minutes. *Cast:* Ben Johnson, Harry Carey, Jr., Joanne Dru, Ward Bond, Charles Kemper, Alan Mowbray, Jane Darwell, Ruth Clifford, Russell Simpson. Kathleen O'Malley, James Arness, Fred Libby, Hank Worden, Mickey Simpson, Francis Ford, Cliff Lyons, Don Summers, Movita Castenada, Jim Thorpe, Chuck Haywood.

RIO GRANDE (1950)

Producers: John Ford and Merian C. Cooper. *Director:* John Ford. *Screenplay:* James Kevin McGuiness (based on the story "Mission with No Record" by James Warner Bellah). *Cinematographers:* Bert Glennon, Archie Stout (second unit). *Editors:* Jack Murray and Barbara Ford. *Music:* Victor Young, songs sung by The Sons of the Pioneers. *Art Direction:* Frank Hotaling. *Production and Distribution:* Argosy Pictures - Republic Pictures. *Release Date:* November 15, 1950. 105 minutes. *Cast:* John Wayne, Maureen O'Hara, Ben Johnson, Claude Jarman, Jr., Harry Carey, Jr., Chill Wills, J. Carroll Naish, Victor McLaglen, Grant Withers, Peter Ortiz, Steve Pendleton, Karolyn Grimes, Alberto Morin, Stan Jones, Fred Kennedy, Jack Pennick, Pat Wayne, Chuck Roberson,

The Sons of the Pioneers: Ken Curtis, Hugh Farr, Karl Farr, Lloyd Perryman, Shug Fisher, Tom Doss.

THE LONG GRAY LINE (1955)

Producer: Robert Arthur. *Director:* John Ford. *Screenplay:* Edward Hope (based on the book *Bringing Up the Brass* by Marty Maher with Nardi Reeder). *Cinematographer:* Charles Lawton, Jr. *Editor:* William Lyon. *Assistant Directors:* Wingate Smith and Jack Corrick. *Musical Adaptation:* George Duning. *Art Direction:* Robert Peterson. *Costumes:* Jean Louis. *Production and Distribution:* Rota Productions - Columbia Pictures. Filmed in Technicolor - CinemaScope. *Release Date:* February 9, 1955. 138 minutes. *Cast:* Tyrone Power, Maureen O'Hara, Robert Francis, Donald Crisp, Ward Bond, Betsey Palmer, Phil Carey, William Leslie, Harry Carey, Jr., Patrick Wayne, Sean McClory, Peter Graves, Milburn Stone, Erin O'Brien-Moore, Walter D. Ehlers, Don Barclay, Martin Milner, Chuck Courtney, Willis Bouchey, Jack Pennick.

MISTER ROBERTS (1955)

Producer: Leland Hayward. *Directors:* John Ford, Mervyn LeRoy, and (uncredited) Joshua Logan. *Screenplay:* Frank S. Nugent and Joshua Logan (based on the play by Joshua Logan and Thomas Heggen and the novel by Thomas Heggen). *Cinematographer:* Winton C. Hoch. *Editor:* Jack Murray. *Assistant Director:* Wingate Smith. *Music:* Franz Waxman. *Art Direction:* Art Loel. *Costumes:* Moss Mabry. *Production and Distribution:* Orange Productions - Columbia Pictures. Filmed in Technicolor - CinemaScope. *Release Date:* July 30, 1955. 123 minutes. *Cast:* Henry Fonda, James Cagney, Jack Lemmon, William Powell, Ward Bond, Betsy Palmer, Phil Carey, Nick Adams, Harry Carey, Jr., Ken Curtis, Frank Aletter, Fritz Ford, Buck Kartalian, William Henry, William Hudson, Stubby Kruger, Harry Tenbrook, Perry Lopez, Robert Roark, Pat Wayne, Tige Andrews, Jim Maloney, Denny Niles, Francis Conner, Shug Fisher, Danny Borzage, Jim Murphy, Kathleen O'Malley, Maura Murphy, Mimi Doyle, Jeanne Murray-Vanderbilt, Lonnie Pierce, Martin Milner, Gregory Walcott, James Flavin, Duke Kahanamoko.

THE SEARCHERS (1956)

Producers: Merian C. Cooper and C. V. Whitney. *Director:* John Ford. *Screenplay:* Frank S. Nugent (based on the novel by Alan LeMay). *Associate Producer:* Patrick Ford. *Cinematographer:* Winton C. Hoch, Alfred Gilks (second unit). *Editor:* Jack Murray. *Assistant Director:* Wingate Smith. *Music:* Max Steiner. *Title Song:* Stan Jones. *Art Direction:* Frank Hotaling and James Basevi. *Costumes:* Frank Beetson and Ann Peck. *Production and Distribution:* C. V. Whitney Pictures. Filmed in Technicolor - VistaVision. *Release Date:* May 26, 1956. 119 minutes. *Cast:* John Wayne, Jeffrey Hunter, Vera Miles, Ward Bond, Natalie Wood, John Qualen, Olive Carey, Henry Brandon, Ken Curtis, Harry Carey, Jr., Antonio Moreno, Hank Worden, Lana Wood, Walter Coy, Dorothy Jordan, Pippa Scott, Pat Wayne, Beulah Archuletta, Jack Pennick, Peter Mamakos, Bill Steele, Cliff Lyons, Chuck Roberson, Ruth Clifford, Mae Marsh, Dan Borzage, Billy Cartledge, Chuck Hayward, Slim Hightower, Fred Kennedy, Frank McGrath, Dale van Sickle, Henry Wills, Terry Wilson, Away Luna, Billy Yellow, Bob Many Mules, Exactly Sonnie Betsuie, Feather Hat, Jr., Harry Black Horse, Jack Tin Horn, Many Mules Son, Percy Shooting Star, Pete Grey Eyes, Pipe Line Begishe, Smile White Sheep.

TWO RODE TOGETHER (1961)

Producer: Stan Shpetner. *Director:* John Ford. *Screenplay:* Frank Nugent (based on the novel *Comanche Captives* by Will Cook). *Cinematographer:* Charles Lawton, Jr. *Editor:* Jack Murray. *Assistant Director:* Wingate Smith. *Music:* George Duning. *Art Direction:* Robert Peterson. *Costumes:* Frank Beetson. *Production and Distribution:* Ford-Shpetner Productions - Columbia Pictures. Filmed in Pathecolor. *Release Date:* July 1961. 109 minutes. *Cast:* James Stewart, Richard Widmark, Shirley Jones, Linda Cristal, Andy Devine, John McIntire, Paul Birch, Willis Bouchey, Henry Brandon, Harry Carey, Jr., Ken Curtis, Olive Carey, Chet Douglas, Annelle Hayes, David Kent, Anna Lee, Jeanette Nolan, John Qualen, Ford Rainey, Woody Strode, O. Z. Whitehead, Cliff Lyons, Mae Marsh, Frank Baker, Ruth Clifford, Ted Knight, Maj. Sam Harris, Jack Pennick, Chuck Roberson, Dan Borzage, Bill Henry, Chuck Hayward, Edward Brophy.

FLASHING SPIKES (1962)

Television Episode for the Alcoa Presents TV Series

Associate Producer: Frank Baur. *Director:* John Ford. *Scenarist:* Jameson Brewer (based on the novel by Frank O'Rourke). *Cinematographer:* William H. Clothier. *Editors:* Richard Belding and Tony Martinelli. *Assistant Director:* Wingate Smith. *Music:* Johnny Williams and Stanley Wilson. *Art Direction:* Martin Obzina. *Costumes:* Vincent Dee. Production and Distribution: Avista Productions - MCA. Filmed in black and white. *Televised:* October 4, 1962. 53 minutes. *Series Host:* Fred Astaire. *Cast:* James Stewart, Jack Warden, Pat Wayne, Edgar Buchanan, Tige Andrews, Carleton Young, Willis Bouchey, Don Drysdale, Stephanie Hill, Charles Seel, Bing Russell, Harry Carey, Jr., Vin Scully, Walter Reed, Sally Hughes, Larry Blake, Charles Morton, Cy Malis, Bill Henry, John Wayne, Art Passarella, Vern Stephens, Ralph Volkie, Earl Gilpin, Bud Harden, Whitey Campbell.

CHEYENNE AUTUMN (1964)

Producer: Bernard Smith. *Director:* John Ford. *Screenplay:* James R. Webb and (uncredited) Patrick Ford (based on the novel by Mari Sandoz). *Cinematographer:* William Clothier. *Editor:* Otho Lovering. *Associate Director:* Ray Kellogg. *Assistant Directors:* Wingate Smith and Russ Saunders. *Music:* Alex North. *Art Direction:* Richard Day. *Production and Distribution:* Ford-Smith Productions - Warner. Filmed in Technicolor - Panavision 70. *Release Date:* October 1964. 159 minutes. *Cast:* Richard Widmark, Carroll Baker, James Stewart, Edward G. Robinson, Karl Malden, Sal Mineo, Dolores Del Rio, Ricardo Montalban, Gilbert Roland, Arthur Kennedy, Patrick Wayne, Elizabeth Allen, John Carradine, Victor Jory, Mike Mazurki, George O'Brien, Sean McClory, Judson Pratt, Carmen D'Antonio, Ken Curtis, Walter Baldwin, Shug Fisher, Nancy Hsueh, Chuck Roberson, Harry Carey, Jr., Ben Johnson, Jimmy O'Hara, Chuck Hayward, Lee Bradley, Walter Reed, Willis Bouchey, Carleton Young, Denver Pyle, John Qualen, Nanomba "Moonbeam" Morton. Dan Borzage, Dean Smith, David H. Miller, Bing Russell. *Narrators:* Spencer Tracy and Richard Widmark.

Index

Compiled by Steven A. Stilwell